UNCHARTED TERRITORY

An Unofficial and Unauthorised Guide to *Farscape*

Also by Scott Andrews:

*TROUBLED WATERS: An Unauthorised and Unofficial
Guide to Dawson's Creek*

UNCHARTED TERRITORY

An Unofficial and Unauthorised Guide to *Farscape*

Scott Andrews

First published in Great Britain in 2002 by
Virgin Books Ltd
Thames Wharf Studios
Rainville Road
London
W6 9HA

A catalogue record for this book is available from the British
Library.

ISBN 0 7535 0704 8

Typeset by TW Typesetting, Plymouth, Devon
Printed and bound in Great Britain by
Mackays of Chatham PLC

Contents

Acknowledgements

My editor, Kirstie Addis, for help and patience this time and last.

Jim Smith, without whom I'd not have got the gig.

Ben and Sue, for lending me the DVDs so I could see what it was I was actually writing about.

Those folks at uk.media.tv.sf.farscape, who answered my occasional questions and pointed me in the right direction a few times.

My friends, who've been very patient with my sequestered silence as I've written this book. Can we *please* go out and have a beer now?

Introduction

Welcome to the Uncharted Territories, where nobody is exactly what they seem, everybody wants to get inside your head or your pants – that is, when they're not trying to kill you – and your best friend probably has tentacles. This book is an episode guide to *Farscape* but it's 'Unofficial and Unauthorised', which means I don't have access to the cast or crew, or to privileged behind-the-scenes info or lots of colour glossy 8×10 photographs with arrows and labels – if you want that stuff there's the official Companion and the bi-monthly *Official Magazine*. All I have access to are the episodes themselves and interviews I happened to stumble across in my travels. So this book is designed as a light-hearted *aide-memoire* to the series, designed to be read alongside the episodes, or kept in the toilet for reading in short spurts. It'll be informative (hopefully), amusing (with luck) and opinionated (definitely), the idea being that you'll find out stuff you may have missed and connections you hadn't made, and you'll sometimes like and sometimes hate what I have to say, which is the way it should be. If you violently agree or disagree with something I've written or, God forbid, think you've spotted an error, get it off your chest by mailing me through my website *www. sixesandsevens.net/unchartedterritory*. So without further ado, here's how each episode will be presented:

Character sections: Each of the central characters will get his, her or its own section, where I note how they develop over time, and draw attention to action or dialogue that really defines them. *Farscape* has masses of regular characters, although they rarely all appear at once . . .

> **Buck Rogers Redux:** John Crichton, our viewpoint character, a stranger in a strange land.

> **You Can Be More:** Aeryn Sun – gun-toting, leather-wearing, all-singing, all-dancing, bad girl turned good.

Big Blue: Pa'u Zotoh Zhaan, the blue skinned mystic and psychopath. Cures whatever ails you, but may then kill you anyway.

I was a Teenage Luxan: Ka D'Argo, sword-wielding, muscle-bound warrior guy, in reality an insecure adolescent. Regularly gets it all horribly wrong.

Buckwheat the Sixteenth: Rygel, the Mekon-type deposed regent is selfish, arrogant, bossy, unpleasant, ruthless and smelly. But we love him anyway.

Everyone's Favourite Little Tralk: Chiana, the black and white character in this most colourful of shows. Sneaky, sexy, self-serving, amoral and untrustworthy.

The Man in the Iron Mask: Stark, the unstable energy being who ends up on Moya. Totally unpredictable.

Jool in the Crown: Jool, the newest recruit. Spoiled brat who screams a lot, irritates everyone, but has skills that save the day more than once.

In the Driving Seat: Pilot, the multi-armed, biologically bonded controller of Moya is far more a character than may at first be suspected.

The Insane Military Commander: Crais, Season One's pursuing nemesis, latterly a reluctant ally of his one-time foes.

Nosferatu in Rubber: Scorpius assumed Crais's role in Season Two and has dominated the show ever since.

A Ship, a Living Ship!: Moya, the Leviathan, home to the 'scapers and just as alive as they are.

Big Baby: Talyn, Moya's child, is an impulsive warrior ship, bonded to Crais, and is far more trouble than he's worth.

The Ballad of Aeryn and John: How their relationship blossoms and flowers and then goes horribly weird and screwy.

The Ballad of Chiana and D'Argo: Likewise for these two.

Worlds Apart: The various planets and civilisations Moya's crew visit.

Alien Encounters: The races that Crichton and co. meet along the way.

Hi, Harvey: Crichton acquires a neural clone of Scorpius inside his head. He names it Harvey.

Disney on Acid: Crichton peppers his speeches with pop culture references that nobody else on Moya could possibly understand. This category will list and explain them.

Get Frelled: Sex is a major component of the *Farscape* world. Everyone's doing it, wants to be doing it, or is regretting having done it. 'If we were stuck on a ship with Aeryn Sun and Chiana for three years, well, I'd be trying to get laid by one of them . . .' David Kemper, *SFX*.

What Does This Do?: Bodily functions are never ignored on Moya, from Rygel's helium farts, to the radiation shielding properties of Zhaan's puke. 'Our people go to the bathroom!' David Kemper, *SFX*.

Seen it all Before: *Farscape* is very good at taking old storylines and twisting them in new and unexpected ways. This section points out where you may have encountered a particular idea before.

Stats: The everyday hardware of the Farscape world, the measurements, rules, facts and figures.

Logic Leaps: Moments when the story asks you to suspend disbelief just that bit too much.

Bloopers: Screw-ups and continuity errors accounted for.

WHAT did you just say?: Memorable quotes and linguistic oddities.

Guest Stars: Who they are and where you've seen them before.

Backstage: Behind-the-scenes info that informs the episode.

The Verdict: A brief, subjective review of the episode.

List of Episodes

Season One

101 Premiere
102 Throne For a Loss
103 Back and Back and Back to the Future
104 I, E.T.
105 Exodus From Genesis
106 Thank God it's Friday, Again
107 PK Tech Girl
108 That Old Black Magic
109 DNA Mad Scientist
110 They've Got a Secret
111 Till the Blood Runs Clear
112 The Flax
113 Rhapsody in Blue
114 Jeremiah Crichton
115 Durka Returns
116 A Human Reaction
117 Through the Looking Glass
118 A Bug's Life
119 Nerve
120 The Hidden Memory
121 Bone to Be Wild
122 Family Ties

The episode list above is taken from the UK DVD releases and is the order they were originally broadcast in the UK, so it's the order I will use for this book. The original Australian transmission order was almost the same, except 'That Old Black Magic' ran between 'Thank God it's Friday, Again' and 'PK Tech Girl'.

The original US transmission order ran:
101 Premiere
102 Exodus From Genesis
103 Back and Back and Back to the Future
104 Throne For a Loss

105 PK Tech Girl
106 Thank God it's Friday, Again
107 I, E.T.

The US DVD releases follow the preferred viewing order:

101 Premiere
102 I, E.T.
103 Exodus From Genesis
104 Throne For a loss
105 Back and Back and Back to the Future
106 Thank God it's Friday, Again
107 PK Tech Girl
108 That Old Black Magic
109 DNA Mad Scientist
110 They've Got a Secret
111 Till the Blood Runs Clear
112 Rhapsody in Blue
113 The Flax

Broadcast

In the US Season One was originally broadcast on the SciFi Channel except for 'PK Tech Girl' which first aired on the USA Network.

In the UK it was shown on BBC2 in an early evening slot. This necessitated some cuts for content. 'You guys edit the hell out of the show! What the hell do they cut out? It's not like we're *Sex And The City*!' David Kemper said in *SFX*. It was then rerun on the UK SciFi Channel.

In Australia it was shown by Channel Nine in a late evening slot, normally 8.30 p.m., although some episodes were shown as late as 10 p.m. It was then rerun on Fox Kids, where it was cut for content.

Duration

Season One episodes ran to over 48 minutes. In Europe they were shown at that length, except for any content cuts deemed necessary for the time-slot. In the US the episodes ran at 44 minutes. So approximately three to four minutes of disposable character material was shot for each episode but was only seen in Europe. It has been reinstated for the DVD releases.

Season Two

201 Mind the Baby
202 Vitas Mortis
203 Taking the Stone
204 Crackers Don't Matter
205 The Way We Weren't
206 Picture If You Will
207 Home on the Remains
208 Dream a Little Dream
209 Out of Their Minds
210 Look at the Princess I: A Kiss is but a Kiss
211 Look at the Princess II: I Do, I Think
212 Look at the Princess III: The Maltese Crichton
213 My Three Crichtons
214 Beware of Dog
215 Won't Get Fooled Again
216 The Locket
217 The Ugly Truth
218 A Clockwork Nebari
219 Liars, Guns and Money I: A Not So Simple Plan
220 Liars, Guns and Money II: With Friends Like
     These . . .
221 Liars, Guns and Money III: Plan B
222 Die Me, Dichotomy

   Again this is the UK order and the order of the R2 DVD releases. In the US there was one difference – 'My Three Crichtons' was shown before the 'Look at the Princess' trilogy.

Broadcast

In the US Season Two was originally broadcast on the SciFi Channel.

In the UK it was shown on BBC2 in an early evening slot. This necessitated some cuts for content. It was then rerun on the UK SciFi Channel.

In Australia transmission was all over the place, with Channel Nine running a set of stand-alone episodes before showing **201**, 'Mind the Baby' and resolving the cliffhanger. All narrative continuity was lost. Fans were annoyed, casual viewers alienated at the shabby treatment of the show and its ever-changing time-slot.

Duration

Unlike the first season, this run of episodes was shot at 44 minutes each, so there is no extra European material. Any cuts in episodes shown in the UK or Australia were therefore only for content.

Season Three

301 Season of Death
302 Suns and Lovers
303 Self Inflicted Wounds I: Could'a, Would'a, Should'a
304 Self Inflicted Wounds II: Wait for the Wheel
305 . . . Different Destinations
306 Eat Me
307 Thanks for Sharing
308 Green-eyed Monster
309 Losing Time
310 Relativity
311 Incubator
312 Meltdown
313 Scratch 'n' Sniff
314 Infinite Possibilities I: Daedalus Demands
315 Infinite Possibilities II: Icarus Abides
316 Revenging Angel
317 The Choice
318 Fractures
319 I-Yensch, You-Yensch
320 Into the Lion's Den I: Lambs to the Slaughter

321 Into the Lion's Den II: Wolf in Sheep's Clothing
322 Dog with Two Bones

Unlike previous seasons the story-arc for Season Three was so strong that it was impossible to change the order of the episodes and so everyone got to see them in the right order.

Broadcast

In the US Season Three was originally broadcast on the SciFi Channel.

In the UK it was shown on BBC2 in an early evening slot. This slot necessitated some cuts for content. 'Scratch 'n' Sniff' was completely impossible to cut for this time-slot and so was shown late Saturday night.

Season Three has, at the time of writing, yet to be shown in Australia.

*'My name is John Crichton . . . I got shot
through a wormhole, now I'm lost . . .
[on] a ship, a living ship,
full of strange, alien life forms . . .
I'm just looking for a way home.'*

Season One

Regular Cast
Ben Browder (Commander John Crichton)
Claudia Black (Aeryn Sun)
Virginia Hey (Pa'u Zotoh Zhaan)
Anthony Simcoe (Ka D'Argo)
Lani Tupu (Voice of Pilot)
Jonathan Hardy (Voice of Dominar Rygel XVI)
John Ecclestone (Head puppeteer for Rygel)
Gigi Edgley (Chiana) **115 'Durka Returns'** onwards

101
Premiere

1st US Transmission Date: 19 March 1999
1st UK Transmission Date: 29 November 1999
1st Australian Transmission Date: 20 May 2000

Writer: Rockne S O'Bannon
Director: Andrew Prowse
Guest Cast: Kent McCord (Jack Crichton), Murray Bartlett (DK),
Lani Tupu (Capt. Bialar Crais), Christine Stephen-Daly (Lt Teeg),
Damen Stephenson (Bio Isolation Man 1),
Colin Borgonon (PK Weapons Officer)

While testing a theory of slingshot space travel, John
Crichton's Farscape module is transported through a
wormhole into the middle of a space battle on the other
side of the galaxy. His module collides with a fighter craft

Uncharted Territory

(a Prowler), which crashes as a result. Crichton is then sucked on board a huge ship, Moya, the crew of which – Zhaan, D'Argo and Rygel – are prisoners in the middle of an escape attempt. They successfully StarBurst to safety, sucking Aeryn Sun's Prowler along in their wake. The leader of their attackers, Captain Crais of the Peacekeepers, discovers his brother was piloting the Prowler that collided with Crichton's module, and he blames Crichton for his brother's death. Crais takes his ship, a Command Carrier, in pursuit of Moya. Moya is damaged in the escape, so the crew find a commerce planet and go to barter for vital fluids to repair her, leaving Aeryn and Crichton locked up on board. They escape, take Aeryn's Prowler down to the planet, and Aeryn signals Crais. Zhaan and Rygel return to Moya, D'Argo stays to recapture Crichton and Aeryn, but they are all captured and imprisoned by Crais. They escape and return to Moya just as Crais's ship moves in to attack. Moya is too weak to StarBurst, but using Crichton's slingshot theory, and Aeryn's piloting skills, they escape.

Buck Rogers Redux: 'I don't know where I am, technically I don't know how I got here, but I'm not going to stop trying to get home.' Commander John Crichton is a scientist first and an astronaut second, and the Farscape project is his baby, in collaboration with DK, a childhood friend. Crichton's been up in the shuttle only twice before. He broke out of quarantine the night before his big test flight so that he could watch the sunrise over the launch pad. His father, a famous astronaut who walked on the moon, gave him a good-luck charm: a puzzle ring he received from Yuri Gagarin. Crichton spends most of his time on Moya being punched, knocked out, locked up and abused, but he still manages to use his scientific skills to save the day and prove his slingshot theory at the same time, demonstrating his usefulness to the crew of Moya. He realises that he must have travelled through a worm-hole and defines his objective – to find another one, or to create one, and use it to get home. He is recording messages for his father on his minidisc player.

You Can Be More: 'It's my duty, my breeding since birth, it's who I am.' Aeryn Sun, an officer and special commando in Peacekeeper command, is caught in the wake of Moya's StarBurst because she disobeys orders and continues attacking. She was bred to be a Peacekeeper, it's all she's ever known, and she doesn't want to be on Moya at all. Crais has branded her 'irreversibly contaminated' by her long exposure to Crichton, so she has no choice but to stay – the Peacekeepers will kill her if they find her. Her piloting skills are essential in allowing Moya to escape Crais.

Big Blue: 'On my home world, even amongst my own kind, I was something of an anarchist. Actually, I was the leading anarchist.' Zhaan is a Delvian priest who was imprisoned, she implies, for being a troublemaker (we discover her true crime in **113**, 'Rhapsody in Blue'). She spent three cycles on a maximum labour planet working with Peacekeeper technology. She can work very fast indeed, her hands fly over the controls at super speed. She establishes her role as mediator between hot-headed D'Argo and selfish Rygel immediately. She meditates nude.

I was a Teenage Luxan: 'I am a Luxan warrior, I have seen two battle campaigns!' D'Argo is thirty cycles old, which is young for a Luxan. He has seen two battle campaigns, and Zhaan states that that's not very many. He has spent eight cycles on Moya and prior to that spent some time working on the 93rd level of the Kemlach mines on Meeka 7, a punishment so brutal Zhaan is amazed he survived. He claims he was imprisoned for killing his commanding officer (we discover in **103**, 'Back and Back and Back to the Future', that he was lying). Aeryn describes the Luxans as a brutal and uncivilised race, 'indiscriminate in their deployment of violence'. D'Argo has a Qualta Blade, basically a big sword, which he sharpens and polishes obsessively. He can stun people with his incredibly long tongue. According to David Kemper the rings through D'Argo's collarbones were put in without anaesthetic 'by the Peacekeepers after he was captured [because] arm restraints weren't enough'.

Buckwheat the Sixteenth: 'I am Rygel the 16th, Dominar to over six hundred billion people. I don't need to talk to you.' Rygel has demonstrated his usefulness to the crew – it was he who bribed the guards for the codes that allowed them to escape, but he's an irritating, smelly, self-centred kleptomaniac. His phlegm (he spits on Crichton) is red. He tells Crichton that his cousin, Bishan, stole the throne while he was asleep, 'a mistake I will soon be correcting'.

In the Driving Seat: After the StarBurst, Pilot has no idea where they are, it's obvious that he and Moya are inexperienced.

The Insane Military Commander: 'You charged my brother's prowler in that White Death Pod of yours!' Captain Crais commands an armada of Peacekeeper ships, but when his brother's Prowler is destroyed after an accidental collision with Crichton's module he goes rogue, leaves the armada behind, and takes his Command Carrier off in pursuit of Moya and Crichton. He promises to rip Crichton apart just to find out how he works, and when Aeryn protests he turns on her and has her locked up too. He is a melodramatic scenery chewer, and someone needs to talk to him about his taste in hats, but he's got a big ship, a crew to back him, and he's ruthless to a fault. Aeryn tells Crichton that he won't stop coming just because Moya's gone outside his jurisdiction.

A Ship, a Living Ship!: Moya, the ship, is a Biomechanoid Leviathan, which means she's a living being. She is bonded with Pilot and he is the only one who can speak to her and for her. She has no offensive or defensive capability, but she can StarBurst, which means that she can zap herself instantly to another seemingly random point in space. She was fitted with a control collar, which restricted her to following Peacekeeper orders, but D'Argo ripped out some synapses from the control console and freed her. To repair the damage, the crew needed to find some Iriscent Fluid. Moya has limitations – she needs to regain her strength for a while after each StarBurst before she can do it again. The ship is maintained by small yellow droids called DRDs – Diagnostic Repair Drones. She can be piloted manually from the bridge, using a joystick (this is seen again, in **103**, 'Back and Back and Back to the Future').

The Ballad of Aeryn and John: The very first thing Aeryn does when she meets Crichton is beat him up, so things can only get better. She tells Crichton she hates compassion, yet when he is about to be taken away and dissected by Crais she intercedes on his behalf, betraying her own weakness. He repays the favour by telling her that she can be more than just a soldier, basing his faith in her on little actual evidence.

Worlds Apart: Moya was transporting the prisoners to Terran Raa, a planet for lifers. Both Zhaan and D'Argo spent time as prisoners on Meeka 7. The commerce planet that the crew visit is never named. Moya flees into the Uncharted Territories (UTs), an area of space in which the Peacekeepers have no jurisdiction. It is, presumably, represented on maps as a big blank, perhaps with 'Here Be Monsters' written on it.

Alien Encounters: The Peacekeepers are a race called Sebaceans. We're not told what the race the dealer Rygel meets on the commerce planet is, but he's got enough teeth that he can pretty much choose for himself – who'd argue with him? If you look closely you can see Zhaan talking to a Sheyang, from **107**, 'PK Tech Girl', when she's on the commerce planet.

Disney on Acid: 'Boy was Spielberg ever wrong. *Close Encounters* my ass.' Poor old Crichton gets upset when he makes first contact and the aliens don't play tunes to him.

Get Frelled: Upon discovering that Zhaan is a Delvian priest, D'Argo's first thought is of sex. He says he's heard about her race's 'appetites' and something they experience called the 'Fourth Sensation'. Zhaan's playful response – that she's experienced that, but 'not lately' – gets the

Luxan all hot under the collar. Later, when Crichton has saved the day, Zhaan gives him a Delvian ear kiss that leaves him cross-eyed and D'Argo jealous. Outwardly Sebaceans resemble humans, and Zhaan, who wastes no time drugging Crichton and ripping his clothes off, indicates that the only way she knew Crichton was not Sebacean was the unusual bacteria in his body. So his reproductive organs must look much like those of Sebacean males, and thus, presumably, he and Aeryn are ... um ... *compatible*.

What Does This Do?: Rygel farts helium, but only sometimes, when he's 'nervous or angry'.

Logic Leaps: Crais is down on the commerce planet before Zhaan and Rygel leave in Moya's pod. This means that for a while at least his Command Carrier was in orbit with an entirely undefended and helpless Moya. So why wasn't Moya crawling with Peacekeepers when Zhaan and Rygel returned? Also, why are D'Argo, Crichton and Aeryn imprisoned on the commerce planet? Why not just bundle them into a ship and take them back to the Command Carrier?

Bloopers: Crichton works for IASA – presumably the International Aeronautics and Space Administration. However, the insignia on his uniform has the stars and stripes on, and the module has United States written on it. How does the broken DRD get on the table in the final scene – can they levitate?

WHAT did you just say?: 'Don't move or I'll ... fill you full of little yellow bolts of light!' Crichton trying to be a hard man with a ray gun and blowing it horribly. Aeryn proves that Crichton isn't the only one who can get it all wrong, by saying that Crichton claims to come from a planet called Erp.

Stats: Distance is measured in Metras (Peacekeeper Frag Cannons have a range of 45 Metras). Speed is measured on the Hetch scale (Moya's maximum speed after StarBurst is said to be 'Hetch II'). Time is measured in Cycles (approximating to years) and Arns (approximating to hours). Translator Microbes are injected into most people at birth. They colonise at the base of the brain and allow people to understand each other (Babel Fish anyone?). In Peacekeeper Territory there is some sort of genetic sieving process (D'Argo refers to it, astonished that Crichton, whom he assumes is an idiot, escaped it), presumably designed to weed out perceived genetic defects. Prowlers can hold three people.

Guest Stars: Kent McCord played Commander Scott Keller in four episodes of Rockne S O'Bannon's show *Seaquest DSV* and prior to that he was Captain Troy in the equally dreadful *Galactica 1980*, plus he's been in a large number of TV movies, such as *Dragnet* and *Beg, Borrow, or Steal*, and in *Adam-12*. Murray Bartlett used to be Luke Foster on *Neighbours*. Christine Stephen-Daly currently appears as Lara Stone in the UK hospital drama *Casualty*.

Backstage: The US DVD release of this episode has a commentary track featuring Rockne S O'Bannon, Brian Henson and Ben Browder. The creation of this episode, and the changes it went through from script to screen, is covered in exhaustive detail in issue one of the official *Farscape Magazine*.

Crichton's Farscape Module (henceforth referred to as the WDP – White Death Pod) was based on the proposed emergency re-entry vehicle for the International Space Station.

When the show began production two episodes were filmed simultaneously (while this is virtually unheard of in the UK or US it is common working practice in Australia, where *Farscape* is filmed), so **101**, 'Premiere' was lensed at the same time as **105**, 'Exodus From Genesis'. This might explain why some confusion has arisen about the production order of the first few episodes and the sequence in which they should be viewed. This method of working was abandoned with **107**, 'PK Tech Girl'.

The Verdict: Not the strongest pilot ever made, it tries to do too much in a short time and comes across as rushed and unsatisfying. The characters are established in broad strokes and seem, at first glance, to be little more than stereotypes. There's also a bit too much of characters being locked up and escaping. When watched for the first time it doesn't really draw in the casual viewer, it isn't different enough to justify instant loyalty. However, when watched in hindsight, with knowledge of how subverted all those initial stereotypes will be, it's much more interesting viewing. Looks great, sounds totally original, and holds promise, but there is little here to indicate the levels of weirdness, perversion, violence and narrative originality that is to come.

102
Throne For a Loss

1st US Transmission Date: 9 April 1999
1st UK Transmission Date: 6 December 1999
1st Australian Transmission Date: 27 May 2000

Writer: Richard Manning
Director: Pino Amenta
Guest Cast: John Adam (Bekesh), Jeremiah Tickell (Kyr),
Zoe Dimakis (Hontovek), Api Bavardra (Nonk)

Rygel is kidnapped from Moya by a race called Tavleks, who believe he is still the ruling Dominar and can be ransomed. During the kidnap one Tavlek, Kyr, is wounded and left behind. Like all Tavleks, Kyr wears a Gauntlet weapon which injects the user with an addictive stimulant that heightens aggression. D'Argo puts on the Gauntlet and becomes unmanageably violent. Crichton and Aeryn knock him out and go to the Tavlek planet to rescue Rygel. In the process, Aeryn puts on the Gauntlet. D'Argo recovers and comes down to help, stunning Aeryn in time to stop her going on a suicidal rampage in the Tavlek camp. By the time they reach Rygel's cell he is already being moved elsewhere. Crichton puts on the Gauntlet and runs to catch the Tavlek party. He convinces the Tavlek leader, Bekesh, that Rygel is worthless, and he is released.

Meanwhile, back on Moya, Zhaan helps Kyr through withdrawal from the Gauntlet stimulant. She gives him the choice of staying clean or returning to his drug addicted ways. He eventually returns home and when Zhaan calls him to see how he's doing he reveals that he's put the Gauntlet back on by choice.

Buck Rogers Redux: Aeryn: 'Somewhere out there's a whole world full of Crichtons. How useless that must be!' Crichton tries to be calm and reasonable among a crew whose first response to any situation is violence (Aeryn), extreme violence (D'Argo), and theft (Rygel). D'Argo and Aeryn concede that Crichton is providing common ground between them, if only by uniting them in their assessment of him as some sort of amusing idiot figure. He calls Jotheb a 'critter' and Tavleks Tavloids, no matter how many times he's corrected.

You Can Be More: Aeryn swears she will 'take out every last Tavlek. No survivors. No mercy.' She is bloodthirsty, violent and a very good shot. Her reaction to every problem is to try and force a resolution, something that lands her in trouble time and again.

Big Blue: 'Am I the only species in creation that doesn't thrive on conflict?' Zhaan is a Pa'u, a priest of the ninth level. She can share others' pain and relieve their suffering by laying on of hands and kissing. Her blood is white and has soothing properties. She's hard as nails, she just chooses not to resort to violence. She can brew up a sleep mist, which would knock most life forms out but fails on D'Argo because of the Gauntlet.

I was a Teenage Luxan: 'Enough of this stupid voting; from now on I make the decisions.' Luxans bleed black when wounded; the wound has to be beaten to encourage blood flow, only when the blood runs clear is the wound cleansed and can heal. D'Argo's Qualta Blade works as a rifle as well as a sword. It was last charged eight cycles ago.

Buckwheat the Sixteenth: 'I'm unloved, unwanted, unpopular . . . unconscious.' Rygel was deposed a hundred cycles ago (this later changes to approximately a hundred and thirty cycles), so he's pretty old. He loves playing emperor, and steals a synaptic processor to adorn his sceptre even though Pilot expressly forbade him to. He is actually killed by Bekesh but Jotheb, the creature in the cell next to him, revives him.

A Ship, a Living Ship!: Moya's synaptic processors are 'trillions of silicon neurons suspended in a crystalline matrix', which is a complicated way of saying they're big, pretty, red crystals. Her sensors are initially blocked by vegetation with a high concentration of Chloroferric compounds, but Zhaan and D'Argo reconfigure them. She must periodically vent supercoolant or the pressure builds to dangerous levels. Moya doesn't have a tractor beam, she instead has a Docking Web, which is what was used to bring the WDP aboard in **101**, 'Premiere'. The ship has a Maintenance Bay.

The Ballad of Aeryn and John: He annoys her so much that she knocks him out with a Pantak Jab. They bicker, squabble, fight and take it in turns to have plans, which the other always derides.

Worlds Apart: Prior to this episode, the crew have visited Porzin II, where Rygel negotiated for some food cubes that turned out to be stale.

Alien Encounters: Tavleks live on an unnamed planet. They are a violent species, living by plunder and kidnapping, but when they realise that Rygel is no use they let him go without any hint of revenge, so they have an honour code. They sustain many wounds, presumably in battle, and patch themselves up with staples and metal plates. The Gauntlet sustains them. (See scifi.com's *Lifeform Encounters* for an explanation of the Tavleks' intriguing backstory.) Jotheb is the 'next in succession to preside over the Consortium of Trao', which is composed of 'ten thousand planets, each averaging some four billion Trao'.

Disney on Acid: Crichton trying to talk Aeryn out of carrying a gun to the meeting with the Tavleks, on the basis that her John Wayne impression will prevent the Tavleks paying them to haul cargo. 'John Wayne, the big guy, *True Grit*, *The Searchers*, *The Cowboys*, *Gengis Khan*. Oh no, look, forget about *Gengis Khan*, everybody makes a bad movie . . . *Kung Fu*! *Kung Fu* never carried a gun!' Then, when Aeryn tells him her plan to recapture Rygel, he says that even Wile E Coyote could have come up with a better plan. And, finally, when being told how to operate the Gauntlet: 'willpower, like the Green Lantern's ring'.

Get Frelled: Zhaan has, for the second episode in a row, a prisoner, and, for the second episode in a row, she strips him while he's unconscious. This is becoming a compulsion. Kyr flashes Zhaan to try and intimidate her but she gives him a good look and replies that he's quite respectable for his age, before stripping off herself and giving him a good look in return: 'Did you think to shock me? Is nudity a taboo in your culture? Are you ashamed of your bodies?' The poor boy's left speechless. It took six hours in make-up to prepare Zhaan for the nude scene.

Bloopers: When Crichton puts on the Gauntlet and the shot cuts back to Aeryn and D'Argo, look in the top left-hand corner and you can see a footbridge in the park where the scene was shot.

What Does This Do?: We get to hear Rygel on the toilet. Lovely.

WHAT did you just say?: Kyr tells Zhaan he's sick of hearing her Plock. Zhaan lets rip with an incomprehensible Delvian curse when she hears that Crichton has a plan to save the day. Crichton definitely says 'shit' at one point.

Stats: Geographic position is given thus: 'Delta 6, Premno 9, Lurg 8'. Aeryn uses Occulars, which are a slim headset that operate as binoculars. Her rifle blows up after Crichton accidentally overloads the pulse chamber. The Tavleks want 'Purity 9 Corvinium' in return for Rygel's release.

Guest Stars: John Adam was Luke Cunningham in *Home And Away* and also appeared in five episodes of the cop drama *Water Rats*.

Backstage: During the scene when D'Argo stuns Aeryn you get a good look at his green contact lenses which were dropped after Anthony Simcoe got make-up removal fluid in his eyes and had to be rushed to hospital with a damaged cornea; the doctor forbade him to wear lenses for six months afterwards, hence his eyes change from green to normal at random during the first four episodes depending on whether a scene was filmed before or after the accident. The blue vegetation was achieved by grading the film in postproduction – the plants were not painted. This episode was filmed at the same time as **104**, 'I, E.T.'. The US DVD release of this episode includes a commentary track featuring Ben Browder and Claudia Black.

The Verdict: The bickering between Aeryn and Crichton is the greatest strength of this episode, and Claudia Black shines. She gets some nice scenes with D'Argo too, as the characters are rounded out and the tensions among the crew emerge more clearly. The crunching guitar-chord background music is trying too hard to be edgy and cool though, and shows that *Farscape* is still trying to find its voice. The production values are excellent, but in the final analysis this is a forgettable tale.

103
Back and Back and Back to the Future

1st US Transmission Date: 2 April 1999
1st UK Transmission Date: 13 December 1999
1st Australian Transmission Date: 3 June 2000

Writer: Babs Greyhosky
Director: Rowan Woods
Guest Cast: Lisa Hensley (Matala), John Clayton (Verell)

Moya rescues an escape pod with two scientists, Matala and Verell, on board. They are Ilanics, a race who are at war, and they are developing weapons. On their pod they have isolated a Quantum Singularity (that's a Black Hole to you and me) and Moya's crew agree to ferry them to a rendezvous with a ship that will take them home where they will use the Singularity as a weapon to win the war. Matala uses her sex appeal to keep D'Argo off balance and use him as a protector and champion while Verell tries to solve the containment problem that led to their ship being destroyed.

Crichton is exposed briefly to energy from the Singularity and becomes unstuck in time, flashing forward into the future. He learns that Matala is an agent of the Scorvians, the race the Ilanics are at war with. She intends to kill Verell once he's solved the containment problem, and the ship they're heading to meet is in fact Scorvian not Ilanic. He tries to persuade D'Argo of this, but the Luxan is too besotted with Matala to believe him. We then see three separate future flashes of Crichton attempting to resolve the situation, but each time it ends in everyone's death. Finally he realises that to save the day he must convince D'Argo of the truth. He does so but Matala still kills Verell and escapes in the pod to meet her ship. Verell is able, just before he dies, to self-destruct the pod, release the Singularity, and thus destroy the weapon, Matala and the Scorvian ship.

Buck Rogers Redux: 'I could just be going plain ol' bonkers here, I guess it's about time for that to happen.' When the flashes start Crichton begins to wander around the ship muttering to himself, convincing everyone he's lost the plot entirely. Aeryn asks Zhaan what's wrong with him and her response is just that he's Crichton.

You Can Be More: When Verell and Matala are suspicious of Aeryn because she's a Peacekeeper, D'Argo tells them that she's an escapee and she's now 'one of us', the first real statement of unity among the group and the first time anyone publicly accepts Aeryn's right to be there. She challenges Matala to a workout which turns into a knockdown fight, and Aeryn doesn't pull her punches.

She's beaten by Matala's Scorvian neural stroke, a manoeuvre which stuns the victim, but which betrays Matala's identity.

Big Blue: Zhaan is more attuned to Moya than the others and is able to sense imbalances in her systems caused by the Singularity. She's the one Crichton turns to when he works out what's happening, cementing her role as calm confidante and emotional centre of the group.

I was a Teenage Luxan: 'I am normally unaffected by females in a crisis, it's just, it's been so long.' Poor old D'Argo; eight cycles without female companionship and the first compatible woman he meets deliberately drives him to distraction and then tries to kill him. He reveals to her that he was not really convicted for killing his commanding officer (as he told his crewmates in **101**, 'Premiere'). Crichton overhears this and asks him what he really did, but D'Argo refuses to tell his true crime. As with **102**, 'Throne For a Loss', a rogue D'Argo following his own agenda, regardless of what the others think, is shown to be the greatest threat to the crew's unity and survival. In one of the possible futures he even goes so far as to run Crichton through with his Qualta blade. He is building something called a Shilquen in his workshop (it is an instrument and is finished in **109**, 'DNA Mad Scientist'). His chin is an erogenous zone.

Alien Encounters: Ilanics are genetic cousins of the Luxans and they 'have been blood allies for a thousand cycles'. The Scorvians declared war on the Ilanics three cycles ago and launched an unprovoked attack on a colony, which left 2 million dead. The Luxans are aiding the Ilanics with hardware and troops.

Get Frelled: Matala is 'leading D'Argo round by his mivonks', the first time that word's used, but I think we all know what it means, don't we? In one of the future flashes she shoves her hand down D'Argo's trousers and the look on his face is priceless. He admits to Crichton he's been off balance because he's gone so long without a woman and

Crichton tells him he knows how that feels – they're both desperately prowling around Moya!

Logic Leaps: Crichton's first few visions are sexually charged flashes of he and Matala 'getting horizontal', but although all his other visions come to pass in some form or another, this one never does and it's hard not to conclude it's simply done to titillate and provide convenient tension between Crichton and D'Argo. Also, he's never actually cured of his time flashes, so presumably they just stop once the situation with Matala resolves itself, which is a bit convenient – it smacks of a 'reset button'.

Seen it all Before: The unstuck in time story is a staple of sci-fi, as are time-loop episodes where events are repeated again and again with slight differences. *Star Trek: The Next Generation* did it with 'Cause and Effect', *Star Trek: Deep Space Nine* did it with 'Visionary', *Stargate: SG1* did it with 'Window Of Opportunity' and even *Buffy the Vampire Slayer* used it a bit in the episode 'Life Serial'. The danger is that repetitive episodes like this can get really boring – 'Cause and Effect' was hailed by some as a masterpiece and derided by others as the height of tedium – but *Farscape* pulls it off with aplomb and the tension builds admirably throughout.

Guest Stars: If you've seen *Tackle Happy*, the documentary about two Australian guys who perform as 'Puppetry of the Penis', then you've seen Lisa Hensley before. She's also been in the movies *Paradise Road* and *Mr Reliable*, as well as many TV movies and mini series. John Clayton has a long career behind him in Aussie TV, including *Chopper Squad*.

Backstage: The design on the floor of the gym where Aeryn and Matala fight is the PK logo and will appear throughout the series. It is taken from a piece called *Beat the Whites with the Red Wedge* by El Lissitzky. The US DVD release of this episode includes a commentary track featuring Ben Browder, who says this is his favourite of the first set of episodes.

The Verdict: Superb. Now that the characters have been established in two action-focused runarounds it's time to start paying more attention to the plotting. Ben Browder gets to do his unhinged Crichton act for the first time and is engaging, funny and believable, providing a hint of the extremes his performance will reach. Anthony Simcoe gets a lot to do too, skilfully showing the tender, immature, impulsive side to D'Argo, already moving him away from the stereotypical hard man presented in **101**, 'Premiere'. But the real plaudits go to Babs Greyhosky for the script, which leads the viewer up the garden path again and again and provides the first inkling of the narrative complexity that *Farscape* will soon achieve. Also, the music's far better than in **102**, 'Throne For a Loss', and the effects, especially when Moya is sucked into a black hole, are excellent.

104
I, E.T.

1st US Transmission Date: 7 May 1999
1st UK Transmission Date: 20 December 1999
1st Australian Transmission Date: 10 June 2000

Writer: Sally Lapiduss
Director: Pino Amenta
Guest Cast: Mary Mara (Lyneea), Cayde Tasker (Fostro),
Boris Brkic (Ryymax)

Moya was fitted with a Paddac Beacon by the Peace-keepers – it's designed to go off when it doesn't receive its regular signal from the Control Collar. In order to muffle the signal Moya lands on a planet and submerges in a bog. The beacon is attached to her Primary Neural Nexus, and the operation to remove it could be painful enough to kill her unless they use an anaesthetic substance called Clorium. Crichton, Aeryn and D'Argo leave to search the planet for some. Hunted by locals, who saw Moya's descent, they split up, and Crichton makes contact with a woman, Lyneea, and her son, Fostro. Lyneea is funded by the military to search for extraterrestrials and is staggered to meet a real alien. She hides him from the military. D'Argo is captured but Crichton and Fostro are able to free him. D'Argo and Crichton take some cooking ingredients which can be used to numb Moya.

Meanwhile Moya, who is not suited to planetary gravity, is being crushed by her own bodyweight. Zhaan decides they have to operate without the Clorium, and Rygel, who is the only one small enough to reach the beacon, begins work. Zhaan absorbs as much of Moya's pain as she can. Rygel succeeds, Crichton arrives with the Clorium and Moya flies away.

Buck Rogers Redux: He understands Lyneea's astonishment: 'You've learned that you're not alone in the universe, that space travel is possible, that a zillion of your empirical facts about science, religion are wrong or ... completely suspect.' The sound from the beacon gives Crichton a nervous tic, or at least that's his story – I think he's just cracking up again. He's fast on his feet, realises what Lyneea's radio dishes mean and tells her he sought her out specifically to make contact. He later admits he lied. He finds the planet very reminiscent of Earth and is fond of Lyneea, seeing much of himself in her wonder and scientific curiosity. His hopes that her star charts will help him get his bearings are dashed.

You Can Be More: 'Look I'm new to all this escaped prisoner crap, all right?' Aeryn is having trouble adjusting to her life outside the Peacekeepers and even regrets telling her crewmates how to remove the beacon. But although her loyalties are still divided she genuinely cares about Zhaan, no matter how much she tries to hide it. She's very sensitive to the idea that anyone would laugh at her.

Big Blue: 'We'll face the pain together.' Zhaan puts her life in serious jeopardy to save Moya.

Buckwheat the Sixteenth: 'I don't know what I'm doing. I've always had others to do for me, even in prison.' Hynerians are aquatic, which seems a little weird given that we've never seen Rygel so much as take a shower, let alone go for a swim. He refuses to operate on Moya till there's absolutely no choice, and even bites a chunk out of Aeryn's arm to stop her forcing him, which leads her to promise that one day his greatest fear will come to pass. He 'will die at the hands of a Peacekeeper'. Zhaan realises it's only because he's afraid of failing and of killing Moya. He comes good in the end – the first time he's done anything vaguely likeable.

In the Driving Seat: This is the first time a member of Moya's crew goes to visit Pilot in his chamber and we finally get a good look at it. Prior to this Pilot could have been a tiny puppet on a screen for all we knew; having him there on screen in all his glory interacting with Zhaan adds greatly to the reality of the character.

A Ship, a Living Ship!: 'When Leviathans are young, they often play with a planet's gravity, see how close they can come. There's a tale about an adult male who once touched down on a planet's surface,' though Moya can't confirm if that's just a myth. Moya comes into her own in this episode and emerges as a character in her own right. She is very scared when she lands on the planet, and the pain she experiences is so intense it nearly kills Zhaan. When she's being operated upon she bleeds a green liquid. Pilot tells Zhaan what happens to young Leviathans captured by the Peacekeepers. A potent sleep agent is administered, which destroys the weak and the old, 'which I suppose is part of its purpose. While the Leviathan sleeps, the control collar is set in place, modifications made in propulsion and guidance.'

The Ballad of Aeryn and John: D'Argo observes that, by their standards, Crichton is a savage, and seems to think this idea bothers Aeryn. Could she already be finding Crichton attractive?

Worlds Apart: Moya lands on a world where the inhabitants, Deneans (although this may not be the name of the species but only the race that inhabits that particular continent or country), are at approximately the same level of technological development as twentieth-century Earth. A well-lit city can be seen below as Moya approaches.

Alien Encounters: The Luxans famously once battled a race called the Grisodians. As the Luxans retreated, the Grisodians massacred thousands of women and children. The Luxans took revenge on the Grisodian women and children. When they reach a certain age Luxans circumcise themselves, or what approximates to circumcision for a Luxan, with a bone knife called a Tokaar.

Disney on Acid: The planet reminds Crichton of Dagobah, where Yoda lives. When Aeryn asks him who Yoda is he explains, 'just a little green guy, trains warriors' and she takes this at face value.

Seen it all Before: The 'we are the aliens' story has been done in the *Star Trek: The Next Generation* episode 'First Contact' (not to be confused with the film of the same name).

Bloopers: The beacon won't let metal anywhere near it and Rygel has to use a non-metal cutting tool to remove it – but he does so wearing his metal comms badge. In **101**, 'Premiere' Crichton can't understand D'Argo and Zhaan until he's injected with translator microbes, which implies that both parties need them to be able to understand each other. However Lyneea can understand Crichton and vice versa, even though her world, as a backward planet with no off-world contact, can't have translator microbes.

WHAT did you just say?: Hezmana = Hell. D'Argo uses it, and Crichton, showing that he can pick up the lingo, replies 'What the Hezmana is it?' When Aeryn says 'crap' the use of a human swearword jars; in later episodes she would use 'dren'.

Stats: There are six cargos that Leviathans are forbidden to carry, one of which is Clorium, 'an atmospherically induced isotope of Twinium', which anaesthetises them. Distance can be measured in Lightcycles, which, given that a cycle is roughly a year, is analogous to a light year.

Guest Stars: Mary Mara was a semi-regular during the second season of *ER*, did a well-received guest shot on *Ally McBeal*, and has appeared in many films, including *K-Pax*.

Backstage: Filmed in the second block of episodes, alongside **102**, 'Throne For a Loss', this really does make more sense, both in plot and character terms, if viewed as the second episode, following on from **101**, 'Premiere'. When Crichton is stunned in Lyneea's kitchen, the arm nearest camera is a rubber fake. The US DVD release of this episode includes a commentary track featuring Claudia Black and Anthony Simcoe.

The Verdict: This episode takes a familiar trope – the aliens are coming! – and turns it on its head with such insight, humour and cleverness that it works on every level. Taking Crichton, a guy who is still dealing with the huge paradigm shift that alien contact has caused for him, and placing him in the position of changing someone else's perceptions and outlook so soon, reflects well the confusions and problems he must be having. Also we get to see increased bonding between the crew as the show continues to evolve – Aeryn cares for Zhaan, Rygel cares for Moya and Crichton refuses to leave D'Argo behind. It manages to be both a terrific character piece and a story of ideas, and it's enlivened enormously by a nice turn from Mary Mara. Oh, and the special effects of Moya's landing are simply breathtaking.

105
Exodus From Genesis

1st US Transmission Date: 26 March 1999
1st UK Transmission Date: 10 January 2000
1st Australian Transmission Date: 17 June 2000

Writer: Ro Hume
Director: Brian Henson
Guest Cast: Damian de Montemas (Melkor), Jodie Dry (Kyona)

Moya evades a PK Marauder ship. A cloud of space bugs infests Moya and begins to raise the temperature. Crichton kills one for study. Replicants of the crew begin appearing, setting the temperature controls to maximum and sealing them with gunk that prevents anyone turning them down again. Rygel finds a huge alien nest with a queen churning out replicants and eggs that hatch into insects. Aeryn reacts badly to the heat (see **Alien Encounters**). Zhaan is possessed by the Monarch of the bugs, which are a race called the Drak. Crichton realises that his killing of the bug was interpreted as an act of war and he talks to the Monarch and explains they want no conflict. The Monarch accepts this and explains that when they have spawned they will leave; it also agrees to lower the temperature to help Aeryn as long as the crew will allow themselves to be confined to one room. The Marauder turns up and five PK commandos board Moya. At first Monarch believes that Moya's crew have broken the truce but Rygel explains and she releases the crew and, on Crichton's instructions, turns up the heat. The Commandos succumb to Heat Delirium and are confronted by lots of replicant Crichtons. Crichton tells the PK leader to return with a message that 'next time Crais sees my face, his crew will be dead and he'll be staring up from a pool of his own blood'. He hopes that the multiple versions of Crichton will convince Crais that humans have special powers and he will abandon his pursuit. The Drak finish spawning and fly off into space.

Buck Rogers Redux: 'I'm getting the hang of a few things.' Crichton is finding life a real problem: even the simple things, like opening a door, give him a hard time. He realises that his chances of survival depend upon his ability to adjust; Zhaan thinks he will do fine in the end. Crichton attended JFK High School, and was beaten up by Eddie Marx in Seventh Grade. When confronted with an alien insect he jumps up on a table like a housewife in a bad 60s sitcom. Wuss.

You Can Be More: Aeryn is still having trouble with her new life as a runaway but her relationship with Pilot seems to be helping her adjust. She had put in for a transfer to a Marauder crew before joining Moya. She had always thought that lesser life forms were for squashing, but Crichton, who she still sees as inferior, is helping her change that view.

Big Blue: 'The answer is a reverence for all living things.' Zhaan dissects the Drak and examines its DNA, so she's quite a biologist. Her solution to all problems is patience and time. She is providing Crichton with emotional support and a sympathetic ear, and she knows that she can lean on him in return.

I was a Teenage Luxan: The problem: how to distinguish between the real crew and the replicants. D'Argo's solution – to 'cut off the tip of our small finger for identification'. When it comes to negotiating with the Monarch, D'Argo wants to fight, and without Crichton's level-headedness he would have consigned the crew to conflict and probably death. He admits that Aeryn and Crichton are now his comrades, and he even acknowledges Rygel's contribution. He has seen Peacekeepers die from heat exposure before and found it 'most enjoyable'.

Buckwheat the Sixteenth: 'I am Rygel, sixteenth of my lineage, Dominar of the Hynerian Empire. I am at once your equal and your humble petitioner requesting an audience.' Rygel's mother had his elder brothers banished because he was her favourite. Again Rygel saves the day because he's the only one small enough to go into the bulkhead and find the Drak nest. He handles the final negotiation very well and effortlessly wins the respect of Monarch.

In the Driving Seat: Pilot cradles the dying Aeryn tenderly and tells her, 'It is strange to be so close to a Peacekeeper I do not fear. That is a compliment.' He agrees that he and Aeryn work well together.

A Ship, a Living Ship!: Zhaan: 'Moya is alive, she's our protector but she's also our servant ... It's a mutual, symbiotic relationship.' Moya has a terrace that is open to space but is protected by a force shield so the crew can go outside; she also has water showers.

The Ballad of Aeryn and John: Crichton thinks that, since they're all stuck on board, they should make the best of it. Aeryn says she wants to be neither family nor friends. At his insistence that she might need someone to be there, her reply is 'No offence, human, but what could I possibly need from you?' 'Oh, I don't know. Manners, personality, stock tips . . .' is Crichton's response.

Aeryn's weakness forces her to rely on others for the first time and Crichton promises to kill her if need be before she enters a coma. He then takes the huge risk of telling Monarch to turn the heat up to disable the PK commandos, even though it endangers Aeryn's life. By taking the risk, and making the promise, Crichton wins Aeryn's respect and even earns a smile from her. He tenderly strokes her cheek when she's ill, which is a dead giveaway.

Worlds Apart: The Luxan planet is called, imaginatively, Luxan, and it's a hot world.

Alien Encounters: Dentics are an insect species which clean your teeth by eating bacteria and food particles. The Drak are a hive insect species with a queen (Monarch) and drones (the aggregate). They live in space but require heat to give birth. They can replicate other life forms perfectly, which helps them infiltrate ships, although they cannot speak and must possess a host to speak for them. They're actually pretty reasonable, and when they've spawned they fly away again, so no harm, no foul. Sebaceans are cold-blooded and heat affects them terribly. First they lose short-term memory, then motor functions, and then long-term memory. At that point they slip into a coma they call 'the living death', upon which their fellows will kill them out of mercy, the only situation in which Sebaceans will do that. The more we learn about Hynerians the dafter the fact that they're aquatic becomes. For example, Rygel is a painter – how exactly does one paint underwater? (Please don't email to say 'with water colours'.)

Disney on Acid: Crichton promises to rent Zhaan a copy of *Animal House*. Which isn't so far-fetched, really, because Blockbuster get everywhere – I can believe they've got branches in the Uncharted Territories, next door to Starbucks.

Seen it all Before: *Invasion Of The Bodysnatchers*; and the nest is very *Aliens*. This is the first time *Farscape* pulls what will become one of its trademark tricks – taking a done-to-death sci-fi standard story and playing it pretty much as expected but then, just when you think you've seen it all before, adding an extra twist in the final third that takes it to new places. *Star Trek: Voyager* would have concluded the story with the truce, but on *Farscape* they throw in the Marauder and explore the ramifications. The writers always push the idea that bit further, which is what enables the show to be original in a genre where most tales have already been told before.

Logic Leaps: So the Drak replicate people, fair enough – they use the DNA to do that, but surely it's a leap too far that they replicate people *with all their clothes on* and, in D'Argo's case, with a Qualta Blade as well. Why do they never replicate Rygel or Pilot?

Bloopers: D'Argo says they could never outrun a PK Command Carrier, but they've done it twice before, once by StarBursting and once using Crichton's slingshot technique.

WHAT did you just say?: Yotz, which basically means Hell, appears, as in 'what the yotz was that?'

Stats: Moya's scanners can detect the Marauder, but the Marauder can't see Moya through the Drak swarm – so the Leviathan has better scanners than PK standard. The Marauder's maximum speed is Hetch 7, and it carries a crew of 5 PK commandos whose success is measured by body count.

Guest Stars: Damian de Montemas plays Jason in the excellent Aussie twentysomething soap, *The Secret Life Of Us*.

Backstage: The Drak queen was originally called the Sultana, until someone pointed out to the American writers that in Britain and Australia a Sultana is a kind of raisin. This episode was filmed at the same time as **101**, 'Premiere'. When Aeryn's replicant kicks Crichton, Claudia Black actually floored Ben Browder on set. This is the only time you'll see Peacekeepers with facial tattoos: the idea was dropped after this episode. The voice of Monarch is Virginia Hey's, treated to make it lower. The US DVD release of this episode includes a commentary track featuring Brian Henson and Virginia Hey.

The Verdict: A key episode for the development of the crew. Zhaan and Crichton bond, as do Aeryn and Pilot, and even D'Argo expresses some regard for each of his crewmates in turn, if grudgingly. It's the character work that really stands out, although the bugs impress, especially when they stand up, and the sense of threat is well established. Not a stand-out episode but not a turkey either and, for a show still finding its feet, perfectly acceptable.

106
Thank God it's Friday, Again

1st US Transmission Date: 23 April 1999
1st UK Transmission Date: 17 January 2000
1st Australian Transmission Date: 24 June 2000

Writer: David Wilks
Director: Rowan Woods
Guest Cast: Angie Milliken (Volmae), Ken Blackburn (Hybin), Tina Thomsen (Tanga), Selina Muller (D'Argo's girlfriend)

D'Argo leaves the ship in a fit of rage and descends to the planet Sykar. The crew follow him but find he is working in the fields harvesting Tannot root, which all the workers also eat. He has a room and a girlfriend, and intends to stay. Crichton and Zhaan try and persuade him to leave. He tells them the next day is a rest day but when dawn comes it is a work day and Zhaan joins D'Argo in the fields. Crichton is ambushed by a group of workers who insert a worm into his naval and he is forced to eat Tannot root to stop the worm hurting him. Zhaan falls under the same influence as D'Argo and tells Crichton she has also decided to stay. The people who ambushed Crichton tell him that the root is addictive – they are naturally immune, but he needs the worm to be so. Mysterious outsiders come to the planet regularly and collect the root, which has led to the breakdown of their society. They gave Crichton the worm so he could help them. The planet's leader, Volmae, asks Crichton to help her steal the last shipment of Tannot root, and he discovers that the ones who collect it are Peacekeepers.

Meanwhile, Rygel's bodily fluids have become explosive as a result of his eating Tannot root and Aeryn takes him to Moya to clear his system. They use his new ability in a confrontation with Volmae – Rygel urinates explosively on the group from above to keep them subdued while Crichton explains to her that the Tannot root is used to fuel PK weapons. She and the immune workers unite, a real rest day is finally called, and they decide to resist the Peacekeepers when they next arrive.

Buck Rogers Redux: Crichton manages to elude all his crewmates for three whole days.

You Can Be More: Aeryn finally encounters a situation her Pulse Rifle can't get her out of and is forced to use her intelligence to diagnose Rygel. She resists, and finds it very hard to focus, but eventually she succeeds and is a little proud of herself, although she does moan to Crichton about how difficult it was: '[it] was like a field strategy exercise, only the enemy wasn't trying to kill me. The enemy was a puzzle and there were lots of different pieces.'

Big Blue: 'My choice to join the Delvian Seek . . . occurred in the matter of a blink of an eye. One moment, I was . . . a savage capable of anything. The next . . . I knew my true path.' This is Zhaan's first time off the ship since **101**, 'Premiere'. When she and Crichton are sharing a room she changes behind a screen. Why? Nudity isn't a taboo for her at all.

I was a Teenage Luxan: D'Argo succumbs to Luxan hyper-rage, which seems to be provoked by the presence of another male, in this case Crichton, who could be a rival. D'Argo tries to find and kill Crichton before eventually leaving the ship. He tells Zhaan that when he was a boy he dreamed of two different lives: 'I would be a magnificent warrior, merciless in battle, fearless, the kind they write shintok sonnets about ... I also wanted a simple life – family, children, a frotash garden.' He had thought that Sykar was that second life but it was an illusion, and he worries that he is destined never to be happy. He can fly Aeryn's Prowler. He admits that he has been a prisoner and fugitive for more cycles than he was a warrior.

Buckwheat the Sixteenth: Aeryn says that it's only people who know Rygel that actually want to kill him. When Rygel is frozen to aid the diagnosis, he appears to be wearing a huge pair of grotty Y-fronts. Glamorous.

In the Driving Seat: Pilot begins to emerge as a character when he admits to Aeryn that he has some weaknesses. A pilot, bonded to a Leviathan, is 'a navigator, a monitor of all the living ship's functions ... Moya was born with a very complete bank of scientific data. I only comprehend a fraction, I'm afraid.' He and Aeryn work well together to diagnose Rygel, and the trust between them, established in **105**, 'Exodus From Genesis', grows.

Worlds Apart: Sykar is a lush world with hot days and cool nights.

Alien Encounters: The inhabitants of Sykar are Sebacean labourers. Aeryn says they are distant cousins of Sebaceans – that's why they can stand the heat. The workers have tanned skins from working in the fields all day, whereas Volmae, who stays indoors, has almost translucent skin.

Disney on Acid: Sykar's city reminds Crichton of *Mad Max Beyond Thunderdome*: 'I think I've seen this one before.

Mel Gibson, Tina Turner . . . cage match! Oh, don't worry, nobody saw the third one anyway.'

Get Frelled: Way to go D'Argo – he finally gets his oats and that seems to put a cap on his hyper-rage, which is probably just a Luxan term for extreme sexual frustration. He tells Zhaan that he was intending to approach her at the next party on Sykar, and she tells him that she would have accepted his advances. Crichton is freaked when Zhaan, sleeping in the same bed, grabs his crotch in her sleep.

What Does This Do?: Only on *Farscape* would the final showdown hinge on a character's ability to piss fire; imagine Harry Kim saving Voyager in such a manner, or Neelix – just doesn't compute, does it?

Seen it all Before: Very similar to *Stargate SG1*'s episode, 'Beneath The Surface', and *Star Trek – Voyager*'s two-parter, 'Work Force'. Happily both those episodes came after *Farscape*, so it got there first.

Bloopers: At the start Crichton is hiding from D'Argo in plain sight. D'Argo must be *incredibly* short-sighted not to have seen him.

WHAT did you just say?: Aeryn on Volmae: 'She gives me a woody [She notices Crichton's expression] . . . I've heard you say it often, when you don't trust someone or they make you nervous . . .' Crichton saves her: 'Willies, she gives you the willies!' Dren = swear word, substitutes for crap, and other excrement expletives.

Stats: Tannot root, when mixed with certain chemicals, produces Chakan Oil, which fuels all Peacekeeper weapons. Presumably there are many planets like Sykar which are similarly enslaved and used to keep supplies flowing. Henta = measure of distance, approximately an inch.

Guest Stars: Angie Milliken, a famous stage actress in Australia, appeared as Jo Moody in *Feds* and returned to

Farscape to voice Yoz in **209**, 'Out Of Their Minds'. Ken Blackburn appeared in the excellent film *The Frighteners*. Tina Thomsen was Finlay Roberts on *Home and Away* before moving to *Shark Bay*.

Backstage: The US DVD release of this episode includes a commentary track featuring Rockne S O'Bannon and Anthony Simcoe.

The Verdict: A colourful episode with good location filming, but it's the marvellous turn from Angie Milliken, under very impressive make-up, that stands out as the episode's most successful element. It's the weirdest performance the show's ever seen – on a planet of junkies she's immune, but still comes across as *way* out of it (many fans have derided her performance as being *too* out there). The development of Aeryn's character is well handled, and D'Argo's becoming more layered too. The only real problem is D'Argo's hyper-rage: it's never explained at all and is a forced and unconvincing way of starting the story.

107
PK Tech Girl

1st US Transmission Date: 15 March 1999 (see **Backstage**)
1st UK Transmission Date: 24 January 2000
1st Australian Transmission Date: 16 September 2000

Writer: Nan Hagan
Director: Tony Tilse
Guest Cast: Alyssa-Jane Cook (Gilina Renaez – PK Technician),
Derek Amer (Teurac), Phillip Hinton (Voice of Teurac),
Peter Astridge (Lomus), Christopher Truswell (Voice of Lomus),
Peter Knowles (Evran), David Wheeler (Capt. Selto Durka)

Moya comes across a derelict ship, the *Zelbinion*, most powerful of all PK ships, lost in battle a hundred cycles ago. They board her hoping to salvage weapons or star charts but the ship has been gutted by Sheyangs. They encounter Gilina, a PK Tech. Crais found the *Zelbinion* and sent Gilina across with a team to investigate its destruction while he continued his hunt for Moya. The Sheyangs killed all her comrades, looted the ship and said they would return for the Defence Shield, which is not badly damaged. Their ship appears and charges weapons to attack Moya but the appearance of a wrathful D'Argo makes them hesitate. Crichton and Gilina work to get the Shield operational and succeed mere seconds before the Sheyangs lose patience with D'Argo's bluffing. There is a spare Shield and Gilina agrees to help them install it on Moya. The Sheyangs launch an assault and one of them breaks through the shield and boards the *Zelbinion*. Aeryn kills him. They broadcast a distress signal to Crais to force the Sheyangs to flee, and Gilina returns to the *Zelbinion* to wait for pickup.

Buck Rogers Redux: 'I try to save a life a day. Usually it's my own.' Crichton got a doctorate in Cosmic Theory. He had a poster of Clint Eastwood from *The Good, The Bad and The Ugly* on his bedroom wall.

You Can Be More: 'Showing pain is a sign of weakness.' At first Aeryn is extremely hard on Gilina and looks likely to kill her, but after Gilina tells the truth, saves their lives and installs the Shield on Moya, they find common ground and Aeryn advises her how to avoid being executed or exiled for having contact with aliens. She even gives Gilina the faintest of smiles. In spite of everything she still longs to go home. She is shocked at the demotion of her unit (see **The Insane Military Commander**) but refuses to show the pain of the loss she feels, except when speaking to Gilina: 'I hope you can only ever imagine how horrible it is to never return to the life that you love.' She grew up entirely on ships like the *Zelbinion*.

I was a Teenage Luxan: 'I spit on your grave, you sons of cowards!' D'Argo loses his temper with the Sheyangs even before they fire on Moya and it's this bravado that convinces them not to attack. He resents Zhaan asking him to mislead the enemy but rises well to the challenge and perhaps learns that some situations are best handled by cunning.

Buckwheat the Sixteenth: Rygel says he was deposed over 130 cycles ago, contradicting what he said in **102**, 'Throne For a Loss'. The *Zelbinion* was the first PK ship he ended up on, and he was tortured by its Captain, Durka. He finds what appears to be Durka's body – he shot himself. Rygel spits on the face of his torturer's corpse and steals back his royal sash and seal.

In the Driving Seat: Pilot and Moya are afraid of fire.

The Insane Military Commander: Although he doesn't appear, Crais is still hot on Moya's trail and is close by throughout the episode. He demoted Aeryn's entire unit and they can only be reinstated upon her death.

A Ship, a Living Ship!: Moya's lack of offensive or defensive capability again lands her in trouble, but now she has a Defence Shield.

The Ballad of Aeryn and John: Aeryn catches Crichton and Gilina kissing and is thrown for a loop – she tells him she doesn't like being 'ambushed'. Crichton asks her whether she's ever 'just "clicked" with a guy'. Her reply changes the nature of their relationship forever: 'Yes, but I didn't let it . . . in the beginning I found you interesting . . . but only for a moment.' Crichton says it's good to clear the air, but Aeryn has again shown a small chink in her armour.

Alien Encounters: Sheyangs are a scavenger race who will attack the moment they sense weakness. They can breathe fire. Peacekeepers are, according to Aeryn, hired by other cultures to keep order and harmony; Rygel says their job is to 'kidnap, torture and assassinate'.

Disney on Acid: Crichton appears to be telling Gilina the plot of *Lethal Weapon 3* before getting sidetracked into describing love stories, which apparently Peacekeepers have as well (this seems unlikely given what we later learn about their breeding habits and the rules against personal attachments of any kind). When D'Argo says the *Zelbinion* was considered invincible, Crichton replies: 'Yeah, well, just ask Leonardo DiCaprio, even the big ones go down'. (On set Ben Browder ad libbed and changed Leonardo DiCaprio to Bill Clinton, but they made him change it back.)

Get Frelled: Crichton finally gets to do some snogging, although what it is that he and Gilina have about each other's eyebrows is food for disturbed thought.

What Does This Do?: Gilina says that human men and Sebacean men are similar. She says this while sitting in his lap doing a little gentle wriggling, so what exact similarity was she remarking on . . .?

Logic Leaps: The ship's been looted first by whoever destroyed it (see **115**, 'Durka Returns') and secondly by the Sheyangs. Yet Rygel found his seal of office just lying in Durka's office?

Bloopers: When Crichton's holding the terminals apart it cuts to Gilina doing rewiring. Watch closely and you'll see that in one shot she's wearing her jumpsuit, the next just her T-shirt, and then she's got her jumpsuit on again.

WHAT did you just say?: Crichton's explanation of humanity to Gilina is that humans are like Sebaceans, 'but we haven't conquered other worlds yet so we just kick the crap out of each other.'

Stats: The invincible *Zelbinion* was famous even on Luxan. Gilina considers it a 'cultural treasure'. Time measurement: a Microt is a second.

Guest Stars: Alyssa-Jane Cook is perhaps best known as the host of *Sex/Life*, although she's also appeared in *E Street* and *Above The Law*.

Backstage: This episode was the first *Farscape* to air. It was shown as a special preview on SciFi Channel's sister channel, USA Network, four days before **101**, 'Premiere' was shown on SciFi. It is also the first episode filmed all at once and not in tandem with another episode, which David Kemper believed heralded a higher level of quality – and he's right. Anthony Simcoe: 'We really found the tone of the show in episode seven . . . as soon as we hit that episode I feel we all discovered, as a company, what *Farscape* was.' In *TV Zone* Claudia Black agreed: 'I also loved "PK Tech Girl" . . . it was the first time we'd expanded the scale of *Farscape* beyond the studio and said "let's make it filmic".' Gilina is the first character that David Kemper rescued: she was to die at the end of this episode but he liked her so much he changed the ending so he could bring her back. Exactly the same thing would later happen with Chiana in **115**, 'Durka Returns'.

The Verdict: Moving effortlessly from atmospheric space mystery, to romance, to action thriller, this is real edge of the seat stuff. Alyssa-Jane Cook is excellent as Gilina and the romance between her and Crichton is moving and believable. The sets are stunning, but to be honest, the Sheyang are a bit daft. They're well realised and fun, but still just fire-breathing Space Frogs at the end of the day. Rygel's subplot is so underdeveloped and unexplored you wonder why they bothered; happily it turns out to be a set-up for future developments. In the end the love story carries the episode and it's nice that Gilina doesn't end up dead in a blaze-of-glory self-sacrifice, which is what would have happened on most shows.

108
That Old Black Magic

1st US Transmission Date: 11 June 1999
1st UK Transmission Date: 31 January 2000
1st Australian Transmission Date: 15 September 2000

Writer: Richard Manning
Director: Brendan Maher
Guest Cast: Chris Haywood (Maldis), Lani Tupu (Captain Bialar Crais), Christine Stephen-Daly (Lt Teeg), Jake Blundell (Lt Orn), Grant Bowler (Shaman Liko), Wadih Dona (Tauvo Crais)

While on a commerce planet Crichton is lured into the domain of a Vampire Sorcerer called Maldis. While his unconscious body is taken back to Moya by Aeryn, his consciousness is in Maldis's realm. Maldis brings Crais to his realm as well and sets him upon Crichton, egging Crais into a murderous rage while Crichton tries to convince him that his brother's death (**101**, 'Premiere') was an accident. Outside Aeryn and D'Argo try to shoot their way in but Maldis freezes them in stasis. Meanwhile Zhaan has met Liko, a priest who tells her that Maldis rules the entire planet, the populace are unable to leave and he kills them at will. He thinks that by uniting their spiritual powers he and Zhaan can defeat Maldis, and he helps Zhaan rediscover how to inflict pain with her mind. Maldis sends Crais back to his ship just as Crichton is about to kill him, and tells Crichton that now Crais will be doubly determined to pursue him, which will bring the PK Command Carrier within Maldis's reach and allow him to wreak havoc. He is about to kill Crichton when Zhaan and Liko succeed in making Maldis momentarily vulnerable and Crichton is able to punch him, although the strain costs Liko his life. Maldis is dispersed by Zhaan, but one day he will coalesce . . .

Buck Rogers Redux: Crichton's mother's maiden name was MacDougal, he skipped Third Grade, and he lost his virginity with Karen Shaw in the back of a truck. This is the first time we see him wearing his yellow flight suit since **101**, 'Premiere'; his uniform must be in the wash. It is Crichton's idea to talk to Crais and try to resolve their differences. He tries his best to convince him that he didn't mean to kill his brother, pointing out the huge technological disparity between his WDP and the Prowler. When that fails he tries to call a truce and get Crais to join him against Maldis. Finally, when all else fails, he accepts that he has to kill Crais, and almost certainly would have had Maldis not spirited Crais away. Crichton dislocated his left shoulder once when he crashed his motorbike, but he snapped it back in again himself. He is not only recording messages for his dad, he talks to his best friend DK too. There's an edge of hysteria in his laughter when he wakes up on Moya, indicating that he's still close to not coping.

You Can Be More: Aeryn scoffs at the idea of Sorcery and shoots at the force-protected wall again and again, even when it's clear it isn't working. However, her idea of overloading her rifle until it explodes would possibly have worked, forcing Maldis to take action, so if nothing else she demonstrates that a big enough gun can solve most problems. She compliments Zhaan on her actions, apologises for doubting her, and calls her a fine warrior. Unfortunately this is the last thing Zhaan wants to hear.

Big Blue: 'I was a savage . . . I thought I'd eradicated it for ever . . . now I have to rid myself of it again and I don't know if I can.' At some point in her past, before she became a priest, Zhaan was in touch with her dark side. She's spent years moving beyond that and it is no longer part of her. She is forced to rediscover her old ways in order to destroy Maldis, reawakens her demons, and is terrified that she may never be able to quell them again. She can inflict pain with her mind, and when she really goes for it can fry someone's brain with crackling blue energy. Her power has a long range too – she inflicts pain on Rygel while he is on Moya and she is on the planet below, something that she admits she 'almost enjoyed'. When Crichton tries to console her back on Moya she lashes out with her mind and warns him off.

I was a Teenage Luxan: D'Argo has a heightened sense of smell and can track Crichton by scent.

Buckwheat the Sixteenth: Rygel has Klendian flu and remains on Moya moaning about it. When the unconscious Crichton is brought to him for care he pronounces him dead, performs a 'Ceremony of Passage' and claims all Crichton's possessions for himself.

The Insane Military Commander: Crais is ordered by the PK Council to return and explain his failure to recapture

Moya. Only he and Lt Teeg know of these orders and she
swears to remain loyal to Crais if he decides to disobey
them. Crais destroys the orders but, according to Maldis,
was seriously considering obeying them. After his fight with
Crichton, however, he is more determined than ever and
kills Lt Teeg because she's the only one aboard who knows
he's disobeying orders. His younger brother was named
Tauvo and their father told Bialar to look after him. They
were drafted into the Peacekeepers as young boys and rose
through the ranks to become officers. Crais's thirst for
vengeance is driven primarily by his own guilt at not
protecting Tauvo better. By the end of the episode he has
gone entirely rogue, driven insane with hatred for Crichton.

Worlds Apart: The commerce planet is unnamed but it is
so hot that Sebaceans could not survive during daytime.

Alien Encounters: Delvian priests can ascend to a twelfth
level, three higher than Zhaan's.

Disney on Acid: Crichton greets Rygel in Oz-style upon
waking: 'It's not Kansas, and you're way too homely to be
Auntie Em, but come here, Toto.'

Get Frelled: No sex this week, although Zhaan looks all set
to jump on Liko to better test his aphrodisiac potions.
Crichton kisses Rygel too, but I think it was strictly
platonic!

Seen it all Before: *Star Trek*'s episode 'Arena' took the
hero and the bad guy and forced them to fight at the behest
of a higher power, as did *Blake's 7*'s rip-off, 'The Duel'.

Stats: Area can be divided into Dekkas, which is a
quadrant or some form of map reference.

Guest Stars: Chris Haywood has a long career in Austra-
lian film and TV behind him, including appearances in
Breaker Morant, *Muriel's Wedding* and *Shine*. Grant
Bowler was the host on the Aussie version of the reality TV
game show *The Mole* and appeared in Russel Mulcahy's
TV version of Nevil Shute's classic book *On The Beach*.

The Verdict: The sets for Maldis's domain are very impressive indeed, as is the opening FX shot of the planet. Although Crais is mentioned in the opening narration, and referred to often, he's not appeared since **101**, 'Premiere', so his reappearance is long overdue. He's given a lot of depth in this episode and Lani Tupu's marvellously unhinged performance serves to re-establish him as a threat. Energy vampires are a sci-fi cliché but making Maldis a virtual sorcerer makes him a formidable opponent, and takes *Farscape* further away from straight sci-fi and into a looser fantasy realm. Also, it's good to see Zhaan getting something to do other than dispense advice and look mellow, her lapse into instability makes her a far more interesting character.

109
DNA Mad Scientist

1st US Transmission Date: 18 June 1999
1st UK Transmission Date: 14 February 2000
1st Australian Transmission Date: 16 September 2000

Writer: Tom Blomquist
Director: Andrew Prowse
Guest Cast: Adrian Getley (NamTar), Julian Garner (Voice of NamTar), Sarah Burns (Kornata)

An alien called NamTar offers Moya's crew maps to their homeworlds. These maps will allow them to avoid areas of PK jurisdiction in return for samples of their genetic material and one of Pilot's arms, which Rygel, D'Argo and Zhaan cut off despite Pilot's protests. Crichton and Aeryn are horrified by their crewmates' actions. The data crystal NamTar gives them contains the three maps but there is too much data – only one map can be downloaded into Moya's databanks, destroying the other two in the process. Rygel steals and hides the crystal to try and force Zhaan and D'Argo to download his map and take him home. They try to lock him in his room but he tricks them and

locks them in there instead while he goes to the flight deck
to download the data. Crichton, finding out from Nam-
Tar's assistant, Kornata, that the crystal is a trap which
will destroy Moya's databanks, manages to destroy the
crystal in time.

Aeryn agrees to give genetic material to NamTar in
return for a map to a non-PK Sebacean colony where she
can settle, but instead of taking a sample from her NamTar
secretly injects her with some of Pilot's DNA. It transpires
that the laboratory is an old research centre that was run
by Kornata. NamTar was a lab rat, whose intelligence she
raised until he took over and used her and her team as
experimental subjects to augment his own genetic make-up
in a quest to become the perfect being. NamTar intends to
use Aeryn to isolate the multi-tasking mental abilities of
Pilot's people which he will then inject into himself. Aeryn
begins to transform into a Sebacean/Pilot hybrid. Crichton
and Pilot help Kornata develop a serum for both NamTar
and Aeryn – NamTar reverts to a harmless lab rat and
Aeryn reverts to her normal Sebacean physiology.

Buck Rogers Redux: Crichton is normally neurotic about
food and drink and analyses it before touching it. However, he's so depressed at not finding Earth in NamTar's
database that he gulps down some alien booze without a
second thought and gets nicely drunk for his pains. He's
astonished that Pilot doesn't seem angry about having his
arm cut off, but unlike Aeryn he never confronts his
crewmates about their actions.

You Can Be More: Aeryn is depressed because she can
never go home, but she knows about some Sebacean
colonies where she could fit in and clutches at this last
straw of hope. When she begins to change she admits to
Crichton that she is scared. She also exhibits the compassion she was so scornful of in **101**, 'Premiere', when she
protests to D'Argo and Zhaan about their treatment of
Pilot, although she excuses it as acceptable if it's compassion for a comrade. Although the forced evolution of
NamTar's experiments is reversed she does evolve as a

person (yes, I know that sounds very *Star Trek*, but it's done well, and with subtlety): she starts the episode telling Crichton that, as a Peacekeeper soldier, she was always 'a member of a division, platoon, a unit, a team. I've never been on my own, John ... Ever.' Yet after her transformation she says that she's always thought of herself 'in terms of survival, life and death, keeping the body alive, but what NamTar did to me ... it was me, inside. The real me.'

Big Blue: This is a different Zhaan to the calm, mellow priest of the first seven episodes. Her experiences in **108**, 'That Old Black Magic' have wrought huge changes in her personality – she's ruthless, vicious, conniving, deceptive, nasty and full of rage. After a mere third of a season *Farscape* has entirely altered the personality of one of its main characters – what other show would do something so brave and risky so soon?

I was a Teenage Luxan: D'Argo again tries to bully others into doing everything his way but Zhaan won't have it and Rygel doesn't trust him. He refuses to apologise to Pilot and admits he'd do the same thing again in the circumstances, even telling Aeryn that he'd do it to any of them if he had to, but he has finished the Shilquen he was building in **103**, 'Back and Back and Back to The Future', and he comes to play it for Pilot.

Buckwheat the Sixteenth: Rygel is again revealed as the negotiator, having made first contact with NamTar and brokered the deal for the maps. He's also the most ruthlessly self-interested one among a crew of self-interested people – he even stored food cubes for himself when the rest of the crew were starving. He had a secret escape route from his cell that the Peacekeepers never found, and he has hiding places similarly concealed.

In the Driving Seat: Pilot tells Crichton that a pilot bonded to a Leviathan gives itself to the service of the 'ship first, then those who travel aboard her ... My species is incapable of space flight on our own ... this is the trade off we make for the chance to see the galaxy.' He feels it is an 'equitable arrangement'. He claims not to be angry about having his arm cut off, but when the data crystal turns out to be useless he sarcastically taunts the crew with barely disguised relish.

The Ballad of Aeryn and John: Crichton offers to take Aeryn home with him, but she replies, 'Me, on a planet full of billions of you?' They emerge as natural allies in this episode, as they are the only two who do not mutilate Pilot and, although that's arguably because they were the only ones who had nothing to gain by doing so, it seems unlikely that they would have in other circumstances. They go drinking together, seem more relaxed in each other's company, and Aeryn is willing to show weakness and ask for his help – something she's been reluctant to do before.

Worlds Apart: NamTar's base is on some sort of asteroid that looks as though it's made of dead animal parts – could it be a calcified Budong (**207**, 'Home On The Remains')? Delvia has at least three moons.

Disney on Acid: Crichton gets homesick for the three stooges: 'Larry, Curly and Moe just found out that they can only use one of the maps.'

Get Frelled: Hynerians are not really 'body breeders' which I assume means they have an egg-based reproduction system like most aquatic life (this seems to be directly contradicted in a host of subsequent episodes, most notably **318**, 'Fractures'), but their ear-brows are very sensitive indeed (these are shades of Ferengi ears on *Star Trek*).

What Does This Do?: A reference is made to Zhaan's Numa, implying that is the name of her reproductive organ, or one of them anyway.

Seen it all Before: Mary Shelley's *Frankenstein* is given a *Farscape* twist and melded with elements of HG Wells's *The Island Of Doctor Moreau*.

Logic Leaps: At first it seems that NamTar can locate a planet by matching a species to information in his database – this is why Earth is not in there, because he's never sampled a human. However, Zhaan and D'Argo's later discussion of the applications of NamTar's work seems to imply that by some magic process he can map a route to a homeworld using information from the DNA itself, which is daft, really. When NamTar is defeated and Kornata is back in charge, why did Moya's crew not ask her to extract useable navigation data from the system for them and fly off home?

WHAT did you just say?: Frell = expletive, meaning to have sex, used most often in exactly the same way as f**k, i.e. 'Frell You', 'Get Frelled' etc.

Stats: NamTar's database contains 11 million life forms.

Guest Stars: Julian Garner was Simon Broadhurst on *Home And Away*.

The Verdict: All the elements that make *Farscape* so unique are here: gross body horror, amazing design from the Creature Workshop, superb effects, bucket loads of real internal conflict and distrust, violence, sex and a unique visual aesthetic. After eight episodes finding its feet this is the point at which the show comes into its own, and this is a cracking episode.

110
They've Got a Secret

1st US Transmission Date: 25 June 1999
1st UK Transmission Date: 21 February 2000
1st Australian Transmission Date: 22 September 2000

Writer: Sally Lapiduss
Director: Ian Watson

The crew are sweeping Moya for leftover PK devices when D'Argo falls into a shaft and finds a PK-installed hatch.

He kicks it loose and releases a stream of particles. He is
blasted out into space and collected by Aeryn's Prowler.
Moya begins to malfunction, systems go down, the DRDs
turn hostile and Pilot passes out. Crichton believes the
particles are a PK virus that is destroying Moya but
eventually they realise Moya herself is causing the crisis –
she is trying to kill them. They are able to switch off the
DRDs and decide to sever the neural connections to
Moya's higher functions to protect themselves. Crichton
goes down the shaft to investigate the hatch and finds a
huge chamber with a Leviathan foetus inside – Moya is
pregnant. By rupturing the hatch D'Argo released the
particles which caused conception. Aeryn stops cutting
Moya's higher functions just in time, they switch on the
DRDs (which the baby needs to survive), and Crichton
convinces Moya that they are not a threat to the child. The
ship returns to normal and Pilot revives.

Meanwhile D'Argo is suffering mental confusion as a
result of his exposure to space, and his secrets are revealed.

Buck Rogers Redux: Crichton is still staggered by the level
of science he's encountering and is in awe of the Peacekeepers' eradication of all diseases, wishing it could be like
that back on Earth. But when Aeryn asks him why he
wants to return to a world with so much disease and
suffering he plaintively replies, 'you guys don't have
chocolate'.

You Can Be More: Aeryn takes over for the unconscious
Pilot with ease, using the controls without difficulty.
Crichton thinks that some of Pilot's knowledge and skill
has remained with her after her augmentation (**109**, 'DNA
Mad Scientist').

I was a Teenage Luxan: D'Argo was married to a
Sebacean, Lo'Laan, and they had a son, Jothee. They fled
to a new world but they were still reviled as outsiders.
Lo'Lann's brother, a Peacekeeper named Macton, was
disgusted by the marriage and killed Lo'Laan. Then, with
his sister's dried blood still on his hands, he arrested

D'Argo for the murder. Before being put on trial D'Argo was able to take Jothee to a secret place where he would be safe, but he's tormented by not knowing whether his son remained safe, or is even still alive. So his true crime, which was referred to in **103**, 'Back and Back and Back to the Future', is revealed. He keeps a hologram of his wife and son in an open wound on his chest. While hallucinating he believes Zhaan is his wife and Rygel his son. He is revealed to be a total softie – all puppy-eyed love for Lo'Laan, and piggyback rides and tickling for Jothee. Now that his constant bad temper and his habit of reacting to everything with violence has been put into context it makes him more a person and less a 'noble warrior' stereotype.

In the Driving Seat: Pilot's arm has grown back already, so either he's a really fast healer or quite some time has passed between episodes. His tendrils run all the way throughout the ship.

The Insane Military Commander: Aeryn mentions that Crais will follow them wherever they go, but she's not seen him at all since **101**, 'Premiere' and he's only appeared when brought into the arena by Maldis (**108**, 'That Old Black Magic'), so either they have had some off-screen encounters or it's just the writer reminding us of Crais, because, for the big nemesis of the series, he's not exactly cropping up every week, is he?

A Ship, a Living Ship!: 'Our beloved ship may be trying to kill us!' Moya can control the DRDs directly, see through them and hear through them too. She also appears able to understand Crichton when he tells her, through a DRD, that they won't harm the child. Moya has a Bio-Polymer structure and can function without Pilot, although life-support and other such functions are controlled by Pilot since Moya doesn't need them – they're only there for the convenience of passengers. Moya takes some serious damage from Aeryn cutting into her connectors. She must be very resilient indeed because you'd expect at least partial brain damage if the connection is partially cut,

wouldn't you? Pilot explains the system malfunctions: 'To
nourish the foetus through the very tenuous period right
after conception, Moya needed to reroute a few resources.'
Pilot has no idea at all what to expect from the pregnancy
or what course it will take.

Alien Encounters: Aeryn reveals that Peacekeepers go in for
racial purity – right from birth they have it trained into
them to keep the bloodlines pure. Unlike humans Delvian
bodies contain no bacteria. Luxans can survive for about
a quarter of an arn in space as long as they are revived
quickly, but leave them too long and they die of interna-
thermia. Zhaan refers to D'Argo's 'pulses', so he has more
than one heart. Peacekeepers are 'born and bred on ships.
We're in a totally controlled environment until we're sent
on our first Peacekeeper mission.' They are given inocula-
tions against diseases and as soon as a new one is
discovered their scientists neutralise it – they're entirely
disease free.

Disney on Acid: When the DRDs look at Crichton he
describes it as 'like the cave scene in a Yosemite Sam
cartoon'.

Get Frelled: Leviathans don't – they appear able to
reproduce asexually without the contribution of another
member of their species.

Seen it all Before: *Star Trek: The Next Generation* had a
similar idea in their final season episode 'Emergence' when
the Enterprise gave birth, despite being a machine and not
a creature, like Moya.

Stats: The DRDs, which are wholly mechanical, can fire
laser bolts that look potentially fatal and squirt purple
glue. Does Crichton really say that he's using a 'urine
solvent' to dissolve it?

Backstage: Moya's pregnancy was revealed in the original
pilot script which was used to sell the series, but was
removed from the final draft and saved for later.

The Verdict: Bottle shows – episodes set entirely on standing sets and using only the regular cast – are often the best episodes of any series because they force writers to deal with the characters rather than rely on SFX and big battles. They're good money savers too. This is one of the best, but it seems to promise little when it begins, after all the 'alien virus infects the ship' story has been done to death. However, that's a double bluff, and when the real reason for the situation is revealed it's one of *Farscape*'s masterstrokes, and introduces another ongoing storyline. Following the redefinition of Zhaan's character in the last two episodes, it's D'Argo's turn – this development promises layers and depths of character that will be most welcome. A low-key highlight that starts slowly but builds to a real humdinger of a climax.

111
Till the Blood Runs Clear

1st US Transmission Date: 9 July 1999
1st UK Transmission Date: 28 February 2000
1st Australian Transmission Date: 23 September 2000

Writer: Doug Heyes Jr
Director: Tony Tilse
Guest Cast: Magda Szubanski (Furlow), Jeremy Sims (Rorf),
Jo Kerrigan (Rorg)

Crichton and Aeryn are in the WDP running tests near a star which has high solar flare activity. They are trying to recreate the conditions that created the wormhole in **101**, 'Premiere' by slingshotting around a nearby planet. To Crichton's surprise he succeeds in creating a wormhole but it's unstable and the WDP is damaged. They land on the planet and give it to a local mechanic, Furlow, to be fixed. In the main square they find a beacon from Crais advertising a reward for D'Argo, Zhaan and Rygel. Aeryn takes the beacon and discovers a personal message for her from Crais, offering honourable retirement if she turns in her shipmates. Two Vorcarian Bloodtrackers, Rorf and his mate Rorg, are on the planet hunting for the fugitives. Crichton pretends to be another bounty hunter and by acting the Alpha Male he manoeuvres Rorf into an alliance to buy time. D'Argo comes down to the planet to fetch Aeryn and Crichton and is captured by Rorf. Crichton is only just able to prevent them torturing D'Argo. Zhaan also comes down to the planet and while Rorf and Rorg hunt her D'Argo escapes. The Bloodtrackers see Crichton and D'Argo together and open fire, realising Crichton's double-crossed them. Meanwhile Aeryn has had a fight with someone she found trying to access the WDP's flight data. During the fight she is exposed to a solar flare and temporarily blinded. She gets Furlow to change Crais's beacon to say that the hunt is called off. The Bloodtrackers see this and decide to cut their losses and leave. Furlow's charge for repairing the WDP is exclusive access to the wormhole data Crichton collected – he reluctantly hands it over.

Buck Rogers Redux: Crichton's dad had two Dobermans, that's where Crichton gets the idea of playing Alpha Male to the Bloodtrackers. He's almost hypnotised by the appearance of the wormhole and only snaps out of it just in time. This is the first time he asserts his rights over his crewmates, insisting that his desire to get home is just as valid a reason for action as theirs. His adoption of Alpha Male status with the Bloodtrackers inspires him to challenge D'Argo's own claim to that role on Moya – he faces down the Luxan and they reach a sort of truce to stop jockeying for superiority all the time in a key scene for the development of their relationship. When Crichton says, 'I have no idea what goes on in that tiny, little brain of yours, D'Argo,' D'Argo comes back with, 'I have no idea why you do *anything* that you do.' Crichton is sick of having his offers of help rejected and they agree that they are both selfish. Crichton bemoans the fact that they'll never be friends and D'Argo agrees that 'Friendship is a lot to ask.' 'Then how about respect? We can be allies,' finishes Crichton.

You Can Be More: Aeryn may be blind but she can still win a battle. Her idea of getting Furlow to change the beacon is a masterstroke, and even though she's blind at the time she strides out into the middle of a firefight and sets it off. She angrily refuses Crichton's help even though she can't see.

Big Blue: On the planet, when she knows she's being tracked, Zhaan chants and appears to cloak herself and her scent in some way.

I was a Teenage Luxan: D'Argo is ready to abandon Crichton and Aeryn at first, then he decides to go get them. After he and Crichton have their little talk, he refuses to abandon Crichton during the firefight with the Blood-trackers because they are 'comrades'.

The Insane Military Commander: Crais has placed wanted beacons on many worlds. Crichton is not on them because Crais wants to kill him personally. Aeryn's not mentioned either because they contain a secret message only she can access using her PK code. His offer of retirement according to Aeryn, probably means, 'a radiation-induced brain fever to bring on the living death'.

A Ship, a Living Ship!: The radiation from the solar flares is within Moya's tolerance, but it may damage her baby.

The Ballad of Aeryn and John: Aeryn is angry that Crichton didn't think to ask her opinion or assent before trying the slingshot manoeuvre. She tells him that next time he wants to do tests he can fly solo. He later tells her that if he does find a way home she is still welcome to come with him, but she dismisses the idea.

Worlds Apart: The planet is called Dam-Ba-Da.

Alien Encounters: Vorcarian Bloodtrackers are pack animals and the females are subservient to the males. They track by scent.

Disney on Acid: Crichton tells the Bloodtrackers that he and Aeryn are Butch and Sundance, the Hole in the Sky Gang. Butch Cassidy and the Sundance Kid were outlaws in America and ran the Hole In the Wall Gang. At first he thinks Rorf is called Worf, like the Klingon in *Star Trek: The Next Generation*. He later calls him Pluto, after Mickey Mouse's dog. Strangely, Furlow quotes *A Streetcar Named Desire* when she says it 'must be hard for someone as invulnerable as you to have to rely on the kindness of strangers'. Is this meant to be a coincidence, or are we supposed to wonder about her origins. Given that she, too, has a special interest in wormholes, could she know Earth?

What Does This Do?: According to Pilot, Delvian females are very sensitive to ionic radiation. This means that when they're exposed to it – literally in this case, as Zhaan once again rips her clothes off at the slightest provocation – they have what is called a 'photogasm'. Rygel's response upon hearing this: 'I'll get a mop and bucket.' Zhaan blisses out and writhes around a lot with a big smile on her face. Lucky her.

Logic Leaps: It's a desert planet and it looks very hot indeed, but Aeryn, whose race suffer heat exhaustion in high temperatures, seems unaffected. So it must be a cold radiation-soaked desert planet.

Bloopers: Crichton's solar goggles vanish when he and D'Argo are attacked by the Bloodtrackers. During the fight in the workshop it's clearly Claudia Black's stunt double in long shots.

WHAT did you just say?: Rygel is horrified that he may see Zhaan nude: 'Help! A mad Delvian exhibitionist is forcing herself on me, visually!'

Stats: According to Furlow, no one has ever created a wormhole and they are only theoretically possible. When Crichton creates one above the planet Furlow registers Brophase radiation, which is what would theoretically be produced by a proto-wormhole, so she knows what he's up to. She also states that wormholes allow you to travel through 'space and time' which could indicate that Crichton may not only be on the other side of the galaxy, he may be in the far past or distant future. So if he returns home he may find an Earth very different to the one he left (the producers have stated in interviews that Crichton has not travelled in time but it has not yet been established on screen). His WDP is now a two-seater and has been souped up with Moya parts.

Guest Stars: Magda Szubanski (who returned in **314** and **315**, 'Infinite Possibilities' I and II) has appeared as Margaret O'Halloran, the dog trainer who solves mysteries in the *Dogwoman* TV movies, but you probably recognise her as the farmer's wife in both *Babe* movies. Jeremy Sims plays Tony Dunne MP in the Aussie sitcom *Corridors of Power*.

The Verdict: An action-packed episode that makes great use of location filming to conjure a believable desert world, giving the episode an epic feel. The make-up for the Bloodtrackers is superb too. A good runaround that begins the show's arc regarding wormholes and will have repercussions far down the line.

112
The Flax

1st US Transmission Date: 16 July 1999
1st UK Transmission Date: 6 March 2000
1st Australian Transmission Date: 23 September 2000

Writer: Justin Monjo
Director: Peter Andrikidis
Guest Cast: Rhys Muldoon (Staanz), John Bachelor (Kcrackic), David Bower (Goon)

Aeryn is training Crichton to fly one of Moya's transport pods when they become ensnared in the Flax – a huge invisible net used by Zenetan pirates to catch ships to loot. They launch a distress buoy but they have to fix the atmospheric mix in order to buy the time they need to be rescued. The cabin is full of oxygen so they can't weld it without blowing up the pod. They decide to jettison the atmosphere, fix the link, and repressurise. However Crichton's space suit is broken and he's the only one who can weld. He teaches Aeryn how to make the repair, teaches her CPR and lets her kill him with an injection, telling her she has four minutes before he's irretrievable. Aeryn runs out of time before she's managed the repair but she stops anyway and revives Crichton. They now have only half an hour of air left.

Moya is boarded by a drifter called Staanz. He was once one of the pirates who run the Flax but now he's solo and he warns ships about it in hope of reward. He tells D'Argo that there's a Luxan ship in the Flax and D'Argo persuades Staanz to take him there so he can retrieve maps that can lead him home. On the way they detect Moya's pod venting atmosphere and D'Argo decides to go and rescue Crichton and Aeryn instead.

Meanwhile, Moya is boarded again, this time by Kcrackic, the leader of the Zenetan pirates. Staanz, who's on the run from Kcrackic, asks Rygel and Zhaan to distract him to give him and D'Argo time. Rygel plays Kcrackic at Tadek and loses, giving the pirate Staanz's location from the computer. Kcrackic leaves in pursuit. In fact Rygel deliberately lost, having planted false information in Moya's computer to send Kcrackic off on a wild-goose chase.

Buck Rogers Redux: Crichton was in a head-on crash when he was nineteen. He's slow to learn how to fly Moya's pods but he's getting there. After Aeryn revives him he reveals that he didn't see any light, or afterlife, just blackness.

You Can Be More: Sebaceans believe that, when you die, that's it, 'You go nowhere, you see nothing.' Aeryn could have finished the repair and saved herself, but at the cost of Crichton's life. Instead she chooses to save him. She says that this is because she doesn't want to die alone – a very un-PK thing to admit to.

I was a Teenage Luxan: As a boy D'Argo dreamed of serving on a Luxan Assault Piercer. He chooses to save

Aeryn and Crichton rather than collect the maps that could reunite him with his son, but his indecision nearly costs his crewmates their lives. He cuts himself no slack because a Luxan warrior should never be indecisive in battle. 'My indecision nearly cost Crichton and Aeryn their lives . . . and by saving them, I may have given up my only chance at seeing my son again. On every front, I failed.'

Buckwheat the Sixteenth: Rygel smokes and is a mean Tadek player. For a time we think he has sold out Staanz and D'Argo, and while many shows use that tactic – make you think a regular character has sold out his friends – it never works because you know they're planning something clever. Only on *Farscape* does that device really create tension, because it's entirely plausible that they – especially Rygel – would sell each other out.

In the Driving Seat: Pilot blasts the crew with a high-pitched noise to get them to stop arguing and get their attention, and then blithely shrugs it off and tells the crew his news. He's getting snide – the crew's influence must be rubbing off on him.

A Ship, a Living Ship!: Kcrackic once tried to seize a pregnant Leviathan. He lost eighty men in the process, so they must have *some* sort of defence mechanism.

The Ballad of Aeryn and John: It had to happen. Lock two people who are attracted to each other in a room together and sooner or later they're going to snap. When Crichton shoves Aeryn out of the way of a falling cable he lands right on top of her. The Aeryn of a few episodes earlier would have punched him, but now she just smiles and wryly asks: 'Are you comfortable? Shall I get you a pillow?' Then when all hope seems to be gone the music swells and before you can say Food Cubes the clothes are coming off. When they're interrupted by D'Argo's rescue Aeryn cries in disbelief: 'Someone's *docking*!?' Back on Moya they both swear it'll never happen again, but when Crichton playfully asks Aeryn if she is the female of her species it looks very much like she grabs his hand off screen and puts it somewhere designed to answer his question. 'I'll take that as a yes,' he says.

Disney on Acid: Crichton imagines he's Tom Cruise while flying the transport pod: 'This is *Top Gun*, this is the need for speed!'

What Does This Do?: Staanz drops his trousers to show his tattoos and prove to D'Argo that he was a Zenetan pirate. This also reveals a singular lack of expected appendages down below, and Staanz explains: 'I'm a Yenen by species. We're not exactly cut from the standard mould.' He later proves this by revealing that he is a she, and declaring her love for D'Argo, much to the Luxan's discomfort.

Get Frelled: So close . . . but Aeryn and Crichton's docking was interrupted by someone else's. Also, D'Argo was on a promise, had he chosen to take poor lovesick Staanz up on it.

Seen it all Before: Name one sci-fi show that hasn't had two lead characters facing certain death only to have them rescued at the last minute after some sort of cathartic life lesson has been learned or feelings revealed. It's a standard, and it's practically impossible to mess it up.

Logic Leaps: Would D'Argo really leave poor old Staanz trussed like a chicken for Kcrackic to find?

WHAT did you just say?: Crichton's southern accent surfaces in this episode. Ben Browder explains that that was down to the writers. 'A decade of trying to lose the accent and they haul it back out for all the world to see. I love my native accent but I don't see Crichton as carrying too heavy a southern accent. I reckon it'll come out sometimes . . . y'all.'

Stats: Staanz's ship doesn't come into Moya's docking port, it actually stays outside and docks the old-fashioned way. The Flax is a Magnadrift mesh, 75 million Zakrons long, and you can't see it till you're snagged in it. Peacekeepers use Kill shots and Nerve shots to first kill then revive each other for battle triage. Crichton is continuing to add Moya parts to his WDP.

Guest Stars: Rhys Muldoon plays Greg Dominelli in *Grass Roots*, an Australian political drama directed by Peter Andrikidis – who directed this episode of *Farscape* – and which also featured Tammy Macintosh who plays Jool from Season Three onwards. David Bower appeared in *Four Weddings and a Funeral*.

The Verdict: A tense episode that begins exactly like its predecessor began – with Aeryn and Crichton out flying and the rest of the crew back on Moya bickering. Rhys Muldoon is hilarious as Staanz, especially at the end, and the Flax works well as a plot device. Rygel gets to do something worthwhile, and D'Argo's burgeoning loyalty to his shipmates is tested and he comes up trumps. But it's the Aeryn/Crichton near miss that caps things. *Farscape* could have gone on milking sexual tension between the two for ever and fallen into the *Moonlighting* trap of relying too heavily on it and ruining the show when it finally dissipated. Instead only twelve episodes in and the writers have cut to the chase, which is both gutsy and risky – typically *Farscape*.

113
Rhapsody in Blue

1st US Transmission Date: 23 July 1999
1st UK Transmission Date: 13 March 2000
1st Australian Transmission Date: 30 September 2000

Story: David Kemper and Ro Hume
Teleplay: David Kemper
Director: Andrew Prowse
Guest Cast: Darlene Vogel (Alexandra/Lorana), Kate Raison (Tahleen),
Max Phipps (Tuzak), Michael Beckley (Hasko),
Aaron Cash (Pa'u Bitaal), Grant Magee (Jothee),
Robert Supple (Young Crichton)

Moya's crew are experiencing dreams of past sexual encounters when Moya StarBursts in response to a distress call from a Leviathan. The call was a ruse to lure Moya to a planet inhabited by a fugitive Delvian sect who need Zhaan's help. The leader, Tahleen, has powers of mind control and can meddle with people's memories. It was she who gave Moya's crew their dreams. Exiled from Delvia, they wish to return and seize power from the Peacekeepers, but in order to do this they will need to master the dark side of their natures. Most Delvians go insane when they release their dark impulses but Zhaan is unique in her ability to act violently and remain sane.

Zhaan shares Unity with Tahleen in order to impart her spiritual control but Tahleen betrays her and takes all her control, leaving Zhaan on the verge of madness. Unfortunately she does not take enough and decides to try again, even though this time it will probably kill Zhaan. Zhaan agrees, intending to kill Tahleen. Crichton is distracted by another member of the sect, Lorana, who appears to him as his lost love, Alex. At the same time D'Argo, Aeryn and Rygel are similarly manipulated on Moya to prevent them interfering. Lorana eventually relents and tells Crichton he can save Zhaan. She distracts Tahleen and Crichton shares Unity with Zhaan instead. Zhaan sees herself through Crichton's eyes and this gives her back her spiritual control. She and Crichton leave Tahleen to her madness.

Buck Rogers Redux: 'Almost everything we see, almost every day, is new to both of us, and it's worthy of response.' Crichton was in love with Alexandra Kimberly O'Connor and was intending to propose but he had a chance at the space programme and she wouldn't come with him, choosing instead to take a job in Stanford.

You Can Be More: 'It amazes me how people mistake theosophy for superiority.' Aeryn is freaked out by the serenity of the Delvians and unimpressed by either their ship/temple or their food source. She seems jaded and uninterested and brings a gun with her into the Delvian ship/temple even though it was strictly forbidden. To distract her they play on her fear of her rifle breaking and leaving her defenceless.

Big Blue: 'I am adrift. As the past is sweeping over me, I must rely on the judgment of someone I trust. Please understand. Please.' On Delvia Zhaan studied under a teacher called Bitaal and they became lovers. At the end of his term of office he refused to stand down and, allied with conservative forces on Delvia, called in the Peacekeepers to maintain his rule. All liberal thinkers and dissidents were rounded up. Zhaan's father was sent to an 'asteroid camp' and may still be there. Zhaan killed Bitaal in revenge for what he had done to her world and people – this is the crime for which she was imprisoned. She then spent seventeen cycles struggling to maintain control and prevent her dark impulses sending her mad. When she shares Unity with Tahleen Zhaan takes some of Tahleen's powers and ascends to the tenth level and is able to extend mental protection to others. She discards her priest's robes before leaving, because she believes she is no longer worthy of them, although she says she will one day be a Pa-u again. She now owes Crichton her life and they have shared Unity, which strengthens the bond between them.

I was a Teenage Luxan: D'Argo refuses to go down to the planet because it would have meant leaving his Qualta Blade behind. The Delvians confuse him with images of his son being carried away by Peacekeepers.

Buckwheat the Sixteenth: 'I like my wives pregnant and my ships cold to the touch. That way my feet stay warm and my slumber is uninterrupted.' Rygel's insecurity about his size is exploited by the Delvians and they make him believe that he has shrunk even smaller.

The Ballad of Aeryn and John: Aeryn still finds Crichton baffling and tells him he is 'the most bizarre creature' she has ever met.

Worlds Apart: We do not know the name of the world the Delvians have inhabited, but the surface is toxic.

Disney on Acid: Unity is apparently 'like Disney on acid'.

Alien Encounters: If Delvians give in to their 'dark impulses' they succumb to madness and their eyes turn red as 'tissue burn' migrates to their brains. They can bond with each other mentally and become one consciousness which allows the sharing of spiritual strengths and mental powers. After Unity the 'essence' remains but specific memories fade. The population of Delvia is 'over a billion'.

Get Frelled: Crichton says that sharing Unity is 'like ten years of really great sex all at the same time'. Wow. I'll have some of that please.

Seen it all Before: There's no avoiding it – Delvian Unity is exactly the same as Vulcan mind melds on *Star Trek*. They even do it the same way, by touching each other's heads.

Logic Leaps: Aeryn enters wearing Crichton's Calvin Klein underwear, but Crichton's got his undies on too, which means that he brought a spare pair of boxers with him in the WDP on his test flight. Wonder why he thought he'd need a spare pair . . . Tahleen easily lures Moya using the distress call of a pregnant Leviathan. Why does Crais not use the same ploy? Tahleen says they have no maps back to Delvia, but they navigated to this world – surely it's just a matter of checking the flight logs and reversing course.

Stats: Delvian ships land, melt the rock and sink beneath the surface allowing it to cool and harden over the ship. This allows peace and quiet as well as providing excellent defence. The Delvians eat an aquatic plant/animal hybrid that Crichton calls a 'half squid-calamari-cucumber' and they let Moya's crew take as many as they want for food supplies.

Guest Stars: Darlene Vogel plays Dr Melanie 'Lanie' MacIver on *One Life to Live*. Kate Raison has been a regular on *Pacific Drive*, *Outriders*, *A Country Practice* and *Home and Away*, which currently features Michael Beckley as Rhys Sutherland. Max Phipps appeared alongside Virginia Hey in *Mad Max II* and also cropped up in *The Cars that Ate Paris* and countless TV movies and series. Aaron Cash appeared in *Titanic* and returned to *Farscape* for the three-part 'Look at the Princess' story in Season Two.

Backstage: Poor old Virginia Hey. She shaves her head and eyebrows to play Zhaan, but when other members of her race are introduced they have hair, and make-up which conceals eyebrows. Why, when her discomfort was discussed, did the scriptwriters not have Zhaan simply decide to grow her hair again, since we know Delvians can? It would have been acceptable within continuity. It took eight make-up artists to handle all the Delvians for this episode.

The Verdict: Zhaan is the most underused character on the show, next to Rygel, and it's about time she got a shot at carrying an episode. Virginia Hey is excellent, Zhaan gets to evolve, and the Delvian race is given a backstory, a wider culture and a lot of depth. Perhaps the lack of any real subplot makes the episode a little too linear, but you could argue it also makes it more focused. Either way it's an intriguing rather than a thrilling episode, and it makes for a nice change of pace.

114
Jeremiah Crichton

1st US Transmission Date: 30 July 1999
1st UK Transmission Date: 20 March 2000
1st Australian Transmission Date: 30 September 2000

Writer: Doug Heyes Jr
Director: Ian Watson
Guest Cast: Natalie Mendoza (Lishala), Kevin Copeland (Rokon),
John O'Brien (Kato-Re), Deni Gordon (Neera),
Tania Mustapic (Maid)

Oh well, here goes . . . Crichton throws a wobbly and goes for a drive in his WDP to cool off. While he's away Moya's pregnancy causes complications and she has to StarBurst away, stranding Crichton. He flies to a conveniently local planet, which, happily, is just like Earth and, luckily, is inhabited by Earth-type people. Here he settles down on a beach, does some fishing and grows a beard. The daughter of the local chief, Lishala, falls for Crichton and the chief hunter, Rokon, gets jealous. He is egged on by his scheming mother, who is head Priesten.

Rokon is about to kill Crichton when D'Argo and Rygel serendipitously appear and save the day. Crichton thinks his crewmates abandoned him but they reveal they've been looking for him for three months. Crichton and D'Argo are captured, accused of attacking Rokon and are about to be sent off to a labour camp when Rygel appears and is, wouldn't you know it, hailed by the tribe as a god.

The gang want to leave but their ships, weapons and Rygel's Thronesled are knackered because there's an energy vortex on the planet that prevents technological devices from working. On Moya, Aeryn and Zhaan locate the source of the vortex and fire its co-ordinates in a canister at the settlement.

Meanwhile, we discover that there is a prophecy relating to Rygel that says he will rise up and lead the tribe into the light. Luckily there's a book around to explain everything, and happily it's in Ancient Hynerian, which of course Rygel can read. It turns out that the tribe were sent to the planet from the Hynerian Empire by Rygel X to spread his influence, and were abandoned. The energy-dampening device was installed to keep them there and the Priestens created a religion based around the Hynerian Dominar. Rygel, of course, can't rise up, and admits this. Crichton and D'Argo run leaving Rygel to be tortured to death for being a false god.

Luckily the capsule containing the map fired by Moya lands right next to them and they return to the village and destroy the device. Rygel's floating chair works again so he sits in it and rises up before the tribe. The Priesten is discredited, Rokon and Lishala make friends and everyone lives happily ever after. Which is nice.

Buck Rogers Redux: 'I'm sick of this whole turd-burb end of the Universe.' Crichton finally loses his cool, storms off

Moya to get some space and then spends three months thinking he was left behind deliberately. He chooses to live outside the tribe because he doesn't want to disturb their ways, but he feels comfortable on Acquara and considers staying even once a return to Moya is open to him: 'I've been hunted, beaten, locked up, shanghaied, shot at. I've had alien creatures in my face, up my nose, inside my brain, down my pants.' Acquara is the first place where he's felt at peace.

You Can Be More: Although she knows there will come a time when their search for Crichton will have to be abandoned, Aeryn sticks at it longer than Zhaan would have.

Big Blue: Zhaan is pricklier and more threatening now that she has abandoned her spiritual quest (**112**, 'The Flax'), and she is the first of the crew who seems willing to abandon the search for Crichton. She is getting on Aeryn's nerves and D'Argo thinks she has become 'cold'.

I was a Teenage Luxan: D'Argo has changed from being the one who always wanted to abandon his crewmates, obviously he's taken his little talk with Crichton, (**111**, 'Till the Blood Runs Clear') to heart. He refuses to stop looking for Crichton, partly due to his own sense of guilt at helping drive him loopy in the first place.

Buckwheat the Sixteenth: Rygel loves being a regent again and has surprisingly enlightened views, defining the highest sacrilege as 'purposely keeping your own people ignorant and subjugated for your own glorification'.

A Ship, a Living Ship!: Moya's pregnancy is continuing to affect her. The technobabble is all a bit confusing, but basically something builds up which she can't vent herself. D'Argo and Crichton try to help but in the end Moya has to StarBurst to prevent some sort of rupture.

Worlds Apart: The Earth-type world is referred to as Acquara by the natives.

Disney on Acid: When Rygel rises up Crichton mutters, 'The Slug Who Would Be King'. *The Man Who Would Be King* was a morality tale by Rudyard Kipling about the dangers of playing God. 'Well, hakuna matata, Masata' says Crichton at one point, referencing a song from *The Lion King*.

Seen it all Before: So many times ... where to begin? *Doctor Who* specialised in advanced-people-who-now-live-as-savages-surrounded-by-relics-of-their-former-glory-which-they-revere stories, to wit: 'Face of Evil' (in which the Doctor is mistaken for a god), 'Death to the Daleks' (which features an energy-draining device that has to be destroyed), 'The Mysterious Planet' ... and many more. *Star Trek*, in all its incarnations, did a few of those too, as has every other sci-fi show. And they were never any good *first* time around.

Bloopers: Crichton's beard is long, but his hair obviously isn't. Sticking a bit more gel in it and making it spiky does not equal three months' growth.

Logic Leaps: If the tribe, who grow hair naturally, have blades sharp enough for Rokon to shave his bonce every morning then surely they could rustle up a razor for poor old Crichton?

Guest Stars: Natalie Mendoza normally appears in musicals, including *Moulin Rouge*, but also appears in *Beastmaster*. Kevin Copeland can be seen in *Muriel's Wedding* and *The One*.

Backstage: John Eccleston, one of the chief puppeteers, appears as a native, running carrying Rygel over his head. This episode hit trouble when a hailstorm, with hailstones the size of cricket balls, hit the Henson workshop and threatened the sets. Ben Browder admitted to *TV Zone* that the pieces didn't seem to fall together with this episode – it 'didn't know what it wanted to be. There was a conflict between what was on paper and what was in the heads of the people executing it, myself included.'

The Verdict: Oh dear, this really is dreadful. 'Space Tribe' episodes are always corny and this one crams every happy accident, freaky coincidence and cliché in town into the mix. The characters are stereotypes, the love triangle is predictable and dull, the Priesten might as well have been rubbing her hands and cackling. And as for 'one of the crew is mistaken for a god', how many times have we seen that hoary old number? For once *Farscape* takes a familiar theme and fails to put a new spin on it, instead churning out tired old nonsense. And that beard . . . shudder.

115
Durka Returns

1st US Transmission Date: 13 August 1999
1st UK Transmission Date: 27 March 2000
1st Australian Transmission Date: 2 December 2000

Writer: Grant McAloon
Director: Tony Tilse
Guest Cast: Gigi Edgley (Chiana), David Wheeler (Captain Selto Durka),
Tiriel Mora (Salis)

Moya collides with another ship and is forced to take it on board. There are three occupants – a Nebari man named Salis, a Nebari girl named Chiana, and Durka, the ex-captain of the *Zelbinion* and the torturer of Rygel (**107**, 'PK Tech Girl'). They wait on Moya for a Nebari craft which is on its way to collect them. Durka faked his own death on the *Zelbinion* (which explains the body Rygel found in **107**, 'PK Tech Girl') and fled in an escape pod, leaving his crew to die. Chiana is being taken back to Nebari for mind cleansing and is locked up at Salis's request. Durka has already been cleansed and is now a nice guy. Nonetheless Rygel wants him dead.

Rygel rolls a bomb into the room where Durka is, not knowing Crichton is in there too. Luckily Rygel mixed the bomb's ingredients badly and it doesn't kill them, but it does break Durka's conditioning, unbeknown to anyone but Rygel. The crew tie Rygel up and leave him in his quarters. Meanwhile, Chiana escapes and Salis is found dead. Durka knows that if they rendezvous with a Nebari vessel he will be recleansed so he seizes Moya's flight deck and holds Aeryn and Rygel prisoner. Durka tells the crew that unless they release the StarBurst controls he will torture Aeryn and Rygel, but he discovers that Moya cannot StarBurst for some time during this stage of her pregnancy. He decides to abort the child.

Crichton and Chiana join forces and she lures Durka into a trap, but it doesn't work and he goes to his ship, intending to shoot Moya's midsection and thus abort the child. Crichton manages to use Rygel's explosives properly and blows Durka's ship out of the airlock and damages it, leaving Durka floating helplessly, waiting to be picked up by the Nebari and recleansed. Chiana stays aboard.

You Can Be More: Aeryn initially regards Durka as a hero, having been taught about all his great achievements.

Big Blue: Zhaan is continuing to be prickly and difficult to handle. She's full of barely concealed anger, and is more than willing to have a go at Salis for his repressive views.

Buckwheat the Sixteenth: Rygel goes totally nuts upon seeing Durka, setting off a bomb in Moya without checking whether any of his friends are around. He has a bomb-making kit in his quarters but he doesn't know how to mix the bombs properly. When Chiana tries to do a deal with him he plays along and then instantly double-crosses her, presumably hoping she'll run off, distract the others and leave him free to kill Durka. Unfortunately she stops to tie him up again first. He's very impressive when held hostage by Durka, calling Durka pathetic for being so eager to maim and kill someone defenceless. He then goes on to call Durka a failure because his torture of Rygel actually made Rygel stronger. 'Even if you kill me, I'll be laughing at you because the last thing I'll think of is you on Nebari Prime for another hundred cycles being ground back down into nothing.' He's very proud at having beaten

Durka at his own game but, as Aeryn points out, he just compared himself to a Peacekeeper.

Everyone's Favourite Little Tralk: 'I left the half-dead sanctimoniousness of my planet the first chance that I got!' Welcome Chiana, a black and white character in a colourful show. At first she's presented as a villain but when we discover that she's going to be mind-cleansed for being a bit of a tearaway she gains our sympathy. She's very good at hiding, managing to avoid Moya's internal sensors, and she's able to crack door locks and release herself from handcuffs and a control collar, so she's a slippery customer. When she can't talk her way out of a situation she will use her considerable sex appeal to try and get her way. She's unaccustomed to trusting people and only allies herself with Crichton when he convinces her that it's her best chance of survival. She's entirely mercenary and will always cut a deal to save her own skin. She may or may not have killed before, and she may have killed Salis.

A Ship, a Living Ship!: Moya's pregnancy is continuing to cause problems – first she StarBursts unpredictably, now she can't StarBurst at all. As Zhaan points out, 'Now I understand why the Peacekeepers tried to prevent this pregnancy.'

Alien Encounters: Chiana: 'Among my people you conform.' The Nebari, from Nebari-Prime, are a hugely powerful race – they have no war ships but one of their standard-class host vessels engaged and destroyed the *Zelbinion*, the most formidable ship in the PK fleet (**107**, 'PK Tech Girl'). Theirs is a culture of bland uniformity – dissension and freethinking of any sort are forbidden. They mind-cleanse anybody they disapprove of, and Salis makes it clear that he'd like to cleanse Rygel and Zhaan. Had they met with the host vessel it seems likely that Salis would have had his way.

Disney on Acid: 'Durka's gone all Hannibal Lecter on us' says Crichton, but Chiana just replies that she doesn't know what he means.

Get Frelled: When Crichton is holding down Chiana and trying to persuade her to help him the sexual tension is through the roof . . . could Aeryn have competition?

Logic Leaps: Durka manages to cut his own hair extremely well using only a sharp knife. Obviously his bad attitude is because he missed his calling in life and he secretly longs to spend his days in a posh salon with a pair of scissors. And why does he wear an eye-patch at the start and not after he's restored? Crichton tells Chiana that they only have food cubes, yet they collected tons of the plant/animal food in **113**, 'Rhapsody in Blue' and lots of fresh fruit and veg in **114**, 'Jeremiah Crichton', so Moya's holds should be chock full of tasties.

Guest Stars: Tiriel Mora appeared in *Grass Roots*. He is also in *Queen of the Damned* with Claudia Black.

Backstage: The shot that wings Chiana was originally intended to kill her but David Kemper decided he liked the character and kept her around for a while on a trial basis to see if she worked. Ben Browder explained in *Cult Times* about the crew's reaction when David Kemper talked about Chiana being a young female character. 'The immediate reaction was, "Oh, no, no, not the Wesley [Crusher] factor. We don't want that. We don't want a boy with a dolphin." ' However, Kemper explained to them that this would be a different character, 'David said "This is a little whore with a good heart." ' Her accent was the cause of confusion as Gigi Edgley explains: 'Originally I was a mid-Atlantic American alien, and the Australian producers wanted an Australian alien . . . by the end of series one, they decided they wanted her back in American.' As many scenes as possible were dubbed over but a few Australian bits still remained. Chiana's exaggerated and stylised movements are all Gigi Edgley's invention, though the contact lenses she wears cause tunnel vision, making her move her head more than normal.

The Verdict: Tony Tilse's trippy, slow-mo, slightly distorted direction adds extra tension and weirdness to an already tense script which puts the crew in real jeopardy and provides an excellent introduction for Chiana. Durka is occasionally a bit too mannered, but he's nicely malicious. The climax is exciting but a bit confused and seems to be a set-up for Durka's inevitable return. So with Crais, Maldis and Durka out there, all with grudges against Crichton, he's fast amassing a little army of bad guys out for his blood.

116
A Human Reaction

1st US Transmission Date: 20 August 1999
1st UK Transmission Date: 3 April 2000
1st Australian Transmission Date: 9 December 2000

Writer: Justin Monjo
Director: Rowan Woods
Guest Cast: Kent McCord (Jack Crichton), Phillip Gordon (Wilson), Richard Sydenham (Cobb)

Moya finds a wormhole that leads to Earth and Crichton takes his WDP through. He lands in Australia and is locked up, examined and interrogated by the military, led by a man named Wilson. Because of the additions to the module's technology and Crichton's translator microbes, they are unsure if he is really Crichton. His dad, Jack, arrives and convinces them to let him out. D'Argo, Aeryn and Rygel follow Crichton in one of Moya's transport pods and are captured and held. Wilson has Rygel dissected and D'Argo is flown away to another base. Aeryn and Crichton escape and hide in a house Crichton once stayed at with his father. Next day Crichton discovers that all the magazines and papers are from before he left Earth, and that everywhere he has been, and everyone he has seen are familiar to him. He realises it's all a trick, runs away from Aeryn, and goes somewhere he's never been before – the women's toilet in a bar he once visited – and finds a swirling void. He returns to the military base and confronts

'Jack', who is an alien who has been testing Crichton to find out about humanity. Rygel and D'Argo are still alive, and they, along with Crichton and Aeryn, are released.

Buck Rogers Redux: Crichton is still recording messages to his dad and still has the lucky charm he was given in **101**, 'Premiere'. He's just pulled out his first grey hair. The WDP's engines were tested in Australia on one of Crichton's three visits there. He also met Cobb and Wilson on one of them. On his tenth birthday, when his family were living in Annapolis, his dad was held late at Houston for tests but commandeered a jet and flew home, woke Crichton up and they went fishing at Sawyer's Mill where Crichton caught a trout. The first thing he does when he's released is to eat chocolate (**110**, 'They've Got A Secret').

You Can Be More: Aeryn likes rain and beer, is unsure about dresses and breaks out of her confinement with great ease. Once she's escaped she's determined that she won't be taken alive. We hear her talk without translation and it makes her seem far more the alien than ever before. According to her, Peacekeepers don't kill their prisoners even to study them. She speaks to 'Jack' in her own tongue before leaving the safe house and he appears to understand her . . . but what did she say?

Big Blue: Zhaan cries when Crichton leaves and tells him that there is a piece of her in him (**113**, 'Rhapsody in Blue') and he must take care of it.

I was a Teenage Luxan: D'Argo seems quite moved when Crichton leaves and gives him the pep talk he needs to help him fly through the wormhole. He even calls him John rather than Crichton, which, from him, is practically as good as a big sloppy kiss.

Buckwheat the Sixteenth: Rygel is outraged when Crichton says he won't leave him his stuff, but he laughs when he realises he's just being teased. The sight of poor dissected Rygel is really horrifying but when he turns up alive and eating Marjools (which look just like snails) he's as annoying as ever.

Everyone's Favourite Little Tralk: Chiana hardly features, but to remind us that she's on board now we open with Zhaan telling her off for stealing. Chiana puts up a fight and says that although she agreed to play by the ship's rules she's now changed her mind.

The Ballad of Aeryn and John: Crichton asks Aeryn to come to Earth with him but she refuses, even though she cries when he leaves. She later admits she was too scared to follow him. When Moya's pod follows Crichton, Aeryn is the pilot and she claims that they got caught in the wormhole's pull and couldn't escape, but it's equally possible that she chose to follow him. When they're alone together, Crichton apologises for entirely changing her life, but she doesn't seem that bothered about leaving the Peacekeepers any more. And then, another kiss and a fade out to next morning which, in light of the explicitness of future episodes seems remarkably coy for *Farscape*. In later episodes it is established that they slept together. They've gone from first kiss to lovers in a mere four episodes, which shows that the writers are reluctant to milk the 'will they, won't they' dynamic as many other shows do. So when they get back to Moya, how will things have changed between them?

Alien Encounters: The Ancient Ones are a hive species who are homeless and whose energy is depleted. They have enough left to make one more trip, so they need to choose the planet carefully. They do not intend to conquer a world, but to cohabit with its inhabitants. They hang around in space testing races they encounter to see whether they will be welcome on their worlds.

Seen it all Before: *Star Trek: Voyager* did almost this exact story in 'Non Sequiter'.

Logic Leaps: The biggest clue that all is not as it seems is that in all of infinite space, when we know that no one has ever discovered a wormhole before (**111**, 'Till the Blood Runs Clear'), Moya should just stumble across one. And that it should lead, of all the places in infinite space, straight to Earth, is just too much of a stretch. Crichton buys it because he wants to, but if it were real it would be lazy writing and *Farscape* rarely suffers from that – the viewer probably assumes it's all a trick of some sort immediately.

Bloopers: If you spray water over a film set to make it look like it's raining it is too clear to show up on camera; the standard way of making rain is to mix some milk in with the water so it registers on film. Obviously the *Farscape* crew got a bit carried away because when Crichton's opening the door to the safe house it looks like someone's poured a pint of milk over his head – just look at the drops hanging off the edge of his nose! One of the indications we're given that Crichton isn't on Earth is that an Australian guard doesn't know who won the Superbowl. What most Americans don't realise is that practically no one outside of America knows or cares about American Football, so while it's intended as a clue, it really isn't to anyone outside America.

WHAT did you just say?: Having us hear Rygel, D'Argo and Aeryn speak in their native tongues adds real class – how nice to have a show where the language barrier is addressed and everyone doesn't speak English. It also highlights the translator microbe blunder in **104**, 'I, E.T.'

Backstage: Aeryn's response to rain – opening her mouth to drink it and saying, 'I like it!' – was improvised on the spur of the moment by Claudia Black. Claudia speaking Sebacean was also not post-synced, but is in fact her speaking in a self-devised alien tongue, which impresses the hell out of me. Rowan Woods, the director, explains how this episode started a change in the look of the show: 'That whole concept of where we were with *Farscape* hit me on episode sixteen last year when we had to shift our emphasis from sunny Australia to dark Australia.'

The Verdict: *Farscape* may be filmed in Australia but most shows would have set the story in California or somewhere in the US; how nice to see a sci-fi show actually set outside America for a change, plus it means they can use the locations to their best advantage. Knowing that this is not the final episode, the audience will be expecting Earth to be fake, but the script does a good job of fooling us. By claiming that the wormhole above Earth is still open it offers an entirely new direction for the show that adds plausibility to the scenario and offers us Wilson as a recurring villain. This double bluff even makes it believable that Rygel has been killed because, after all, a puppet is easier to fire than an actor. The ending is a bit of an anticlimax, but that was inevitable, and the Ancient is a disappointing puppet that doesn't really work. One of the very best episodes to date.

117
Through the Looking Glass

1st US Transmission Date: 10 September 1999
1st UK Transmission Date: 10 April 2000
1st Australian Transmission Date: 16 December 2000

Writer: David Kemper
Director: Ian Watson

Moya's pregnancy is inhibiting her ability to StarBurst, increasing the risk of capture. Pilot overhears the crew discussing the possibility of abandoning ship and Moya responds by trying to StarBurst to persuade them to stay. Unfortunately she is too weak and rams the ship halfway into another dimension, creating four separate versions of Moya that inhabit the same space – normal, Red, Blue and Yellow. In order to escape the crew have to travel between the different Moyas and put the engines on all four into reverse. Meanwhile a creature appears to be trying to rip its way into the ship from the other dimension. When putting the engines into reverse doesn't work Crichton realises that the monster's scratches are all prime numbers – it's trying to communicate. He talks to it and it tells him they must instead go forward and it will push them back into normal space. This works and Moya is reintegrated.

Buck Rogers Redux: 'Whatever happens, we go together.' Crichton is the lynchpin that binds the crew together, formulating the plan, taking the leap of faith needed to save the day and co-ordinating his crewmates, and that includes Moya, into an effective unit.

You Can Be More: Aeryn reveals herself as the most competent team player of the bunch, probably due to her PK training. When all the others question Crichton and challenge his decisions, Aeryn accepts his orders without question because she trusts him entirely.

Big Blue: 'I've kicked more arse than you've sat on!' Zhaan fears they are all going to die and puts her Pa'u vestments on again because she realises that, though she thought she'd forsaken the priesthood, it was still in her soul.

I was a Teenage Luxan: At the start D'Argo has decided to leave Moya and will not be swayed. By the end he's resolved to remain.

Buckwheat the Sixteenth: 'Should I disrobe so it's memorable?' Rygel is hilarious stuck in the Yellow Zone, but true to form he only thinks of food. Hynerian Dominars never travel in reverse.

Everyone's Favourite Little Tralk: Chiana may be on board but she's far from being a member of the crew. Every time she tries to speak the others tell her to shut up, and when a crisis hits she immediately tries to jump ship. Crichton says that he thought she was 'Junior Miss Tough Chick of the universe,' and Chiana's response is 'Yeah, when I can kiss or kick or cry my way out of it. This is way, way, way, way different.' However, when she realises she has no choice she joins the team, and by the end she seems to have integrated a little more.

In the Driving Seat: Pilot fails to understand why the crew laugh so much when they have reassembled Moya. Laughter's clearly not a tension release for his race, then.

A Ship, a Living Ship!: Rygel: 'Moya has been . . . our protector, our home, our companion, and our friend . . . however, as relationships grow, they also change. Do you think we can trade her for a faster vessel?' Moya wants to demonstrate her ability so as to reassure the crew and prevent them leaving but she messes it up. It's the first time Moya's insecurity has driven a storyline. In order to try and make up for her mistake she offers to lose the baby to gain more power to try and break free, but Crichton refuses. After the ordeal she reveals that the pregnancy has entered its final, most stable phase and she can StarBurst again.

The Ballad of Aeryn and John: No reference is made to the fact that they slept together in the last episode but there is a closeness and rapport there which seems deeper than before. When he returns to the Blue Zone for Aeryn she says she was worried he wasn't coming back. His reply – 'I'd never leave you' – raises a smile.

Alien Encounters: The creature Crichton meets is a guardian that hangs around between dimensions cleaning up things that break through. It communicates using prime numbers and has the power to reroute them back to normal space only when they fully leave it and enter the space between dimensions. The Nebari have experience with other dimensions – Chiana relates a time when the weapons scientists 'poked a hole through another dimension. Once it widened, they lost control . . . the whole solar system, four populated planets, dissolved into tiny chunks.' When Zhaan hurts her arm she says the 'fibres' are torn.

Logic Leaps: If Moya is split into four why aren't the crew? The script addresses the problem by saying that it's to do with relative densities and the crew are too small to be fractured, but if that's the case shouldn't things like Rygel's painting and the food, which we see on different Moyas, remain only on the original?

Bloopers: Aeryn and D'Argo disappear from the same spot but end up on different Moyas. When Crichton goes through that same space he doesn't disappear, but from that point on the doorways are always in the same place on each version of Moya and are reusable. Pilot explains that StarBurst 'is technically the seam between space-time dimensions. Moya's power cells allow us access and we simply ride out the energy stream until we're pushed out at random', but if that's the case how did she answer the distress call in 113, 'Rhapsody in Blue', which required her to StarBurst to a specific destination?

WHAT did you just say?: Crichton declares that he needs to leave before he ends up like Rygel. Rygel's typical comeback is: 'What? Handsome with a great sexual prowess?'

Backstage: Ben Browder explains Chiana's nickname: 'It just came out one day. I looked at her and just said "Pip"! There was another nickname scripted, but I just looked at her and said "Pip". And it's her.' According to Gigi Edgley, she was actually called Pip when she was young.

The Verdict: For a sci-fi show *Farscape* is more often fantasy space action rather than the technobabble-fuelled sci-fi of *Star Trek*, but this episode is the exception that proves the rule: it's entirely predicated upon inter-dimensional gobbledygook. But David Kemper, executive producer of the show, uses it as a team-building exercise, showing the division within the crew and then forcing them to work together and realise that as a unit they have great strength. It's managed well and avoids becoming the corny 'life lesson of the week' type episode that can be so stomach churning: 'You see captain, I realised that if we just love each other we can be better spacefarers.' The sound design of the various Moyas, as well as the visual effects in the Red Zone, are excellent and give the episode a really trippy feel. A strong character piece for which the technobabble is merely an excuse, and a necessary bonding experience for the crew before the trauma that comes next . . .

118
A Bug's Life

1st US Transmission Date: 17 September 1999
1st UK Transmission Date: 17 April 2000
1st Australian Transmission Date: 23 December 2000

Story: Doug Heyes Jnr
Teleplay: Steven Rae
Director: Tony Tilse
Guest Cast: Paul Leyden (Larraq), Richard White (Thonn),
Zoe Coyle (Hassan), Michael Tuahine (Rhed)

A damaged PK Marauder approaches Moya. Crichton persuades everyone to pretend they are still prisoners while he and Aeryn pretend to be Peacekeepers. The ship is carrying a four-person Special Ops team, under the command of Captain Larraq. They are transporting a captured Intellent Virus to a hidden PK Gammak base (a science/military installation) deep in the Uncharted Territories. Crichton and Aeryn try and gather information about the PK base and its mission. Chiana and Rygel, believing the cargo to be valuable, open the casket and release the virus. Thonn interrupts them, is possessed by the virus, and immediately shoots Rhed. The infection then leaps to Chiana. Chiana/Virus tells everyone that Rygel is the one possessed and Peacekeepers and supposed prisoners unite, hunt him down and freeze him. Meanwhile the virus leaps to Crichton and he increases Moya's speed towards the PK base. Zhaan decides to try and develop an antibody with the help of Hassan, but Crichton/Virus kills Hassan first. Zhaan realises the virus was in Chiana, not Rygel, and is therefore still loose, so she and D'Argo abandon the pretence of being prisoners and storm the command deck. She realises the virus is in Crichton, everyone starts fighting and in the confusion the virus leaps elsewhere, so that everyone is standing in a circle pointing guns at each other, no one knowing who is infected. Since the virus cannot re-enter a host, Crichton and Chiana are clear. They all go to the medical bay and Zhaan whips up an injection which will force the virus to reveal itself. It turns out to be in Larraq, who takes Aeryn hostage then makes a run for his ship, stabbing Aeryn badly during the escape. Crichton lets him escape. The damaged Marauder is still leaking fuel so Crichton moves Moya's StarBurst engines into the trail of fuel, ignites it and blows the ship up.

Buck Rogers Redux: Crichton adopts a cod English accent as the PK captain and bluffs brilliantly. Pretending that Moya was a PK ship carrying prisoners was his plan and the others only go along with it reluctantly.

You Can Be More: Aeryn is again confronted by the life she's lost when Larraq offers to have her transferred to Special Ops. She and he get on very well, and there's a hint of romantic interest. When Larraq/Virus stabs her Crichton says, 'he missed your heart' and Aeryn wistfully replies, 'closer than you think'.

She started flying 'Scrub Runners' at fourteen, then a KL-80 and a KL-81 before starting Prowler school at sixteen, which is late for a PK, but her feet didn't reach the pedals until she was sixteen.

I was a Teenage Luxan: D'Argo allows himself to be chained up in order to fool the Peacekeepers but he is humiliated and angry about it. After it is all over he destroys the chains and swears never to allow himself to be chained again by anyone.

Buckwheat the Sixteenth: Rygel knows there are Peacekeepers on board and that the crew are all in great danger but he still breaks out of his cell using his secret exit and goes to try and steal the Peacekeepers' cargo. The crew, especially D'Argo, are less than sympathetic when he gets frozen.

Everyone's Favourite Little Tralk: Chiana poses as Crichton's servant and flirts with Thonn to get what she wants – in this case an impression of the key to the cargo pod from pressing it into a food cube.

A Ship, a Living Ship!: Crichton tells Larraq that he and Aeryn are with PK New Tech, testing a way of controlling Leviathans without Control Collars using Neural Control of Pilots. Larraq reveals that this has been tried before, but each time the ship and crew have been lost.

The Ballad of Aeryn and John: Aeryn is frustrated by Crichton's plan and only lets him play Captain because the uniform they find won't fit her. Crichton is very distressed when she nearly dies from the stab wound, and she thanks him for staying by her bedside, but she's distracted by her attraction to Larraq.

Alien Encounters: The function of the Intellent Virus is to incubate in a host for one hour and then release a million spores. It wants to get to the PK base because that will give it the best vector for mass infection. During infection the host acts almost normally. It is an acid-based life form. After possession a host's body displays high acidity and dizziness as a reaction to the mild hallucinogenic left behind by the virus to prevent the host remembering its possession. The Peacekeepers want to use it as a weapon. A Delvian colony world was once wiped out by such a virus.

Disney on Acid: Ben Browder delivers another ad lib and quotes *Ghostbusters*: 'You might think your magic pill worked, and then Rygel's up walking around the ship, coughing up the spores, cats and dogs living together . . .'

Get Frelled: Out of left field comes sexual tension between Chiana and . . . Rygel? Gross! Though Rygel denies he's had fantasies about her, Chiana declares, 'Oh, I've seen you looking at me. You want to be a pervo, you ought to practice subtle . . . oh, well don't get your shivvies in an uproar. Like I care.'

Seen it all Before: *Invasion of the Bodysnatchers*, all three versions, but perhaps most directly John Carpenter's *The Thing*, in which all the crew take a test to establish which of them is the alien. It's a classic scene that's been replicated in countless films and TV shows. The finale, where Crichton lights the ship's fuel, is just like the end of *Die Hard 2*.

Logic Leaps: It's a bit of a stretch to accept that Zhaan can whip up an antibody to such a complex creature in almost no time at all, with no samples to work from. Moya's DRDs put on an impressive display of firepower to persuade Larraq to be nice, a defensive measure very effective here but rarely used in other episodes. For example, since all the doors have little hatches to allow DRDs to enter why didn't Pilot simply send a few into the command deck to shoot Durka in **115**, 'Durka Returns'?

Guest Stars: Paul Leyden plays Simon Frasier in *As the World Turns*.

The Verdict: It would take a spectacularly bad show to mess up such a familiar storyline, but by adding a bunch of Peacekeepers to the mix *Farscape* spins an old chestnut just enough to get away with over familiarity, and the tension is racked up nicely to an exciting conclusion. It feels as though the show is going somewhere at last; before, they've been wandering around talking about Crais and the Peacekeepers but rarely bumping into any. The introduction of the mysterious Gammak base and the threat of a PK presence out in the Uncharted Territories offers renewed threat, and when Chiana grabs Larraq's ID badge during a fight it's an indication that it'll be used in future episodes, promising a running storyline. That is what we finally get . . .

119
Nerve

1st US Transmission Date: 7 January 2000
1st UK Transmission Date: 8 May 2000
1st Australian Transmission Date: 30 December 2000

Writer: Richard Manning
Director: Rowan Woods

Guest Cast: Lani Tupu (Capt. Bialar Crais), Alyssa-Jane Cook (Gilina), Kent McCord (Jack Crichton), Wayne Pygram (Scorpius), Paul Goddard (Stark), Imogen Annesley (Niem), Stephen Leeder (Commander Javio), Anthony Kierann (Lt Heskon)

(NB: this is almost a direct follow-on from **118**, 'A Bug's Life'.)

Aeryn's stab wound damaged her Paraphoral nerve and her body cannot filter out toxins – she has two days to live. Crichton decides to visit the secret PK Gammak base, masquerading as Larraq, and get the tissue sample Aeryn needs to survive. Chiana gives Larraq's Ident Chip to Crichton and volunteers to come along and help divert attention. At the base they are contacted by Gilina (**107**, 'PK Tech Girl'), who has recognised Crichton. She obtains a hypodermic which can cure Aeryn. A PK scientist called Scorpius realises Crichton is an impostor and he is captured, but not before he hides the syringe. Crichton is tortured in the Aurora Chair, a device which rips into its occupant's memories. Scorpius discovers Crichton's history and sends a message for Crais. When the chair finds memories of his encounter with The Ancients (**116**, 'A Human Reaction') it encounters a neural block. It transpires that The Ancients secretly planted the equations needed to create wormholes in Crichton's subconscious to help guide him to the knowledge that will get him home. Crichton cannot directly access the memories, and they're too well protected for the Chair to extract. Since the purpose of the Gammak base is to try and create wormholes, Scorpius assumes that Crichton is there to spy on their research. While recuperating in a cell, Crichton meets Stark, a prisoner who appears to have been driven insane by the Aurora Chair. Gilina patches into the cell's comms unit and Crichton tells her where the syringe is. Gilina programs a blind spot in the base's scanners and gives Chiana a safe route out. Chiana collects the syringe and escapes.

Crais arrives and demands that Scorpius hand Crichton over, but Scorpius cuts a deal – Crais is to help him explore

Crichton's mind in return for Scorpius handing over Crichton afterwards. Crais says he's captured Moya and that Crichton must submit to the Chair if he wants his friends to live. Crichton knows Crais is lying because he doesn't know Aeryn's ill, but to buy time for Chiana he agrees and is strapped into the Chair and the torture continues.

Meanwhile Zhaan and D'Argo connect Aeryn to Moya and use the ship as a sort of dialysis machine to filter out the poisons in Aeryn's body and keep her alive until Chiana returns and she is cured.

Buck Rogers Redux: Crichton initiates the plan to get the graft for Aeryn and refuses to take no for an answer – even Rygel eventually endorses the plan. He's like a man possessed, undertaking what is, in effect, a suicide mission to save Aeryn. If not for Chiana's possession of the Ident Chip, and Gilina's fortuitous presence, chances are he'd have been dead in an arn. He holds up to torture very well: no matter how much Scorpius hurts him in the Aurora Chair he still laughs in his face every time he's allowed to draw breath. Gilina can tell immediately how much Crichton has changed from the happy-go-lucky, still-learning space cadet of **107**, 'PK Tech Girl', to the stressed out, self-possessed undercover agent he is here.

You Can Be More: 'If a warrior can't die in battle she can at least die alone.' Knowing that she is dying Aeryn at first plans to take her Prowler and die alone in space. D'Argo knows, however, that she doesn't want to die, especially alone (which she proved by reviving Crichton in **112**, 'The Flax').

I was a Teenage Luxan: D'Argo comes up with the plan to use Moya to filter Aeryn's toxins but won't take credit for it because he believes it's disrespectful of her desire, as a warrior, to be left alone. He sits by her bed and holds her hand, unexpectedly paternal and caring, and she thanks him.

Everyone's Favourite Little Tralk: 'The more they look at me the less they look at you.' Unlikely as it may seem

Chiana does not have a hidden agenda – she really does want to help Crichton save Aeryn. She's an 'accomplished burglar and distraction causer' and she drives all the men on the base wild within minutes of arriving. She can fly a Prowler. Her manipulation of the base's captain is masterly, but he recognises her when she tries to leave and she ruthlessly burns him alive. The long lingering close-up of his smouldering corpse is a memorable, if gruesome, sight. Chiana seems rather to enjoy the killing. Maybe she did kill Salis (**115**, 'Durka Returns').

The Man in the Iron Mask: Welcome Stark. Why Scorpius keeps torturing him in the Chair we don't know but it's driven him nuts. He even begs to be given more time in the Chair, appearing to enjoy his torture. He banishes Crichton to the other side of the cell.

The Insane Military Commander: Crais never filed a report of Crichton's existence and still maintains that he never received recall orders from First Command (**108**, 'That Old Black Magic'). He tries to order Scorpius about but gets nowhere – he's only kept in the loop because he can help Scorpius coerce Crichton. Already he seems neutered.

Nosferatu in Rubber: 'I long ago learned the value of patience.' Welcome our new nemesis. He will actually appear in the show from time to time, unlike the rarely seen but oft-mentioned Crais. He's a wrinkly skinned, S&M, PVC nightmare. The Aurora Chair is his toy, the base is his domain, and although he is an ally of the Peacekeepers, we do not yet know what official position he holds, if any. He is trying to create wormholes and in Crichton he sees the opportunity to avoid cycles of research and cut straight to the chase – if only he can get the Ancients' equation out of Crichton's head. He is able to detect Crichton's alien nature simply by being close to him.

A Ship, a Living Ship!: Moya experiences contractions that threaten Aeryn's dialysis process, but Pilot is unsure if this heralds the birth of her child.

The Ballad of Aeryn and John: Gilina is in love with Crichton and would do anything for him, but although he doesn't tell her of his feelings for Aeryn he tries not to lead her on. However, when Gilina realises that Crichton is willing to die for Aeryn, she knows things have changed. Chiana, keen to keep Gilina on side, tells her Crichton loves her and that Aeryn's just a shipmate, so Gilina plans to leave with Crichton when Chiana returns with reinforcements.

Worlds Apart: The Gammak base is in what appears to be an abandoned mining station on a moon in orbit around a gas giant.

Disney on Acid: Lying in the cell, all Crichton can say is, 'Danger Will Robinson, danger! Beware the Chair . . .' lapsing into *Lost In Space* land. He mimics Connery's Bond from *Goldfinger* when he says, 'but of course you are . . .' when Scorpius introduces himself. He quotes Monty Python's Spanish Inquisition sketch (you didn't expect that, did you?) when he cries 'fetch the comfy chair!' Some of these are ad libs, a not uncommon occurrence on the *Farscape* set: ' "Danger Will Robinson" was me. "Fetch the comfy chair" was Ricky Manning. And I reckon those are two rippers,' Ben Browder told *TV Zone*.

Guest Stars: Wayne Pygram was a regular as a fireman on *Fire*. Paul Goddard played Simon Armstrong on *Sons and Daughters,* came to the UK to play Stephen on *Coronation Street* and was Agent Brown in *The Matrix*.

Backstage: Scorpius's half-Sebacean half-Scarran nature was revealed in the original script, and it was established that he wiped out the Scarran race with a virus. Happily this was cut, because the Scarrans go on to become a regular element on *Farscape*. Also, Scorpius was at one point conceived as an entirely animatronic creation. This episode had Crichton getting laid, but Ben Browder disagreed. 'I said "you can't do that! I'm down here to save Aeryn. I'm going to get laid while I'm down there? No way man, I don't see it happening!" ' (*TV Zone*)

The Verdict: After a series of stand-alone episodes designed to give the characters room to breathe, establish the rules of the show and draw in viewers, the writers suddenly feel confident enough to start playing with the continuity they've established and reward loyal fans with a stunning episode that begins the story arc which will dominate the show from this moment on. Scorpius is instantly more menacing than Crais ever was and raises the threat level hugely. The revelation about the wormhole equations comes entirely out of the blue but it works. Gilina is a welcome returnee, Chiana finally earns her place on the ship and Crichton goes to extraordinary lengths to show his devotion to Aeryn. We even get introduced to Stark who at this stage seems to be only a minor background character. Another sign of *Farscape*'s class is the design on the Gammak base. On any other show it would be gleaming and shiny, but here it's dark, grungy and partly built of stone – at some points it's obviously filmed on location. Ben Browder pulls out all the stops and delivers an excellent performance. Everything, absolutely everything, about this episode works. From here on it only gets darker and more dangerous as the stakes get ever higher.

120
The Hidden Memory

1st US Transmission Date: 14 January 2000
1st UK Transmission Date: 15 May 2000
1st Australian Transmission Date: 6 January 2001

Writer: Justin Monjo
Director: Ian Watson
Guest Cast: Lani Tupu (Capt. Bialar Crais), Alyssa-Jane Cook (Gilina),
Wayne Pygram (Scorpius), Paul Goddard (Stark),
Imogen Annesley (Niem), Anthony Kierann (Lt Heskon)

Crichton is blocking a memory from the Aurora Chair and Scorpius is killing him trying to break through to it, thinking it's about wormholes. In fact it's the memory of kissing Gilina, which would give her away as his accomplice. Gilina alters the Chair so that when he does think of the kiss it plays false memories that make it look as though Crichton has given all the wormhole secrets to Crais. Scorpius throws Crichton back in the cell with Stark and puts Crais in the Chair. Crais is also blocking a memory. Scorpius again assumes it's about wormholes, but in fact it's the murder of Lt Teeg (**108**, 'That Old Black Magic'). Aeryn, Zhaan and D'Argo fly through Gilina's safe route and land on top of the Gammak base. Aeryn makes contact with Gilina while the others remain on the roof. Aeryn and Gilina free Crichton and Stark and make for the roof, but they are cut off and have to hide. They need an Ident Chip from a senior officer to get out and Aeryn goes to find one. She discovers Crais in the Aurora Chair, takes his chip and switches the Chair to full power, leaving him to die. Gilina finally realises that Crichton loves Aeryn and decides to stay behind. On the roof the crew are reunited just as troops attack. There is a gun battle and Scorpius grabs Crichton. Gilina appears, having changed her mind, but she's too slow and is shot by Scorpius, although the distraction allows Moya's crew to flee. Back on the ship, Gilina dies, but we learn that before she left the base she scrambled their sensors so Moya can escape undetected (**121**, 'Bone to Be Wild' implies that she didn't do a very good job of it.).

Meanwhile Moya gives birth to a boy with some help from Chiana, but it is a warship – the first Leviathan with weapons.

Buck Rogers Redux: Crichton is willing to die to protect Gilina, much as he was to save Aeryn. His resistance to the Chair is nothing short of incredible, and without rescue it would surely have killed him before long.

You Can Be More: Aeryn hasn't recovered from her nerve damage but she goes charging in to save Crichton, even with her hands shaking. She thanks Gilina and urges her to come with them. Her encounter with Crais is marvellous and she confronts the PK past that was still troubling her in **118**, 'A Bug's Life' and lets it go once and for all, telling Crais that she's no longer a Peacekeeper. 'You know what I learned when I was away from you? Everything I lost isn't worth a damn, and I don't want to go back to your past.' As she leaves him to die on the Chair, not one shred of doubt is visible on her face.

I was a Teenage Luxan: Zhaan calls D'Argo's Qualta Blade 'unconventional', which leads to quite a speech about a race a long time ago who were even more feared than the Peacekeepers – the Telloks. They laid siege to D'Argo's planet for more than a hundred solar days. 'When the final assault came all our warriors had were these unconventional weapons ... When the final days come Luxans believe that the Qualta Blade will lead us to freedom.'

Buckwheat the Sixteenth: 'I've conceived hundreds of progeny, and those are only the official ones with my wives ... My progeny were ... tiny and handsome, like their father.' When Moya's giving birth she has to equalise pressure with the outside, which means creating a vacuum on her inside. Rygel and Chiana shelter in a tiny pressure chamber and Rygel loves being that close to Chiana. He's lecherous and gross, and when he's not farting he's obviously copping a feel, to her disgust.

Everyone's Favourite Little Tralk: For the second time in two episodes Chiana earns her keep. She goes haring into the birth chamber to help deliver Moya's baby, at great risk to her own life. Chiana – intergalactic midwife!

The Man in the Iron Mask: Stark has been in the Chair over a hundred times but his insanity is a ploy – he acts mad to keep them off his back. He's been held there for two cycles and in that time he's built a magnetic crypt encoder out of pieces of metal, which allows him to try combinations that might open the cell door. Peacekeepers killed most of his people – the Banik slave race – but he interested them so they didn't kill him. He can hide thoughts from the Chair. ... 'Outsiders think that we do not feel, but it's only that our feelings don't always show.

Just as this [indicates his mask] can hide our feelings, we're also able to cloud thoughts from our minds.' When he removes his mask half his head is a mass of glowing light which soothes Crichton's pain. He can share thoughts with others in order to calm them, and he gives Gilina a memory of a place he saw once as a boy – the memory he was keeping from the Chair – to help her die more easily.

The Insane Military Commander: Crais gets his comeuppance. His murder of Lt Teeg is revealed, his crew abandon him to Scorpius and he's tortured in the Chair. It doesn't break him, though – when Aeryn confronts him he still rants: 'I will track you down and kill you, Officer Sun, on that, I give you my vow.' When we last see him, he's unconscious but still alive, so he's not out of the way yet. His parents were farmers.

Nosferatu in Rubber: Scorpius is determined not to let Crichton escape. He turns on Crais and gets away with it, so he must be very confident of the strength of his position with PK command.

A Ship, a Living Ship!: Moya's baby is not normal – the Peacekeepers altered her reproductive system to produce a warship. Because it's an unusual child it cannot be born normally and Chiana has to get it to fire one of its guns on low power and cut its way out of Moya. It is born healthy and it's a boy, but it's unique and its loyalties uncertain.

The Ballad of Aeryn and John: 'That is the radiant Aeryn Sun.' Gilina asks Crichton if he wants to be with Aeryn but he doesn't have time to answer. She then asks Aeryn the same question and she also dodges the issue. By the end Gilina knows Crichton loves Aeryn, but he admits he could have loved her had things been different. She dies while he's kissing her.

Disney on Acid: Crichton refers to Scorpius's assistant as 'Peacekeeper Barbie'. Rygel's hand on the steamed up window of the pressure capsule is a visual reference to *Titanic*. There are more ad libs in this episode too. Ben

Browder told *TV Zone* that, 'When I'm in the Chair "It looks like an episode of *Melrose Place*" was me, and it's me taking a shot at myself because I did an episode of *Melrose Place*.'

Logic Leaps: The Gammak base has no sensors up top because they would reveal its location – in other words, the Peacekeepers have chosen secrecy over defence. So they can't develop hidden sensors? Come on. Then again, perhaps that's not too unbelievable, since all their technology seems to use simple jack plugs!

Bloopers: Zhaan spends time mining the top of the Gammak base in preparation for a PK attack, but when the attack comes she doesn't use the bombs at all.

Backstage: Like Gilina and Chiana before him, Stark was only intended to appear in these two episodes but Paul Goddard so impressed the team that they began plans to work him into Season Two immediately.

The Verdict: The second part of a two-parter is always tricky – rarely does resolution work as well as build-up – and although this is a gripping instalment it lacks the punch of the first half. Gilina's death is affecting but something of a surprise because it's such an obvious thing to do. The scene with Aeryn and Crais is a classic, but the drama of Moya's birth is far more exciting even if it does play like the B Plot. Still, it's nice to see a good old-fashioned laser-gun battle with glowing pulse blasts and silly gun sound effects like you used to make in the school playground (go on, admit it). No one seems to do those much any more, except *Farscape*.

121
Bone to Be Wild

1st US Transmission Date: 21 January 2000
1st UK Transmission Date: 22 May 2000
1st Australian Transmission Date: 20 January 2001

Writer: David Kemper and Rockne S O'Bannon
Director: Andrew Prowse
Guest Cast: Lani Tupu (Capt. Bialar Crais), Wayne Pygram (Scorpius),
Francesca Buller (M'Lee), Marton Csokas (Br'Nee),
David Franklin (Lt Braca)

Moya and her baby are hiding from Crais's Command
Carrier in an asteroid field when they receive a distress call,
which takes D'Argo, Crichton and Zhaan off Moya to a
lush asteroid with no animal life. A creature called M'Lee
is hiding from a monster, Br'Nee, who she claims ate her
family. They take M'Lee back to the transport pod but
Br'Nee attacks, damaging the pod. Zhaan is taken by
Br'Nee, who is a botanist and warns that M'Lee is a bone
eater and ate all the other members of his expedition.
Zhaan is revealed to be a plant, which fascinates Br'Nee.
M'Lee tells Crichton that her people were planted on the
asteroid to eat all animal life and thus protect the plants so
that Br'Nee and his team could harvest the world. They
had assumed that all of M'Lee's people would be dead
when they returned but she survived by eating her fellows.
She restrains her hunger and begs to be rescued. Br'Nee
miniaturises Zhaan to keep her as a sample for study.
Crichton releases Zhaan and kills Br'Nee. M'Lee eats
Br'Nee's bones and when the Peacekeepers arrive in
pursuit of the already departed Transport Pod she is taken
to the Command Carrier. Crichton and co. return to Moya
with Br'Nee's charts which will enable them to navigate
safely out of the asteroid field.

Aeryn remains on Moya at Pilot's request and goes
aboard the baby to help it trust Moya and her crew.

On board the Command Carrier, Scorpius wrests control from Crais.

Buck Rogers Redux: Crichton unwittingly offends Zhaan
by accusing Br'Nee of sacrificing M'Lee's people just to
preserve 'some stinking plants', and expresses amazement
that Zhaan is a 'vegetable'. Tactful, isn't he? He also makes
some terrible puns, most notably 'bone appetit' when
M'Lee eats Br'Nee.

You Can Be More: Aeryn is tender towards Moya's baby and has an instant rapport with it. She's almost motherly!

Big Blue: Zhaan considers the asteroid, a world exclusively populated by plant life, to be paradise, and she's upset that she will never visit it again.

I was a Teenage Luxan: D'Argo has bad allergies to plant life. He has always been suspicious of doctors because he's mostly been treated by charlatans, but he's amazed by the effectiveness of Br'Nee's herbal remedy. D'Argo comes over all philosophical when consoling Zhaan about leaving the asteroid, and it shows how far his character has progressed and deepened during the season. He says that, if Zhaan can't go back, then 'those miracle plants will be found by someone else. In the great scheme of things, it's all the same,' and Zhaan notes the reversal of their roles.

Buckwheat the Sixteenth: Rygel spends his time being cold and bundling up with Chiana, which he uses, again, as a chance to grope her. D'Argo has taken to calling Rygel 'your flatulence'.

The Insane Military Commander: Crais fights Scorpius to retain control of his ship but by the end he realises he has lost and tells Lt Braca, his new second in command, to follow Scorpius's orders.

Nosferatu in Rubber: At first Scorpius tries to influence events by offering suggestions to Crais but, when Crais rejects them, he takes more direct action: Scorpius threatens to report Crais's actions to First Command, then takes command, promising to strip Crais of rank. This provokes Crais to violence but Scorpius exhibits great strength and a much deeper voice when enraged: 'Why must you force me to display my physical superiority to your kind, as well? If you want to fight anyone, attack your executioner.' There are rumours among the Peacekeepers that Scorpius can sense other people's weaknesses and fears which would explain how he knew Crichton was a spy in **119**, 'Nerve'. His reception of M'Lee is very surprising and hints at greater depth of character than expected: 'We must know when to be strong and when to show compassion . . . as a matter of honour, sometimes we must be willing to give of ourselves.'

A Ship, a Living Ship!: Aeryn, the only one among the crew whom Moya and Pilot feel they can really trust, thinks the offspring is 'amazing and frightening'. The child realises he is different and is reluctant to talk to or trust his mother, but when Aeryn comes aboard he answers her every request and need, showing her the right controls to use and allowing her to help him stay hidden from the Peacekeepers. He has a Sonic Ascendancy cannon that Aeryn brings online. Moya is grateful for Aeryn's help and tells her she can choose a name for the child. Rygel and Chiana both point out to Aeryn that they may have no choice but to use the baby as a weapon to help them escape the Peacekeepers. Aeryn refuses even to consider it.

Alien Encounters: Delvians are plants. Twenty-one episodes and we only find that out now, but it all makes perfect sense. First Zhaan has white sap for blood (**102**, 'Throne For a Loss'), then photogasms in intense light (**111**, 'Till the Blood Runs Clear'), then we discover that Delvians eat life forms that are half animal, half plant (**113**, 'Rhapsody In Blue'), and finally when Zhaan hurt her arm she didn't say her bone was broken, she said the fibres were torn (**117**, 'Through the Looking Glass'). Zhaan also makes herself invisible at one point, a skill similar to the cloaking effect she utilised in **111**, 'Till the Blood Runs Clear'. David Kemper has stated that it was because she was surrounded by so many plants, which explains why it is not a skill we see her use again. Her temperature is self-regulating in all but the most extreme climates.

D'Argo is hurt and suffers from internal bleeding. Presumably this is very serious for a Luxan: to make the blood run clear the wound needs to be violently punched or somehow stimulated, and how do you punch an internal injury?

M'Lee's people are calcivores – bone eaters – but they are passive and calm after eating. When they are hungry they sprout spines and thorns and present themselves as a feral beast. Br'Nee's people can live for over two hundred cycles.

Disney on Acid: When they're getting ready to leave for the asteroid Crichton tells Pilot 'four to beam down', although it's doubtful whether Pilot has ever seen *Star Trek*. He says of Br'Nee: 'Swamp Thing here ain't the "Mr Rogers" scientist we thought he was,' which manages to reference DC Comics and American children's TV in one sentence.

Logic Leaps: Scorpius knows about Moya's baby, and since Crichton didn't know Moya had given birth when he was in the Chair, Scorpius must have seen the child when the Command Carrier was in pursuit of Moya. Plus they haven't travelled far, because in **122**, 'Family Ties' they are back at the Gammak base in no time. Thus it's implied that immediately following **120**, 'The Hidden Memory' there was a chase which resulted in Moya hiding in the asteroid belt, otherwise how would the Command Carrier have known Moya was in there? So . . . where on earth did Stark get to? He was on the ship at the end of the last episode and there hasn't been time for them to drop him off anywhere. (Executive Producer Richard Manning admitted that they screwed up, but they offer an excuse in **216**, 'The Locket'.)

A world that's only inhabited by plants couldn't survive because there'd be nothing to enable pollination. Zhaan states there are no insects on the asteroid – so alien plants don't need pollination?

Crichton shared Unity with Zhaan (**113**, 'Rhapsody In Blue'), what are the chances that he could entirely share her consciousness and not realise she was a plant?

Stats: PK scans are keyed to look for energy sources, so Moya switches off all but essential systems to help her hide. This makes the ship very cold indeed. She can establish a direct laser comms link with the baby – to intercept it someone would have to be directly between them.

Guest Stars: English actress Francesca Buller, who is also Ben Browder's wife, appeared as Minnie Chaplin in

Richard Attenborough's film *Chaplin*, and returned to *Farscape* in both Season Two (playing ro-NA in **211**, 'Look at the Princess II: I Do, I Think' and **212**, 'Look at the Princess III: The Maltese Crichton') and Three (playing Raxil in **313**, 'Scratch 'n' Sniff'). Marton Csokas played Borias in *Xena: Warrior Princess* and plays Celeborn in Peter Jackson's first *Lord Of the Rings* film. David Franklin played Brutus in *Xena: Warrior Princess* and will be a semi-regular on *Farscape* from now on.

Backstage: This is the first episode to feature Gigi Edgley in the main title sequence.

The Verdict: The M'Lee storyline plays on *Beauty and the Beast*, making us think it's a standard parable, so at first we think the beast is bad, then it's reversed and M'Lee is supposedly bad, which seems predictable, but then it's reversed again. M'Lee's race have horrible eating habits – eating only the bones and leaving the flesh to rot – but that is just her nature and everything she does she does to survive, so despite some revulsion she earns the crew's sympathies. Francesca Buller and Marton Csokas are both very good, and their costumes are marvellous. Scorpius is emerging as a very threatening character indeed and Crais gets more interesting the more pathetic he becomes. The control room of the offspring is a beautiful set, all lights and red flashes, looking like a huge pinball table. Rarely does *Farscape* so completely separate its A, B and C storylines, but this works, although it seems that the B and C threads – Scorpius and the baby – are groundwork for the imminent season finale.

122
Family Ties

1st US Transmission Date: 28 January 2000
1st UK Transmission Date: 5 June 2000
1st Australian Transmission Date: 27 January 2001

Writer: David Kemper and Rockne S O'Bannon
Director: Tony Tilse

Guest Cast: Lani Tupu (Capt. Bialar Crais), Wayne Pygram (Scorpius), David Franklin (Lt Braca)

'You told me that every man has a chance to become his own kind of hero. Well, I don't think I'll be coming home . . . but I think I know what you meant.'

Moya is still trapped in the asteroid field. Rygel takes a Transport Pod to the Command Carrier and tries to sell out his shipmates. Scorpius indulges him but gives orders for him to be killed as soon as Crichton is captured. Crais, now persona non grata on his own ship, allies himself with Rygel and convinces Scorpius to let him go to Moya and persuade them to surrender. In fact he defects and asks Moya's crew for asylum and sanctuary, which they give him – perhaps too amazed to do otherwise. Moya could StarBurst free but won't leave her baby – which Aeryn christens Talyn, after her own father. D'Argo and Crichton fill a Transport Pod with explosives and fly it into the oil-covered moon which houses Scorpius's Gammak base. Scorpius has the Command Carrier follow the pod to recapture Crichton. Crichton and D'Argo bail out, ready for Aeryn to collect them in her Prowler and return them safely to Moya before she StarBursts free with Talyn close by and thus being pulled through as well. The moon catches fire and the Gammak base is entirely destroyed. Unfortunately Aeryn cannot get to Crichton and D'Argo without being spotted by other Prowlers, and Crais steals Talyn and takes off into the asteroid field, leaving Moya to StarBurst alone. Crichton and D'Argo are left floating in space. D'Argo is unprotected and is dying, Aeryn can't reach them, and even if she does Moya has gone, perhaps for good.

Buck Rogers Redux: 'I can tell you this for free – I will not be taken alive.' It's Crichton's idea to pilot a Transport Pod into the Command Carrier, in effect a kamikaze run, and unless D'Argo had suggested the alternate plan he probably would have gone ahead with it. He calls Rygel a 'soulless bastard', but still forgives him his selfishness. He tells Crais that he's 'desperate for human male to male

conversation' about football and cars, but his rapport with
D'Argo has never been stronger. They crack jokes at each
other even as they fly to almost certain death, and Crichton
tells him, 'I love hangin' with you, man.' He manages to
resist Chiana's come-on, which was the right thing to do,
but must have required superhuman self-control.

You Can Be More: When Aeryn was young, she remembers
a soldier appearing at her bunk one night. It was her
mother, and from her she learned, 'I wasn't merely an
accident, or a genetic birthing to fill the ranks, that she and
a male that she had cared about had chosen to yield a life
– mine.' Aeryn actually cries because she's so honoured by
Moya's decision to let her name the baby. She never
thought she would live as long as she has, and is withering
of D'Argo and Crichton's macho determination to go
down fighting: 'just to be in the warm glow of all this
testosterone'. She is reluctant to stay on Moya, but accepts
that she's the one with the strongest bond to Talyn. She's
incandescent with fury when Crais steals the child.

Big Blue: 'The instant I committed murder, I sacrificed my
right to exist. Since then, I view every microt as a generous
yet undeserved gift from the goddess.' Zhaan, chief anarchist, is the one who comes up with the explosive that
Crichton and D'Argo use, again harking back to her
revolutionary past. She tells Crichton that the crew of
Moya are now her family; Crichton agrees: 'Well, it's a
Jerry Springer kind of family, but for what it's worth,
Zhaan, you are family.' Happily Zhaan does not respond
by chanting 'Je-rry! Je-rry!' and we don't get a closing
thought from Rygel.

I was a Teenage Luxan: 'Fear accompanies the possibility
of death. Calm shepherds its certainty.' D'Argo takes great
satisfaction in kicking the hell out of Crais for keeping him
locked up. He insists on piloting the Transport Pod with
the explosives, and leaves the holo-image of his wife and
child with Zhaan. He is certain he will die, but goes to his
death without a moment of hesitation. He always believed

he'd live longer than this. He admits he has become fond of Chiana.

Buckwheat the Sixteenth: 'I am a Dominar of action!' Rygel tries to sell out his shipmates for his freedom but realises he's overplayed his hand and returns to Moya with Crais. He is unrepentant, though, and when Zhaan accuses him of going to sell them out, he calmly replies, 'You bet your shiny blue ass I did!' He's lucky they don't kill him on the spot. Crichton leaves Rygel his stuff if he dies. Rygel admits his selfishness, but seems grateful for Crichton's forgiveness. At the end he talks about abandoning Crichton, Aeryn and D'Argo but when it comes to the crunch he suddenly refuses to do so, proving that he's not really as self-serving as he appears . . . sometimes. Crichton loses all control of his nickname compulsion and calls Rygel 'Sparky, Spanky, Fluffy, Buckwheat the Sixteenth'. When he's bathing . . . is that a tail?

Everyone's Favourite Little Tralk: 'Don't tell me how to lie, it's one of the best things I do!' D'Argo wants Chiana to play prisoner and pretend that she was forced to help them in **119**, 'Nerve' and **120**, 'The Hidden Memory', but she refuses, preferring to rely on her wits and charm. She shows her appreciation for her crewmates by cooking them all their favourite dishes as a farewell meal.

The Insane Military Commander: 'It should've been about my brother. Somewhere along the way my priorities decayed. I realise I became more concerned with my own image and career.' Crais keeps severed Hynerian heads in his office as trophies. He realises he's lost his ship to Scorpius, but his decision to defect to Moya is hugely risky. He knew that D'Argo was innocent of Lo'Laan's murder (**110**, 'They've Got a Secret') but kept him locked up anyway because it requires a tribunal to overturn a murder conviction. He apologises to Crichton for his pursuit of him, which is another massive character shift, and agrees to advise and help Moya's crew. But when he sees an opportunity to flee in Talyn he takes it. It's love at first sight for him – that ship is everything he's ever wanted and he grabs it with both hands. His final message to Aeryn hints that he is secretly attracted to her. He has been officially designated 'irreversibly contaminated' and can never return to the Peacekeepers.

Nosferatu in Rubber: 'I cannot risk killing the knowledge that [Crichton] possesses and he knows that.' Scorpius has sent M'Lee (**121**, 'Bone to Be Wild') off in a transport but the security guard he assigned to guard her has vanished. Hope he was crunchy! He lets Crais go to Moya even though he knows he won't return, probably hoping that he will be classified irreversibly contaminated and command will fall to himself – which is exactly what happens. He doesn't care about Moya, Talyn, Crais or his Gammak base, only Crichton and the knowledge he possesses. But we still don't know why wormholes are so important to him (it only becomes apparent in Season Three). He admires Crichton's strategy (although it's really D'Argo and Crais's plan) and knows that he has been beaten as soon as the plan is put into effect. We see more evidence of his ability to tell when people are lying while he's interrogating Rygel.

A Ship, a Living Ship!: Moya refuses to leave her baby behind until Crichton persuades her that the best chance of rescuing the child is to StarBurst to safety and live to fight another day.

Big Baby: Talyn can support a pilot but doesn't require one. Instead he has been bred to respond to direct voice control. The Peacekeepers have tried many times to breed such a ship but each time both mother and child have died. Talyn and Moya survived because she gave birth free, and without a Control Collar. Moya can StarBurst free using Br'Nee's maps, but Talyn is still too young to StarBurst on his own.

The Ballad of Aeryn and John: Crichton and Aeryn don't say goodbye to each other. When she asks Crichton about the version of his father that she met in **116**, 'A Human

Reaction', she settles once and for all that it was really her that spent the night with Crichton in the safe house and not some phantom replica.

Worlds Apart: The moon on which the Gammak base is situated is covered in oil. It would have been nicer if they'd mentioned that in **120**, 'The Hidden Memory' rather than dropping it in here, because as it is it seems a bit deus ex machina.

Alien Encounters: Scorpius is a Scarran half-breed, according to Crais. During their conversation, Crais and Crichton discuss whether it really is a coincidence that Humans and Sebaceans should be so alike. Crais regrets that it is a mystery he may never solve.

Disney on Acid: As he and D'Argo are about to jump into space, Crichton calls them both 'Kirk and Spock! Abbot and Costello!' Ben Browder explained these pop culture references to *SFX*: The first 'is a homage to science fiction. But then I'm saying we're more like Abbot and Costello, which is more like a comedic/serious reference — we're a team but we're a different kind of team.'

Get Frelled: Chiana offers Crichton sex before he leaves because it's the only way she knows how to thank him. He replies 'never before the big game', but she gets a kiss out of him, and definitely slips him some tongue!

What Does This Do?: Typical of the attention to detail in the show – when Rygel is bathing in the mist bath on the Command Carrier he lets rip and farts a jet of steam into the air.

Logic Leaps: Aeryn can't move in to collect Crichton and D'Argo because the other Prowlers will see her and realise what she's doing . . . so why doesn't a Prowler from the Command Carrier pick them up? Why doesn't D'Argo have a space suit? Perhaps because none of the PK suits would fit him, but if so it should have been mentioned. In fact, why is D'Argo on the Transport Pod at all? Crichton could have executed their plan on his own quite easily. And although he has some bargaining power, isn't Rygel's treatment aboard the Command Carrier – he's fed, groomed and bathed – stretching credulity a bit too far? Crais has already lost command of his own ship to Scorpius, so why, when the episode begins, is Scorpius still keeping him around and discussing strategy with him? And although he surrenders, and offers some help to their plans, would the gang really allow Crais to sit down and eat with them?

Bloopers: When D'Argo passes out and lets go of Crichton's father's good-luck charm it would not fly away as it does because there's no gravity to attract it – it would float alongside them.

WHAT did you just say?: Both D'Argo and Crais speak in their native tongues in this episode, but we don't find out why the translator microbes don't handle it.

The Verdict: As the first year ends the two people most responsible for the direction of the show, Rockne S O'Bannon and David Kemper, take the opportunity to present what is in effect a restatement of the characters and an assessment of how far they have changed and grown since the first episode. We are given 35 minutes of two-hander character scenes as all the relationships are put under the spotlight and thrown into sharp relief, making it clear how much they have all come to care for each other, and us for them. Crais is entirely reinvented and a new character, Talyn, is introduced. Perhaps there are elements of the plot which don't quite hang together, but this is primarily a character piece, and as such it works beautifully. There is a strong sense of doom around the characters, and the cliffhanger is a genuinely gripping one with no immediate resolution apparent.

Season Two

Regular Cast
Ben Browder (Commander John Crichton)
Claudia Black (Aeryn Sun)
Virginia Hey (Pa'u Zotoh Zhaan)
Anthony Simcoe (Ka D'Argo)
Gigi Edgley (Chiana)
Lani Tupu (Voice of Pilot)
Jonathan Hardy (Voice of Dominar Rygel XVI)
Tim Mieville (Head puppeteer for Rygel)

201
Mind the Baby

1st US Transmission Date: 17 March 2000
1st UK Transmission Date: 12 June 2000
1st Australian Transmission Date: 5 December 2001

Writer: Richard Manning
Director: Andrew Prowse
Guest Cast: Lani Tupu (Capt. Bialar Crais), Wayne Pygram (Scorpius),
David Franklin (Braca)

Scorpius allows Aeryn to collect Crichton and D'Argo because he knows Crichton will not be taken alive (**122**, 'Family Ties'), but Aeryn evades capture and flies back into the asteroid field. Crais contacts her from Talyn and directs her to an asteroid with a breathable atmosphere and an abandoned installation on it where they can hide. In return for this help she agrees to assist Crais in winning Talyn's trust. When D'Argo and Crichton discover what Aeryn's done, D'Argo stuns her and Crichton takes the Prowler, boards Talyn, and removes Crais by force. Meanwhile, Moya has returned to the asteroid field following a distress call from Talyn. Crichton takes Crais to Moya and locks him up then collects the others. Talyn panics and flees the asteroid field and fires on Moya when she pursues. He demands that she provide a captain, and so Aeryn and Crais fly to Talyn to take command. Talyn implants Crais with a neural transponder and together Talyn and Crais throw Aeryn off the ship. Before Scorpius's Command Carrier can intercept either ship, both Talyn and Moya StarBurst away.

Buck Rogers Redux: Crichton's behaviour when he removes Crais from Talyn is manic and over the top, far more so than normal – has the Aurora Chair driven him a little bit nuts? He can now fly a Prowler.

You Can Be More: Aeryn is willing to lie to her friends and give up Crichton and Moya to be with Talyn, whom she cares for deeply. She fights Crais for him but loses and is distraught at her failure.

Big Blue: Zhaan is driven nearly insane by the loss of Crichton, Aeryn and D'Argo. She resumes the Delvian Seek and intends to devote the rest of her life to detached meditation. When Crichton returns she believes he's a spirit or hallucination, but she gives him a Delvian ear kiss anyway. It takes Aeryn to shock her out of her retreat – by accusing her of being selfish and abandoning her friends. However, Zhaan does not abandon the Seek, merely slows it down so that she can better help and cherish her friends.

I was a Teenage Luxan: D'Argo was in a coma for many days after being left in space too long, and when he wakes up he at first believes he is dead. He is hugely pleased to see Aeryn again, but he tongues her as soon as she tells him of her deal with Crais, just to save time arguing about it. He even admits to being pleased to see Rygel. He loves playing Scissors/Paper/Rock, even with himself, and he strongly disapproves of the name Talyn.

Buckwheat the Sixteenth: Rygel suffers from the Intons – a constriction of the airways brought about by strong emotion – when he is reunited with Crichton, Aeryn and D'Argo. When heading back to the asteroid he almost agrees to jump ship with Chiana, but decides against it.

Everyone's Favourite Little Tralk: Chiana is so glad to see Crichton that she actually *flies* across the maintenance bay. In interviews at the time, cast and crew referred to this as the first hint that Chiana had supernatural powers.

The Insane Military Commander: Aeryn: 'His goals and ours may no longer conflict.' Crais helps Aeryn rescue Crichton and D'Argo to gain her trust and offers to let her share command of Talyn. When he stands next to Crichton and tells Aeryn to make her choice, it seems he's indicating more than just a choice of ships, harking back to the hints in **122**, 'Family Ties' that he was romantically interested in her. Initially he contacts Scorpius from Talyn and strings him along, trying to stall for time. Later, when Crais leaves, he tries to convince Scorpius that he's killed Crichton, which could be a dig at Scorpius or an attempt to buy some time for Crichton. He is re-examining everything he was ever taught by the Peacekeepers, and wants to find a new path. Aeryn seems to believe that Crais can change; Crichton isn't so sure. Crais beats Aeryn in a straight fight and throws her off Talyn, but doesn't kill her even though he could. Now that he's rejected PK teaching and methods he's a more interesting character and has embarked with Talyn on a search for enlightenment.

Nosferatu in Rubber: Scorpius is very patient with Crais, and when Moya and Talyn emerge from the asteroid field he expects that there is some strategy being implemented. After the destruction of his Gammak base he won't underestimate them again. He knows Crais is lying about Crichton being dead and resumes the hunt. He has some sort of rod that emerges from his head, revolving and dripping with blood, that has glowing cylinders placed in it (explained in **212**, 'Look at the Princess III: The Maltese Crichton'). He has redecorated Crais's quarters and removed the gruesome trophies of past kills, replacing them with a shield incorporating two crossed maces.

A Ship, a Living Ship!: Moya runs back into danger to help Talyn, regardless of her own personal safety or that of her crew. When Talyn runs in panic she pursues him, which panics him even more, but Moya refuses to stop, believing she can talk her offspring down. The defence shield which was fitted in **107**, 'PK Tech Girl', is still in place, but it is severely damaged when Talyn fires upon Moya. In the opening sequence we see Moya fired upon and hit by a Sheyang vessel, but we never see her escape – presumably she StarBursted away.

Big Baby: Talyn can be panicked and confused by random broadband transmission beamed at him. He chooses Crais as Captain and implants a Neural Transponder in his neck, which allows him to share Talyn's mind and systems in much the way Pilot shares Moya's. He has guns that can be deployed in the control room. He is now mature enough to StarBurst on his own.

The Ballad of Aeryn and John: Crichton asks Aeryn how many times they've been close and she whispers 'just that once', embarrassed that D'Argo might hear. She must be referring to the night they spent together in **116**, 'A Human Reaction'. Crichton's embarrassed too and only meant it in terms of being friendly. When she leaves for Talyn they again refuse to say goodbye, but they lock hands and their look says everything. When she's back on Moya at the end she and Crichton sit in Pilot's den and discuss Talyn. They're cuddled up together, Crichton's playing with her hair and they're relaxed in a way they've never been before.

Worlds Apart: This asteroid field is full of surprises: first a lush plant world and now a mining colony with a breathable atmosphere.

Alien Encounters: From references made by Chiana and Zhaan they have had an adventure off screen. There was some sort of trial on a planet called Litigara when Moya refused to abandon her remaining crew. This adventure will be seen in **208**, 'Dream a Little Dream'; also see **Backstage**.

Disney on Acid: Crichton after Talyn fires on Moya: 'Let's get that boy some guidance before he turns into a full-blown Menendez brother.' The Menendez brothers were two boys who killed their own parents in the US and were the subject of a high-profile trial.

Logic Leaps: Scorpius's strategy seems flawed: he let Aeryn collect Crichton and D'Argo because he was afraid Crichton would not be taken alive, but how could Crichton have killed himself stuck in a spacesuit, short of removing the helmet? And why is he more likely to be taken alive during a forced boarding of Moya by lots of troops, when he will presumably be armed and likely to shoot himself rather than be taken? It seems that his strategy was devised as an excuse to get out of the cliffhanger and it doesn't hold up.

Bloopers: In the originally broadcast version a hand can be seen holding the cable with Talyn's neural transponder on it. It has been painted out for repeats, video and DVD releases.

WHAT did you just say?: D'Argo: 'As Crichton once said, "I would rather go down on a swing".' Crichton: 'Swinging, you wanna go down swinging.'

Backstage: The first episode filmed for Season Two, which was intended to be the season premiere, was 'Re:Union'. At the last minute the second episode, 'Mind the Baby', was brought forward to start the season. 'Re:Union' was recut and eventually emerged as **208**, 'Dream a Little Dream'. As a special treat the original cut of 'Re:Union' was shown by the SciFi channel in the US and there is an examination of the differences between it and **208** in the episode guide for 'Dream a Little Dream'. As originally planned, the season would have begun with Chiana, Zhaan and Rygel alone, searching for their shipmates and Crichton and the others would only have appeared in dream sequences. The references made to Litigara (see **Alien Encounters**) relate to this adventure.

The Verdict: This is all as expected. All the cliffhangers are resolved, some more satisfactorily than others, and by the end the series has embarked on a new direction. Again they are fugitives, and again Crichton is being pursued by 'an insane military commander', but this time it's Scorpius, and he's not after revenge, but the wormhole knowledge in Crichton's head. Talyn is out there too, which adds a nicely unpredictable element to the proceedings. There's bags of emotion on display as the crew are all overjoyed to reunite and heartbroken when they may have to part again Talyn emerges as a character in his own right, and Scorpius looms large too. However, it's hard not to conclude that beginning the season with 'Re:Union', postponing the resolution of the cliffhanger, and toying with our expectations, would have been a more courageous and satisfying thing to do. As it is this feels like a lot of boxes are being ticked but not many risks taken – then again, that's always the problem with the concluding part of multi-episode stories, and this is by no means a bad episode.

202
Vitas Mortis

1st US Transmission Date: 24 March 2000
1st UK Transmission Date: 19 June 2000
1st Australian Transmission Date: 14 July 2001

Writer: Grant McAloon
Director: Tony Tilse
Guest Cast: Melissa Jaffer (Old Nilaam),
Anna Lise Philips (Young Nilaam)

A rumour heard on a commerce planet leads Moya to Nilaam, a female Luxan Orican (holy woman) who is nearing death alone on a forgotten world. She asks D'Argo to help her through the Ritual of Passing and he agrees, but as she prepares to die she senses great strength from D'Argo and instead performs the Ritual of Renewal, turning herself back into a young woman. While she and

D'Argo celebrate with lots of energetic sex, Moya begins to disintegrate and show the signs of extreme old age. Realising that she was in fact draining strength from Moya and not D'Argo, Nilaam tries to save the ship without sacrificing herself, but fails. Eventually she and D'Argo perform the Ritual of Passing, she kills herself, and Moya is healed.

Buck Rogers Redux: Crichton is over the top with his initial objections to D'Argo taking part in the Ritual of Passing. Why does he argue so loudly and so long about this? That makes two episodes in a row where he's exhibited uncharacteristically extreme behaviour . . .

You Can Be More: Aeryn, realising that Nilaam is the cause of Moya's problems, catches her and opens fire without even yelling at her to stop, which is extremely hot-headed, even for her. She's irritated that Chiana won't do her laundry for her.

I was a Teenage Luxan: The tattoos on D'Argo's face and chin mark him as a general even though he is not. This comes from his second campaign. 'My General was badly wounded. I knew he wouldn't survive interrogation if he were captured, so I took on the tattoo of his rank to protect him.' He knows that he has to help Nilaam die in order to save Moya and he cries in front of Crichton because of how hard it is for him to do the right thing. His Qualta Blade is the instrument of her death. Zhaan says that a Luxan who assists in the Ritual of Passing goes partway into the other realm and gets a glimpse of the other side, but D'Argo makes no reference to this after the ceremony.

Buckwheat the Sixteenth: Rygel physically plugs a hull breach with his backside, which is stuck out in space for quite some time: it's a miracle his innards weren't sucked out. Now there's a lovely thought. Chiana refers to him as Froglips and Toadface.

Everyone's Favourite Little Tralk: Chiana does D'Argo's washing but won't do Aeryn's. She looks mighty jealous when D'Argo returns to the ship with fresh young Nilaam. She seems to sense the Ritual of Renewal, even though it's happening down on the planet and she's up on Moya – another hint of supernatural Chi.

In the Driving Seat: When Pilot is affected by Moya's ageing he turns to Aeryn for support, re-emphasising the strong bond between them. Pilot's species live for an average of one thousand cycles, Leviathans only live three hundred. When a Pilot is bonded to a Leviathan they realise it will cost them seven hundred cycles of life. Pilot says he would not have it any other way.

A Ship, a Living Ship!: The crew do their washing in Moya's Amnexus fluid, a substance that solidifies in old Leviathans. Unfortunately for Chiana it solidifies while she is standing in it doing the washing and nothing can dissolve it to free her until Nilaam reverses her drain of Moya's energy.

Alien Encounters: Assisting an Orican in the Ritual of Passing is the highest honour a Luxan can receive. Female Luxans do not have chin tentacles. Nilaam actually sticks her hand inside D'Argo's chest and has a rummage, thereby reading his soul and thoughts; he is unharmed by this. She also zaps a gun out of Crichton's hand, diverts a gunshot, and freezes Crichton and Aeryn in crystal suspension. So Luxans can obviously achieve great spiritual powers, much like Delvians, if they so wish.

Disney on Acid: 'So, if she wants to rip out your liver, snack on it with a Chianti, she can do that?' Crichton refers to *Silence of the Lambs*.

Get Frelled: D'Argo and young Nilaam go at it like rabbits, but the look of a bashful cat-who-got-the-cream on D'Argo's face when he realises he's about to get laid is priceless.

Seen it all Before: This is the first time we've seen another Luxan and the episode is reminiscent of the first time we saw another Delvian, **113**, 'Rhapsody In Blue' – a holy female who spiritually joins with one of Moya's crew and takes something she shouldn't.

Logic Leaps: Nilam says she could lead Moya's crew to their homes, but there's no mention of her passing charts or anything like that to D'Argo, so presumably she was going to sense her way home somehow. Rygel would have frozen solid and died if he were stuck half out in space unless, like D'Argo, he can survive in a vacuum, which seems a bit of a stretch.

Guest Stars: Melissa Jaffer has a long career behind her, including appearances on many Aussie soaps and mini-series including *Head Start*, *G.P.* and *Kings*. She voices a pilot in **205**, 'The Way We Weren't' and returns as a different character in **322**, 'Dog with Two Bones'.

The Verdict: It's nice to see another Luxan, and D'Argo gets more depth, but this is a predictable episode that doesn't deliver much in the way of thrills or laughs. It's competent, and it looks great, but not a classic. Still, it's a nice pink corset Nilaam gets to wear, and women the world over swooned at Crichton in the full black leather PK garb, which reflects the darker tone of the show this season.

203
Taking the Stone

1st US Transmission Date: 31 March 2000
1st UK Transmission Date: 10 July 2000
1st Australian Transmission Date: 6 December 2001

Writer: Justin Monjo
Director: Rowan Woods
Guest Cast: Anthony Hayes (Molnon), Peter Scarf (Das), Michela Noonan (Vyna), Natasha Beaumont (Janixx)

Chiana discovers that her brother is dead but when she tries to talk to Crichton he's distracted and gives her the brushoff. Upset, she leaves Moya in Aeryn's Prowler and lands on a Royal Cemetery planet where clans of young people live in underground caves. In the caves is a deep pit, at the bottom of which is a sonic net that uses the sound of the jumper's voice to generate sound waves to cushion their fall. The clans live a highly ritualised life, and when they are 22 they jump into the pit in silence and die, which they call Taking the Stone. Crichton discovers this is because there is a lot of radiation in the caves, which the pit amplifies, and after 22 cycles they begin to suffer radiation poisoning. He explains the radiation to them but the clans vote to remain in the caves and continue their ways rather than move to the surface where they could live longer and healthier lives. Chiana joins the clan and is determined to jump into the pit both to prove her independence and to feel alive. Crichton tries to force her back to Moya but Aeryn persuades Crichton that Chi must be free to stay or go as she chooses. Eventually Chi jumps, the sonic net breaks her fall, and she returns to Moya.

Rygel steals treasure from a royal grave and decorates his quarters on Moya with it. Unfortunately it is cursed and begins to fly around the room, so he reluctantly returns the artefacts.

Buck Rogers Redux: Crichton's unusually gung-ho approach and increasingly erratic behaviour continues. In **202,** 'Vitas Mortis' he tried to force D'Argo to leave the Orican, now he tries to force Chiana to leave the clans. Both times it was apparent that they needed to be left to their own devices to work through whatever was annoying them. Molnon, leader of the clan, offers to tell him why he wants Chi to jump if Crichton eats one of four magic mushrooms, one of which is deadly. Crichton does so and gets lucky, but it's a stupid thing to do. He then challenges Molnon on the very edge of the pit and seems willing to jump with him. He asks Aeryn if he's seemed a little crazy lately,' to which she replies, 'What do you mean, "lately"?' Since they don't know any other humans, how are any of the others to gauge Crichton's behaviour? It's established that he baffles his shipmates at the best of times. The only ones aware of Crichton's increasing unpredictability are the viewers and Crichton himself. Crichton the scientist makes a brief return: he spends his spare time disassembling bits of Moya's control systems so that he can find out how they work.

You Can Be More: 'I'm not good at nice.' Aeryn is surprisingly insightful and sensible with Chiana, she knows that she needs space to work things out and refuses to let Crichton kidnap Chiana back to Moya. This is because she says she understands loss (Crichton says he does too, but it's not clear who he's referring to). This amazes Crichton because she is 'the pin-up girl for frontal assault'.

Big Blue: Zhaan chants over the objects Rygel plundered, to try and lift any curses, but gives up when he tells her to get lost.

Buckwheat the Sixteenth: Rygel stoops to a new low – grave robbing. Despite his initial refusal to believe in curses he eventually relents and returns the items, but will he have learned his lesson? Fat chance.

Everyone's Favourite Little Tralk: 'I never had any courage. As a kid, Nerri gave me everything. I just followed him.' Nebari, and some other races, use surgically implanted Life Discs to maintain a link with loved ones. When the disc stops functioning it means the other person is dead; Chiana's disc links her to her brother, Nerri. Prior to Crichton and Aeryn's arrival on the planet she performs the first ritual required to join the clan – running naked through rings of fire. She then hangs upside down between two big stones which exert some magnetic force – no one's ever lasted longer than fifteen microts, but she beats the record. Chiana's deeply hurt that Crichton brushed her off when she tried to talk about her brother, but it's interesting that she went to him: in **202**, 'Vitas Mortis' it seemed clear that D'Argo was her favourite shipmate. After all, she did his laundry.

Worlds Apart: Rygel implies that there are many Royal Cemetery planets. He considers it disgusting to bury the dead near the living.

Alien Encounters: We don't know what race the clan are but when the females become pregnant their stomachs turn transparent.

Disney on Acid: Crichton asks Molnon, 'Are we having a failure to communicate, here?' which is a reference to the classic Paul Newman film, *Cool Hand Luke*.

Get Frelled: Chiana makes out with Molnon, but it's not clear how far that particular encounter goes.

Seen it all Before: A world of young people who die at a certain age and think anyone over that age is old and worn out is reminiscent of *Logan's Run*.

Logic Leaps: When Aeryn and Crichton begin exploring the caves they're wearing their coats, but they're coatless for the rest of the episode, until they leave. Presumably the clan have some kind of handy coat-check service. How does the Life Disc work? It must send and receive some kind of signal, so we must assume no one on Nebari Prime knows Chiana has one, otherwise it surely would have been used to track her down by now.

WHAT did you just say?: Rygel calls Earth 'Erp', like Aeryn did in **101**, 'Premiere'. Crichton tells Aeryn to call Zhaan: 'Let's get her on the dog and bone,' though, not surprisingly, Aeryn doesn't know what he means. It's cockney rhyming slang for telephone, and Crichton is very well educated about London dialects for a good ol' southern boy.

Stats: Sonic Nets are used by Peacekeepers in aerial combat training.

Backstage: Nerri was originally intended to be a sister, but Gigi Edgley, who has an elder brother, asked for it to be changed to a brother because she found it easier to connect emotionally to Chiana's loss.

The Verdict: This episode looks great – the planet is spooky and foreboding and the design of Chiana's hair is especially cool, although Crichton's hair seems to be suffering from gel overload. Rowan Woods does a great job and it's clear that the show's darker, grittier aesthetic is now well established and working wonders. The relationships between the characters are also played out nicely, especially the interplay between Crichton and Aeryn, and Crichton and Chiana. Gigi Edgley finally gets to carry an episode and she does a marvellous job. It expands and deepens the character, and avoids her becoming the domestic homebody she threatened to become in **202**, 'Vitas Mortis'. The only downside, apart from the total irrelevancy of Rygel's subplot, is that it's all a bit predictable and nothing unexpected happens – a problem **202**, 'Vitas Mortis' also suffered from. (Happily the next set of episodes alleviate any worries there may have been about the show's scripts becoming routine.)

204
Crackers Don't Matter

1st US Transmission Date: 7 April 2000
1st UK Transmission Date: 17 July 2000
1st Australian Transmission Date: 10 December 2001

Writer: Justin Monjo
Director: Ian Watson
Guest Cast: Wayne Pygram (Scorpius), Danny Adcock (T'raltixx)

While visiting a commerce planet Moya's crew find that Scorpius has seeded it with wanted beacons. They buy a thousand units of crackers and leave with a technician called T'raltixx who promises to make Moya invisible to scans if they take him to his home planet. He builds a small demonstration device which successfully turns the WDP invisible. On the way they have to pass three pulsars and T'raltixx warns them that the light may affect their judgment. The crew turn on each other; D'Argo nearly kills Rygel before teaming up with Chiana; Aeryn and Rygel also team up. Pilot stops talking to anyone, and Zhaan writhes around in the light having photogasms.

Crichton begins to hallucinate Scorpius but realises that they are past the pulsars and it must be T'raltixx who is affecting them. He manages to capture all his shipmates and persuade them to work together and help him kill T'raltixx, who is barricaded in the sluice chamber making Moya bathe him in light. Using T'raltixx's invisibility device Crichton enters the chamber and kills the bad guy.

Buck Rogers Redux: Pilot tells Crichton what he thinks of him: 'You're not particularly smart, can hardly smell, can barely see, and you're not even vaguely physically or spiritually imposing. Is there *anything* you do well?' Crichton's got the worst eyesight of anyone on board and, since it's light that makes the crew nuts, he is the one best able to keep it together.

Howie Lewis beat him up when he was twelve, but he got revenge by pouring sugar in Howie's Harley's petrol tank. He doesn't like Italian food, has blue eyes and better than 20/20 vision. After three episodes in which Crichton's behaviour has become increasingly erratic he finally goes entirely off the deep end, but only because of T'raltixx. Still, he is *very* nuts. Can it only be the light? Also, his initial distrust of T'raltixx, before he has anything to back it up, is just that bit too vehement even before the light takes effect.

You Can Be More: Aeryn barricades herself in command with Rygel and their share of food cubes. She shoots at Crichton when he comes to talk and calls him a 'self-important, deficient little man' which provokes him to call her 'a frigid, flat-butted Peacekeeper skank'. It must be love.

Big Blue: Pilot: 'She's a plant – put her in the light, watch her smile.' Zhaan is least affected. At first she tries to pick a fight with Aeryn but in the end decides it's too much hassle and goes to sit in the light and get her jollies.

I was a Teenage Luxan: D'Argo allies himself with Chiana, tries to kill Rygel by forcing crackers down his throat, stings Zhaan unconscious because he thinks she's in league with Crichton, and tries to run away with Chiana in the WDP. He also takes a gunshot in the leg, from Crichton. He later apologises to Rygel and tells him how ashamed he is, but Rygel can't forgive him.

Buckwheat the Sixteenth: As ever, in a crisis Rygel's thoughts turn to food, but after D'Argo attacks him he hides in a conduit until Aeryn finds him. He attacks Aeryn when he thinks she's going to betray him and gets knocked out for his pains.

Everyone's Favourite Little Tralk: Chiana's distrust of Aeryn surfaces first, then she joins forces with D'Argo. Crichton captures her and for a dodgy moment it looks like he's going to rape her, but instead he calls her a slut and knocks her unconscious.

In the Driving Seat: T'raltixx capitalises on Pilot's distrust of his shipmates, and gets him to admit that he neither likes nor trusts them that much.

Hi, Harvey: When Crichton hallucinates Scorpius it's assumed that it's just the affects of the light . . . but is it?

A Ship, a Living Ship!: T'raltixx implies that his race specifically needs Leviathans to provide the kind of light-rich environment they require. Moya's bio-luminescence is so increased that the ship actually glows.

Alien Encounters: T'raltixx says that there are thousands of his race in dormancy who will be revived by Leviathan light and will swarm around killing everybody. He is blind but has a strong internal radar that is just as good. He can shoot bolts of light from orifices on his face where eyes should be. He can climb walls like Spiderman.

Disney on Acid: Scorpius's comment 'Revenge is a dish best served cold,' gets a frustrated response from Crichton: 'Shut up! I *hate* when villains quote Shakespeare!'

There are simply too many references to list, as mad Crichton goes into pop-culture stream-of-consciousness mode.

What Does This Do?: Zhaan pre-digests some food to make a paste that will protect Crichton from the radiation in T'raltixx's light room. So he goes into battle smeared in light-green puke. Lovely.

Logic Leaps: It was a bit daft of T'raltixx to tell the crew that the light from the pulsars would affect them, because by doing so he revealed his own techniques and gave them the information they needed to defeat him. Oops.

WHAT did you just say?: Crichton's vision of Scorpius tells him to shoot D'Argo: 'Then we can go to the beach. I know a place with naked Sebacean women and margarita shooters!'

Guest Stars: Danny Adcock appeared alongside Wayne Pygram in *Fire* and returned to *Farscape* as Co-Kura Strappa in Season Three.

Backstage: There's a deleted scene on the Region 2 DVD release of Scorpius singing '99 Bottles of Beer on the Wall' with Crichton. It's covered extensively in issue five of the official *Farscape* Magazine. David Kemper, in *Cult Times*, revealed that the appearance of Scorpius in this episode directly inspired the creation of Harvey: '[It] told me what I wanted to do with the year. It suddenly became so clear ... We developed that aspect and it became what the season is about.'

The Verdict: The best episode of the season so far and one of the best *Farscape* episodes ever. All the cast have a whale of a time acting silly, but Claudia Black and Ben Browder get the best lines and get to have a big gunfight that's loads of fun. It's almost a mirror image of **117**, 'Through the Looking Glass' – a ship-bound show with an enemy that the crew have to work together to fight in spite of forces pulling them apart. Except this time there's no happy ending. Lots of old wounds are reopened and harsh truths voiced, and even though they eventually unite and win the day, the crisis pulls the crew apart rather than bringing them closer together. Wayne Pygram has a blast as Scorpius, and seeing him in a Hawaiian shirt rambling about margarita shooters is laugh-out-loud daft. But it's still topped by the sight of Crichton in that absurd outfit, daubed in Zhaan's puke. After two episodes that looked great but perhaps lacked inspiration, this is a sparkling return to form with a script that's crammed full of brilliant one-liners.

205
The Way We Weren't

1st US Transmission Date: 14 April 2000
1st UK Transmission Date: 24 July 2000
1st Australian Transmission Date: 11 December 2001

Writer: Naren Shankar
Director: Tony Tilse
Guest Cast: Alex Dimitriades (Velorek), Lani Tupu (Capt. Bialar Crais),
Melissa Jaffer (Voice of female Pilot)

Then: Three cycles ago a Peacekeeper called Velorek, who specialised in bonding pilots to Leviathans, was contacted by Crais and instructed to secure a pilot. He visited the pilot race's world and convinced one youngster, who had been judged unfit to be bonded, to agree to be bonded to Moya. Moya's original pilot, who had resisted PK servitude, was no longer needed and was executed by PK troops at Crais's command. One of the troopers was Aeryn, who had been taken off Prowler duty and assigned to assist Velorek. Pilot was then forcibly grafted into Moya. Velorek realised that Crais's secret project – to breed a Leviathan gunship – would probably kill Moya, so he secretly installed the shield that prevented conception (which D'Argo shattered in **110**, 'They've Got a Secret'). He and Aeryn were lovers but she betrayed him in order to secure a posting back to Prowler duty. Velorek was tortured to death but never revealed the measures he had taken to thwart Crais's project. Moya never conceived, was reassigned as a prison transport . . . the rest is history.

Now: Chiana finds a recording of the previous pilot's execution and discovers Aeryn had a part in events. The crew confront her and she admits it, but insists she didn't realise Moya was the same Leviathan. D'Argo hides the tape, but Rygel steals it and shows it to Pilot. Pilot nearly kills Aeryn in fury and stops Moya dead, refusing to move until Aeryn leaves. Crichton goes to see Pilot to talk him down but Pilot rips himself out of Moya's system, breaking the bond and leaving Moya uncontrolled. Eventually Pilot will starve and the life support will fail. He then commands the DRDs to adopt defensive position and keep out the crew. Crichton and Aeryn break in and Pilot admits his own culpability in the death of his predecessor. Aeryn and Pilot make peace and Pilot is naturally rebonded to Moya.

You Can Be More: 'Things were very different then: my priorities, my values, and my relationships.' We've always known Aeryn was a PK but now we are confronted with the harsh reality of what that means – she was a traitorous, cold-blooded killer. She was in love with Velorek but she still betrayed him for her own ends, although she tells him to change his mind about sabotaging the breeding programme just before his arrest, so perhaps she relented at the last moment. Her relationships back then were 'painful' but Velorek is the only one she ever loved.

She has been on hundreds of Leviathans.

Big Blue: Zhaan was on board when the pilots were switched and we glimpse her being led along a corridor in one of the flashbacks. She turns on Aeryn too, but soon realises she's being too harsh: 'You had no choice back then ... In that world, that was the only kind of Peacekeeper you could be.'

I was a Teenage Luxan: D'Argo still loses whenever he and Crichton resolve a question by playing Rock/Scissors/ Paper.

Buckwheat the Sixteenth: Rygel was on board Moya when the pilots were changed and his fury at Aeryn is something to behold. He shows Pilot the tape because he says he has a right to know, but the others believe he did it so Pilot would owe him a favour.

Everyone's Favourite Little Tralk: Chiana takes the pragmatist's view to the revelations about Aeryn, wondering if the others had thought Aeryn had been 'out picking Rawliss Buds while all the other mean Peacekeepers did all the really nasty stuff?'

In the Driving Seat: Pilot was voted unworthy of being bonded to a Leviathan but his hunger to see the stars led him to agree to Velorek's deal. He now blames himself for the death of his predecessor and the consequent suffering endured by Moya, and feels unworthy of his role on Moya. For a pilot to bond naturally with a Leviathan takes one or two cycles, but Pilot was forcibly grafted into Moya, and so is in constant pain. After he severs his connection he instructs D'Argo on how to reattach minor, temporary connection to give him rudimentary control. He will now bond naturally with Moya; this will take a cycle during which he will have less control than before, but he will never feel the pain again. When his arm was cut off in **109**, 'DNA Mad Scientist', he only got slightly annoyed, so the fury he displays when strangling Aeryn is entirely unexpected and opens the character up immensely.

The Insane Military Commander: Now we know why Crais went into raptures when he saw Talyn – it was the culmination of a project he had instigated. It was not just the death of his brother that sent him over the edge, the flashbacks reveal he was quite mad and utterly ruthless already.

A Ship, a Living Ship!: Before the current pilot, Moya had a female pilot for 21 cycles. She was anaesthetised while the change was made and awoke to find herself being tortured into accepting a new pilot. The crew aren't weightless because of 'Internal Gravity Bladders'. Crichton and D'Argo are trying to repair the defence screen (**201**, 'Mind the Baby') they took from the *Zelbinion* (**107**, 'PK Tech Girl') but they're not sure they can make it work again.

The Ballad of Aeryn and John: Aeryn tells Crichton that Velorek told her she could be more than just a PK, and Crichton told her the same thing the day they first met (**101**, 'Premiere'). Crichton says, 'And you say you loved this man?' Aeryn doesn't reply, but their looks say it all. She as good as admits that she and Crichton would be lovers were she not both afraid of the consequences and conditioned against such attachments. Crichton's a little floored and momentarily jealous about Velorek, and he has to adjust his image of Aeryn.

Alien Encounters: Pilot's home world is wreathed in mist (a convenient way to avoid showing the operators underneath the puppet), but the sound effects and the scene seem to imply that Pilot's race are aquatic. Their language is so complex that translator microbes can't handle it – one sentence can contain hundreds of meanings (this reflects the unique multi-tasking abilities referred to in **109**, 'DNA Mad Scientist'). Pilot has to train himself to speak in short simple sentences so others can understand him. The elders of their race decide who is worthy of being bonded to a Leviathan.

Disney on Acid: 'Pilot . . . Let's hash this out, right here, right now. Five cents, the Doctor is in.' Crichton obviously reads the comic strip *Peanuts*. If someone's acting irrationally his 'Etch-a-Sketch isn't operating with all its knobs'.

Get Frelled: Peacekeepers are bred for military service and they breed on command. They do not have life partners and their relationships are brief and recreational. This way the best officers can be assigned where needed without High Command having to worry themselves about keeping couples together.

Seen it all Before: In many ways this is similar to the *Star Trek: Deep Space Nine* episode, 'Things Past' that shows us Odo's behaviour when he worked under the Cardassians.

Guest Stars: Alex Dimitriades has been a regular on *Neighbours*, *Heartbreak High* and stars in *Young Lions*.

Backstage: This episode's covered extensively in issue two of the official *Farscape* Magazine. Claudia Black told *TV Zone* that she was very proud of 'The Way We Weren't' because it showed why Aeryn's been burned and why she's difficult with Crichton, as well as tying the past into the present. 'I just grabbed hold of that opportunity with both hands and almost died when I came home every night from work because I poured myself into every ounce of that script.' Lani Tupu also told *Starlog* that he relished this episode, as it becomes clear that Pilot's decision to bond with Moya was a conscious one: 'That for me was a turning point. There was a lot of pain in what was happening. It's great to play that side of Pilot. It gives me something to work with.'

The Verdict: Stunning. Chock-full of revelations, extreme character examinations, explanations to long unanswered questions and, most impressively, giving Pilot a back story and a fully rounded character. This is *Farscape* at its very best. On every other show you can think of the initial revelation that Aeryn was a murderer would have been wormed out of some way – possession, or a trick, or something lame. Not on *Farscape* – she was a cold-blooded killer and that's that. How refreshing to have a show unafraid of muddying the waters and taking the characters, in this case both Aeryn and Pilot, to deep, dark places. Claudia Black is superb in this instalment, taking Aeryn's hard exterior and allowing us the tiniest glimpses of the person underneath all the defences.

206
Picture If You Will

1st US Transmission Date: 21 April 2000
1st UK Transmission Date: 31 July 2000
1st Australian Transmission Date: 21 July 2001

Writer: Peter Neale
Director: Andrew Prowse
Guest Cast: Chris Haywood (Kyvan/Maldis)

Chiana, Rygel and Aeryn visit a trader, Kyvan, who gives Chiana a portrait of herself and tells her it is a window into time. First it shows her a missing necklace moments before a DRD finds it, then it shows her with a broken leg just before she trips over the DRD and breaks her leg. When it shows her dying in fire she panics and believes she is burning up. Her shipmates put her in the freezer but the door jams with her inside, a fire starts from nowhere and by the time they open the door Chiana is burnt to ashes. They burn, smash and eject the picture into space but each time it comes back.

Zhaan tells Crichton that they are in great danger and he must trust her and do what she says without question when the time comes; he passes this message on to Aeryn. Rygel and Aeryn return to Kyvan who tells them she was forced to make the picture on the orders of Maldis (**108**, 'That Old Black Magic').

D'Argo is next to die, but after being impaled he vanishes. Zhaan telepathically tells Crichton that she has a plan and he must distract Maldis. Crichton is electrocuted and vanishes. D'Argo, Chiana and Crichton are trapped inside the surreal world of the picture. Maldis has not yet recorporealised, but he has enough power to lay this trap and extract enough fear from the crew to fully reintegrate. Zhaan is next to die and joins them in the picture. Her fear gives Maldis the power to materialise a doorway from the picture into the Maintenance Bay. Pilot passes a message to Aeryn from Zhaan instructing her to shoot Kyvan and leave, which she does. Kyvan was in fact a manifestation of Maldis, and her death weakens Maldis and allows the crew to escape through the doorway. Maldis attempts to follow but they shoot him with Aeryn's Prowler and his power is broken; the picture shatters.

Buck Rogers Redux: He suggests locking Moya's doors and not letting anybody in or out. 'That way we get no alien critters, no shape-shifting bugs, no mind altering viruses, no freaky-deaky artefacts.' When Zhaan tells Crichton to trust her completely and without hesitation he demonstrates his faith in her and agrees. Given Maldis's power Crichton doesn't seem terribly frightened by him, he's all flip remarks and irreverent humour. Admittedly he's supposed to be distracting Maldis, but the devil-may-care Crichton of **201** 'Mind the Baby' to **205** 'The Way We Weren't' is still in control. Maldis threatens to go and visit Earth, which he says could keep him fed for quite a while. This is the first real threat to Earth in the series – if Maldis were to go there it would be Crichton's fault.

You Can Be More: Aeryn openly considers throwing Rygel and Chiana off the ship on the basis that they cause more trouble than they're worth. Crichton is annoyed and offended by this and walks out. When Pilot tells Aeryn to kill Kyvan she doesn't even blink: the cold-blooded killer of **205**, 'The Way We Weren't' is alive and well; no matter how much she may have changed in other ways, she's damn good at taking orders and carrying them out without hesitation.

Big Blue: 'I've never been more scared in my life.' Because they shared Unity (**113**, 'Rhapsody In Blue') Zhaan can commune telepathically with Crichton by touching heads. She senses Maldis's presence, and knows that it is she he has come to revenge himself upon. Even though she's terrified she manages to save the day, but just by the skin of her teeth.

I was a Teenage Luxan: D'Argo's protectiveness towards Chiana grows and he tries to persuade her to get rid of the picture before it harms her. He admits that he cares about her. When he believes he is about to die he tells Crichton 'You've been a good friend. Whatever happens, it's been a pleasure to know you.'

Buckwheat the Sixteenth: Rygel believes that a Hynerian Royal Tiara from the Neltoth era which he buys from Kyvan for one food cube, is genuine – unfortunately it vanishes when Maldis does. Rygel on Chiana: 'She was quite a lot like me, you know. She had spirit, ambition, large appetites. She would have made an excellent Hyner-an. I'm actually going to miss her.' Nonetheless he still uses her death as a way of trying to squeeze punitive damages out of Kyvan – always on the lookout for the main chance.

Everyone's Favourite Little Tralk: Chiana lost her favourite necklace some time ago and Pilot assigned a DRD to look for it. She's more fragile than she looks – it only takes a trip over a DRD to break her leg.

The Ballad of Aeryn and John: Aeryn feels guilty about Chiana's death because she was dismissive of the painting's warning and of Chiana's usefulness, so she goes to Pilot to try and establish what started the fire. Crichton tells her not to blame herself and she pretends not to understand, provoking him to shout, 'Are you always gonna do this? Keep the entire world at a distance, keep everybody away?'

The Ballad of Chiana and D'Argo: The flirting between them is becoming more open. D'Argo doesn't want the portrait to give them a glimpse of their future, and Chiana queries, 'Why? Because of what it might not show? Or what it might?' Still no action though.

Disney on Acid: In **108**, 'That Old Black Magic' Maldis and Crichton alluded to *The Wizard Of Oz*. This time it's *The Sound Of Music*: Maldis refuses to do requests when Crichton asks, 'Could you do that farewell/goodbye song the kids sing? It's one of my favourites.'

Seen it all Before: Maldis has become *Farscape*'s version of *Doctor Who*'s Master – he turns up to claim revenge, sets elaborate traps, dons disguises, assumes terrible accents (is Kyvan's lingo bad Irish or mangled Jamaican?) and is never conclusively killed off at the end.

Logic Leaps: When Crichton, Zhaan and D'Argo die there's nothing left of them – but when Chiana dies there is a pile of ashes and a necklace left behind . . . why?

The Verdict: This starts off as a spooky ghost story, turns into a revenge thriller and ends up surreal and bizarre as the distorted world of the picture wobbles across the screen. From the opening shot of the trading post through to the giant Maldis hand that emerges from the picture to swat Moya's crew in the Maintenance Bay, this episode is bursting with visual flair and style. Maldis is a great villain and his return is a nice surprise, assuming you didn't recognise Chris Haywood under Kyvan's make-up. Each of the episodes in Season Two, bar the opener, have placed the emphasis on one character, emphasising the ensemble cast, and now Zhaan gets her moment in the spotlight, which is good as she's been underused so far this season. A good sequel to **108**, 'That Old Black Magic' and as Maldis is merely banished again, he's bound to return.

207
Home on the Remains

1st US Transmission Date: 16 June 2000
1st UK Transmission Date: 7 August 2000
1st Australian Transmission Date: 13 December 2001

Writer: Gabrielle Stanton and Harry Werksman Jr
Director: Rowan Woods
Guest Cast: John Brumpton (B'Sogg), Justine Saunders (Altana),
Rob Carlton (Vija), Hunter Perske (Temmon), Gavin Robins (Keedva)

Moya is out of food, and Zhaan is so hungry that she is beginning to bud, so Chiana leads them to the corpse of a Budong (see **Alien Encounters**) and its mining colony. She is intending to renew her acquaintance with Temmon, a miner she lived with and stole from, when she was last there, but he has been attacked by a Keedva and sprayed with acid so she kills him to stop his suffering. Temmon's brother, B'Sogg, declares the mine closed until the Keedva is killed.

B'Sogg, whom Chiana once rejected in favour of Temmon, agrees to feed Moya's crew with fungi and lichen, but will not help Chiana. The lichen will not help Zhaan, who is now too far gone to survive without meat. B'Sogg has meat, but it is hidden in the mine and he won't give it to Crichton without being paid in crystals. Chiana's old

friend, Altana, has found a rich seam but cannot mine it
because B'Sogg has closed the mine – she and Chi suspect
B'Sogg of sending the Keedva to kill Temmon, giving him
an excuse to close the mine so he can jump Altana's claim.
Altana and D'Argo go to mine crystals to buy food, but the
Keedva kills Altana. Crichton follows B'Sogg to his meat
locker but B'Sogg is controlling the Keedva, and sets it on
Crichton. Crichton kills the Keedva, Chiana kills B'Sogg.

On Moya, Zhaan's budding releases so much pollen and
so many spores that it threatens to blind Moya permanently. Zhaan becomes psychotic and leaves her quarters.
Aeryn locks herself in command and Pilot vents Moya's
atmosphere into space to expel the spores and save Moya.
Luckily Zhaan is also in control, hiding. Aeryn knocks her
out and then Crichton and the others return, cook the
Keedva, and chow down, saving Zhaan.

You Can Be More: 'Oh, that's just great. I get to stay on
board with the blooming blue bush, and you get to play
with your favourite little tralk'. Aeryn's opinion of Chiana
is obviously not high. She tries to help Zhaan by mixing a
salve, but it burns her; she bathes Zhaan in light because
she thinks it'll help, but of course it accelerates the process.

And again that streak of ruthlessness: when Moya's on
the verge of permanent damage she gives the order to vent
the atmosphere even though she knows Zhaan will almost
certainly die as a result. She does ask for forgiveness, but
she's not exactly crying about her decision. And when
Zhaan does reveal herself to be alive and more than a little
angry, Aeryn headbutts her unconscious as soon as her
guard's down.

Big Blue: 'It wasn't pleasant reverting back to such a
primitive, vicious state.' All Zhaan's repressed savagery
surfaces as she buds, and she begins to distrust Aeryn. She
later apologises for almost killing her and Aeryn accepts
that she wasn't responsible.

I was a Teenage Luxan: D'Argo's allergies reappear (**121**,
'Bone To Be Wild'). He tries to protect Chiana but she

resents it, telling him she doesn't need another brother. For a guy who's so decisive in battle, he certainly takes his time plucking up the courage to tell Chi how he feels.

Buckwheat the Sixteenth: Crichton's new name for Rygel: Slug-Monkey. Rygel refuses to eat the lichen and gambles at a game called Deemo, even though he has no money. His opponent, Vija, throws him into the mine to get some crystals to pay his gambling debt. When Crichton's running from the Keedva he hangs on to Rygel's Thronesled and it's powerful enough to keep them both just out of reach for a little while. Rygel wants Crichton off, though, so he bites his fingers. Crichton retaliates by biting Rygel's ear and then headbutting him.

Everyone's Favourite Little Tralk: 'I do what I have to do to survive ... I can only let go when I feel safe.' Chiana spent some time in the Budong mining colony with her brother Nerri, and she was originally intending to use his death (**203**, 'Taking the Stone') as a means of getting Temmon's sympathy. She kills Temmon without a moment's hesitation because she knows how gruesome the acid death is, but when it comes to killing B'Sogg she can't shoot him in cold blood and he knows it. Her decision to shoot an acid pustule, drench him in the stuff and then walk away as he dissolves, though, is way, way worse and settles once and for all the question of whether Chiana is a killer. She had good friends in the camp too – the fact that Altana is willing to share her crystals with Chiana speaks volumes for Chiana's loyalty. Altana says she's 'a wild one, but she's got a heart of gold'.

The Ballad of Chiana and D'Argo: D'Argo's jealous when he sees how Chiana uses her sexuality to get what she wants, but he's put off because of the way she treated Temmon – loved him, stole from him, left. He quizzes Altana about Chiana to help him decide upon his next move. Back on Moya he tells her that she is safe and kisses her – which elicits a stunned 'woah'.

In the Driving Seat: Pilot's connection to Moya is still 'less than optimal' (**205**, 'The Way We Weren't').

A Ship, a Living Ship!: Moya is hugely allergic to Zhaan's micro-pollen and spores. It takes an arn to repressurise the ship once it's been opened to space.

Alien Encounters: Budongs are huge animals that live in space. Although their flesh is poisonous they are a source of valuable Nogelti crystals and prospectors set up mining colonies deep inside their gargantuan carcasses. Carnivorous creatures called Keedvas also live inside Budong corpses and feed on the miners. Budongs develop acid-filled pustules as they decompose, and miners must be careful to avoid them, for once touched by the acid it is a slow, painful and certain death.

Disney on Acid: When fighting the Keedva, Crichton keeps up a flippant monologue until he decides 'no more Captain Kirk chitchat'. When Rygel goes gambling he calls him Maverick, after the TV show starring James Garner.

Get Frelled: Chiana is willing to trade sex for food if that's what's required to help her shipmates.

What Does This Do?: When threatened by famine, Delvians begin to bud. This process attracts animals, but the buds are poisonous. The animals are killed, the Delvians eat the animals, and the protein stops the budding process and saves their lives. Delvians can also levitate, as Zhaan does on the Command Deck. This may be something they can only do during budding, however.

Logic Leaps: How does the Budong support both gravity and an atmosphere? Why not freeze Zhaan like Rygel was frozen in **106**, 'Thank God It's Friday, Again'? Or put her in a spacesuit and zip it up?

WHAT did you just say?: Things you won't hear Vija call Rygel on the BBC: 'You little green ass, stinking, horny little bastard, I'm gonna kill you!'

Stats: You can't eat Dentics, even fried. Keedvas, however, are finger-lickin' good.

Guest Stars: John Brumpton played Magoo in the controversial film *Romper Stomper*. Justine Saunders is probably best known as Pamela Madigan in *Prisoner: Cell Block H*.

The Verdict: Again the show looks a million dollars, and the Keedva is that rarest of things – a TV monster that actually looks good when it steps out of the shadows. Crichton's fight with it is good old-fashioned Captain Kirk action, as he admits, and the bite-fight between him and Rygel is hilarious and not a little brutal. In fact this is not an episode to watch while eating your lunch, featuring as it does acid wounds, dissolving flesh, bursting pustules, skewered monsters, the graphic deaths of Altana and Temmon, and a lot of headbutting. No wonder it was the first, and to date only, episode of *Farscape* to get an 18 rating in the UK. Zhaan's budding process is fun and threatening, as is watching Aeryn trying to help and getting it all wrong. The Budong is a good idea too, and will appear again in **208**, 'Dream a Little Dream'. But somehow the episode is less than the sum of its parts and drags at times, takes a little too long to get to the point, and B'Sogg is an all-too-obvious and strangely stilted bad guy.

208
Dream a Little Dream

1st US Transmission Date: 23 June 2000
1st US Transmission Date as 'Re:Union': 1 June 2001
1st UK Transmission Date: 14 August 2000
1st Australian Transmission Date: 28 July 2001

Writer: Steven Rae
Director: Ian Watson
Guest Cast: Steve Jacobs (Ja Rhumann), Sandy Gore (Judge),
Simone Kessell (Finzzi), Marin Mimica (Dersch), Peter Kowitz (Tarr),
Jeremy Callaghan (Bartender)

Note: *This episode is a long flashback to events that took place while Moya was searching for Crichton, Aeryn and D'Argo after 122, 'Family Ties'.*

Zhaan, Rygel and Chi are searching for their lost shipmates on the planet Litigara when the planet's ruling law firm frames Zhaan for the murder of a civil rights lawyer they bumped off themselves. She is going to be executed, but Rygel and Chiana step forward to act as her defence counsel, even though this means that they will suffer Zhaan's fate if they are found to have lied at any point during the case. The ancient book of Litigaran law contains a section about the Light Of Truth – a flaming torch which burns more brightly when held next to someone who is lying. Using Moya to beam light down into the courtroom onto a burning chair leg, Chiana and Rygel manage to convince the court that Ja Rhumann, head of the ruling law firm, is guilty. Zhaan is freed.

Big Blue: Then: Zhaan's grief at the loss of her shipmates drives her to the brink of madness, and when she is locked up she begins to hallucinate the spirits of Crichton, Aeryn and D'Argo. Crichton's spirit appeals to her reason; Aeryn's reflects her guilt, and D'Argo's her spirituality. She sees herself as a mother looking after two children as well as Moya and Pilot, and the stress of it is too much for her to bear. She nearly kills her first lawyer in her rage, but by the end of the trial, during which she tries to sacrifice herself to save Chi and Rygel, she has detached herself so completely from her predicament that she won't even acknowledge her friends. She will only chant and stare.

Now: Zhaan is still tortured by dreams of Aeryn, Crichton and D'Argo dying.

Buckwheat the Sixteenth: Then: Rygel lets his mask slip and reveals how much he cares for his friends by getting blind drunk and challenging Zhaan when she suggests they give up the search. He is pathologically incapable of telling the truth in court and keeps launching into elaborate deceptions until Chi reminds him of the consequences. It is Rygel who comes up with the plan to save the day, though, and who realises that the victim was murdered elsewhere. The little softy holds Zhaan's hand in the cell when no one else is around. His second, fifteenth, and twenty-third wives had blue eyes.

Now: Rygel stored some of his barbequed Keedva (**207**, 'Home on the Remains') in the Nav Linkages of one of Moya's Transport Pods.

Everyone's Favourite Little Tralk: Chiana uses her sex appeal to, um, pump the policeman for information, helping them win the case. She gets drunk doing it and takes some pills to clear her head. Her space cadet performance in court after popping too many pills is laugh-out-loud funny.

In the Driving Seat: Pilot is unable to prevent Moya leaving to search for Talyn.

A Ship, a Living Ship!: Moya is very patient during the search for Crichton, Aeryn and D'Argo but when they reach Litigara she runs out of patience and is prepared to abandon her crew to go and search for Talyn. Luckily she overhears Chiana being threatened by Ja Rhumann and decides to stay and help. From orbit she can focus her bio-luminescence on to a very precise location on the ground.

Worlds Apart: Litigara has two moons.

Alien Encounters: Ninety per cent of Litigarans are lawyers, the remaining ten per cent are Utilities and have no rights. The world is run by ruling Law Firms, the current leader being Rhumann, Willian and Mandel. They kill a lawyer, Wesley Kenn, who wants to give the Utilities rights. Blue-eyed Litigarans do not go out during a double full moon, because it burns their skin. The basis of their law is a small book called the Axiom, but over the centuries ancillary laws have grown up around this central text and made Litigaran law immeasurably complex. If a lawyer uses a 'bad faith' defence, that is if they put forward a defence they suspect to be false, they share the defendant's sentence. The minimum penalty for jaywalking is ten days in jail.

Disney on Acid: Zhaan's obviously been paying close attention to Crichton's speech because her hallucination of him makes a reference to Disneyland.

What Does This Do?: Rygel farts helium in the courtroom when Chiana is trying to address the court: 'I'm nervous, it happens. We're in court, so sue me.'

Seen it all Before: Every show has done a courtroom episode, and they're rarely anything to write home about, because there's little tension: you know a regular character isn't ever going to be thrown into prison and left to rot, so the only tension comes from *how* they're going to get off, not whether they will or not.

WHAT did you just say?: Rygel thinks he may have a solution, but it 'will require lashings of deception and trickery.' Chiana: 'Finally, you and I get to play to our strengths!'

Stats: Chiana is captured in an Electro-Net, and she cures her hangover with Nashtin Cleansing Pills.

Guest Stars: Jeremy Callaghan was Pompey on *Xena: Warrior Princess*. Steve Jacobs can be seen in *The Man Who Sued God*. Sandy Gore was Kay White on *Prisoner: Cell Block H* and a regular on *Grass Roots*. Simone Kessell has been a regular on both *Medivac* and *Greenstone*.

Backstage: This episode was the first to be filmed for Season Two and was intended, under its original title 'Re:Union', to begin the year. It's easy to see why it was eventually moved to deeper in the season: it would have annoyed fans who had waited so patiently for a resolution to the cliffhanger and the episode's many strengths would probably have been ignored in the uproar. However it's hard not to think that it would have been marvellously risky to taunt fans with resolution and not deliver it.

This version of the episode is exactly the same as 'Re:Union' except for the two bookend scenes set on the Transport Pod. In the original cut the episode begins with Zhaan comforting Pilot about the loss of Aeryn, Crichton and D'Argo. It's established that they have searched 24 planets and many moons and asteroids. The sequence of Aeryn and Crichton's deaths is not Zhaan's dream, but

Rygel's, and he dreams it in the Litigaran bar before waking up and then passing out as Chiana enters and we discover that she has been frelling her way through the local men. At the end of the episode Chiana kisses the bartender goodbye, obviously having added another notch to her bedpost; Pilot announces that Zhaan is resuming the Delvian Seek, and Chiana tells Rygel to accept that their shipmates are gone and it is time to move on. It ends with 'To Be Continued'. The US Sci-Fi channel showed the original cut of 'Re:Union' once only in the break between Seasons Two and Three, but the original opening and closing scenes can be found as extras on the R2 DVD release.

The Verdict: For a piece dealing with a planet entirely populated by lawyers it's surprising that the serious, almost dour episode we get isn't played more for laughs; it would have been a lot more fun. Still, there are laughs to be had watching Chiana and Rygel try to save the day without lying. Virginia Hey is very good at mixing the savagery, tenderness, grief and spirituality of Zhaan's increasingly complicated character without making her seem inconsistent or unsympathetic, and Gigi Edgley is obviously having a ball. Visually the cityscape shot is stunning, and the gruesome effects of Crichton's head being sucked out of his decompressing spacesuit are commendably gross. In plot terms it would have been a lot easier to care about the case if we'd been shown Wesley Kenn arguing for civil rights, and had a few more scenes of the Utilities being repressed to give the case a wider context.

209
Out of Their Minds

1st US Transmission Date: 7 July 2000
1st UK Transmission Date: 4 September 2000
1st Australian Transmission Date: 4 August 2001

Writer: Michael Cassutt
Director: Ian Watson

Guest Cast: Lani Tupu (Capt. Bialar Crais),
Angie Milliken (Voice of Yoz), Dominique Sweeney (Tak),
Thomas Holesgrove (Yoz)

Zhaan boards a Halosian ship, which has targeted Moya.
It transpires the ship has skirmished with Talyn and holds
Moya responsible. The defence screen saves Moya but in a
freak accident everybody swaps bodies: D'Argo inhabits
Pilot's body, Pilot Chiana's, Chiana D'Argo's, Crichton
Aeryn's, Aeryn Rygel's, and Rygel Crichton's.

Zhaan persuades the Halosian Captain, Tak, to board
Moya and check that she is unarmed, on the understanding
that if she is he will leave her alone. He tours the ship but
he throws up some acid vomit to destroy the defence screen
because he intends to destroy Moya anyway. Back on his
own ship he fires on Moya again, but the defence screen
has been reactivated by the crew. Everyone changes bodies
again: Aeryn into Crichton, Crichton into Rygel, Rygel
into Aeryn, Pilot into D'Argo, D'Argo into Chiana,
Chiana into Pilot.

Zhaan talks Tak's second in command, Yoz, into killing
Tak and taking command, but Yoz decides to destroy
Moya too. Zhaan kills Yoz and takes control of the
Halosian ship. Everyone resumes the positions they had
when first hit and Zhaan fires on Moya again. Everyone
goes back to their own bodies.

Big Blue: Zhaan can willingly mangle her hand in order to
extricate herself from manacles, but she risks permanent
damage by doing so.

Buckwheat the Sixteenth: 'You all say I'm paranoid, but
it's true – no one ever frelling listens to me!' Rygel's
inferiority complex is borne out when Crichton/Rygel is
ignored by Zhaan but Aeryn/Crichton is listened to. Each
ship in his royal fleet had a hundred cannon. He lives only
to see his usurping cousin deposed and executed.

In the Driving Seat: Pilot/Chiana describes how to control
Moya to D'Argo/Pilot. He says to focus on a distant
high-pitched sound which you can visualise as a dark red;

this represents life-support and all the ship's other functions hang off it like a rope. D'Argo can hardly handle the multi-tasking required but keeps it together, Chiana fares less well, and panics. Chiana's body tries to reject Pilot's consciousness and goes into seizures which abate when she calms down. D'Argo's body cannot handle Pilot at all, and passes out. Pilot envies D'Argo's memories of love and friendship and feels that D'Argo has had richer life experiences, while D'Argo envies Pilot's memories of seeing the birth of stars, and countless planets.

The Insane Military Commander: Crais and Talyn were approached by the Halosian ship and Crais said that they travelled in peace. Only when fired upon did they retaliate, and even then they did not destroy the Halosian ship, though they could have done. So it looks as if Crais is acting honourably and may be trying to find that new path he talked about after all.

A Ship, a Living Ship!: I know it would have been difficult to pull off, but wouldn't it have been amazing to have Moya jump into someone's body and vice versa? Missed opportunity. The defence shield that they took from the *Zelbinion* (**107**, 'PK Tech Girl') and were attempting to fix in **206**, 'Picture If You Will', is finally working again.

The Ballad of Aeryn and John: 'You were in my shoes, I was in your pants.' Having reminded themselves of each other's physical attributes they are all over each other at the end, play fighting on the bridge and chasing after each other laughing. It's like a couple at school – I expected him to pull her pigtails and run away giggling.

The Ballad of Chiana and D'Argo: Their final exchange is a masterpiece of double entendre when D'Argo says, 'I really, really enjoyed being inside your body.' He then follows it up with, 'I really like your body.' And with that they run off in search of privacy and the inevitable consummation of their blossoming crushes.

Alien Encounters: Halosians are huge taloned bird creatures (very similar to the Skeksis from the Henson film *The
Dark Crystal*) that have no interest in other races
other than as targets. They accumulate kills in order to
'evolve', but it's never clear if that is merely a term to
describe a rise in rank or an actual physical evolution. If a
ship's captain fails in a task he or she can be killed
by a challenger who will then evolve in their place. They
can vomit intelligent acid gel, which can be used to
cripple ships' systems. The dangling, erogenous tentacles
on D'Argo's chin are called tenkas.

Disney on Acid: Crichton/Aeryn smacks Rygel/Crichton to
stop him complaining and then moans, 'It's the three-
freakin-Stooges, I'm hitting myself!'

What Does This Do?: 'Yotz, creeping vomit!' Rygel/
Crichton has to pee but doesn't know how to hold it in so
Crichton/Aeryn has to give him directions on unzipping,
pointing it like a gun, and letting go. Rygel's enormously
impressed by how good it feels, but forgets to replace the
member completely before zipping back up. Every male in
the audience crosses their legs and grimaces. Crichton/
Aeryn takes a quiet moment to unzip his vest and gives his
newly acquired boobs a good old jiggle, but when he sticks
his hands down his/her pants he goes cross-eyed. When
Chiana/D'Argo and Aeryn/Rygel see what he/she is doing
Crichton's unashamed: 'Oh, come on, man ... they're
right here! They've been here for a couple of arns ... I'm
a guy, a *guy*. Guys *dream* about this sort of thing!' David
Kemper and Claudia Black discussed what she thought
Crichton would do when left to his own devices in Aeryn's
body. So, though it was scripted that the rest of the crew
would catch him in the middle of something, Black 'just
went for it! ... Crichton's actions were improvised. It
certainly gave me an opportunity to do something John
Crichton wouldn't normally get to do,' she told *SFX*.
Chiana/D'Argo wants to flee the ship and tries to get
Rygel/Crichton to come with her. She tries her standard
trick of using sex to persuade her prey, which leads to the

bizarre sight of D'Argo's body grabbing Crichton's mivonks and doing all sorts of things off camera which lead Rygel/Crichton to exclaim: 'Normally you have to rub my eyebrows to make me feel like this.' She promises she'll do anything he wants to the body once they're off Moya, but he refuses. Aeryn later admits to Crichton that when she was in his body she was also in his pants. Rygel enjoys picking Crichton's nose and sniffing Aeryn's armpits. Pilot can't make Chiana's legs move. When D'Argo gets his body back his tenkas are sore and he wonders what Chiana was doing to make them that way. Only *Farscape* would use intelligent evil vomit as a plot device. When Tak throws up Rygel/Crichton just dismisses it: 'We do that sort of thing all the time here on Moya. I just peed in the Maintenance Bay.'

WHAT did you just say?: Crichton, on being targeted by the Halosian ship: 'Have we sent the "don't shoot us we're pathetic, transmission" yet?'

Stats: Moya is well stocked with food for the first time in ages. DRDs can take photographs and print them out.

Guest Stars: Angie Milliken played Volmae in **106**, 'Thank God it's Friday, Again'.

Backstage: This episode got an 'S' rating in the US, denoting sexual situations. Obviously the episode was as fun to make as it is to watch: 'I was pissing myself all through the rehearsals,' Ben Browder said in an online chat. This episode was written by a freelancer and then remodelled by Justin Monjo, who had deeper knowledge of the characters. While imitating Chiana's irregular breathing patterns, Anthony Simcoe succumbed to the heat on set and had an attack that led to his being rushed to hospital. This is covered in issue three of the official *Farscape* Magazine.

The Verdict: An utterly ludicrous plot device – weapons + defence shield = body swapping – is used to great comic effect in the funniest episode yet, and the cast have the time of their lives imitating each other and playing out of character. Anthony Simcoe's impression of Chiana is hilarious, but Claudia Black and Ben Browder's takes on Rygel are also deeply silly. Crammed full of one-line gems, huge scary puppets and evil mobile vomit, *Farscape* has never been this much fun. Pure joy from start to finish.

210–212
Look at the Princess Trilogy

Writer: David Kemper
Guest Cast: Wayne Pygram (Scorpius), Felicity Price (Princess Katralla), Bianca Chiminello (Jenavian Charto), Matt Day (Counsellor Elka Tyno), Tina Bursill (Empress Novia), Felix Williamson (Prince Clavor), Aaron Cash (Dregon Carzenonva), Gavin Robins (I) and Thomas Holesgrove (II & III)(Cargn), Francesca Buller (ro-NA), Jonathan Hardy (Kahaynu)

210
Look at the Princess I: A Kiss is but a Kiss

1st US Transmission Date: 21 July 2000
1st UK Transmission Date: 11 September 2000
1st Australian Transmission Date: 11 August 2001

Director: Andrew Prowse and Tony Tilse

Moya encounters an independent Sebacean colony in the Uncharted Territories and the crew are allowed to visit their Royal Planet to join the celebrations of the impending coronation. Here they become embroiled in political intrigue. Pay close attention, this gets complicated . . .

The law states that the firstborn heir, Princess Katralla, must marry a DNA-compatible Sebacean before the anniversary of her birth, otherwise the throne is given to the second in line, her brother, Prince Clavor. Clavor has forged an alliance with the Scarrans, who have sent a delegate, Cargn. With Cargn's help Prince Clavor has poisoned his sister's DNA to ensure that she is not compatible with any Sebacean male, thus ensuring the throne will be his.

Unfortunately for Clavor, Crichton is revealed to be compatible, offering Princess Katralla a chance to become Empress if she can persuade him to marry her. The current Empress, Novia, does not want her son Clavor to be Emperor because he will ally their worlds with the Scarrans and ensure a PK invasion. She puts pressure on Crichton to marry her daughter. At this point Scorpius finally catches up with Crichton and his Command Carrier enters orbit. The Empress tells Crichton that if he does not marry Katralla she will turn him over to Scorpius so Crichton is forced to agree to the marriage.

Cargn believes that Crichton and Aeryn are Peace-keepers working with Scorpius to prevent the colony allying itself with the Scarrans, and promises Clavor that he will have Crichton assassinated before the marriage can take place.

Other pertinent information: the fact that Crichton is not Sebacean is kept a state secret to allow the wedding to go ahead. Katralla secretly loves Counsellor Tyno, but cannot marry him because of her poisoned DNA. Prince Clavor has a fiancée, Jenavian, who appears to be some-thing of an airhead, and a personal attendant, the meek, blue-skinned ro-NA. A royal cousin, Dregon Carzenonva, is interested in Aeryn. Immediately after the marriage Crichton and Katralla will be frozen as statues and placed in the senate for eighty cycles, able to hear and see. They will absorb all they need to know about the laws of their world, and then, when the Empress dies, they will be defrosted and assume the throne.

Meanwhile, Zhaan has remained on Moya to meditate. When the Command Carrier enters orbit Moya StarBursts to try and lure it away from Crichton and co. Unfortunate-ly Scorpius does not take the bait. Moya is about to return when she picks up a signal that she cannot help but follow. It leads her to the Builders, the mysterious race who built Leviathans.

Buck Rogers Redux: 'Hope, D'Argo. It's what keeps you going. You're gonna see your son, I'm gonna get home.

Hope. I have hope or I have nothing.' Crichton is horrified by the idea of marrying without love, but accepts he has no choice. When a machine shows he and Katralla what their children will look like he suddenly becomes massively broody and affectionate – he'd obviously make a good dad. He asks D'Argo to be his best man, but D'Argo misinterprets this and reminds Crichton that he's with Chiana now. Crichton decides that his statue will adopt the British Queen's royal wave.

You Can Be More: Aeryn lets Cargn believe that she is working for Scorpius, presumably so as not to tip their hand too early. When he tries to force information out of her she tries to fight but luckily the Empress interrupts before the Scarran can kill her. The Empress warns them both not to fight again.

Big Blue: Zhaan feels she has had too little time to pursue her priestly devotions and chooses to stay on Moya for the solitude it affords her.

I was a Teenage Luxan: Post-coital D'Argo is amazingly mellow and philosophical with Crichton – the endless aggression and anger he's displayed all this time was definitely due to misdirected sexual frustration.

Buckwheat the Sixteenth: Rygel's royal lineage is what persuades the colony to allow Moya's crew to visit. He tells Crichton he's their best negotiator. Crichton won't let him speak which, even though he is a self-serving slug, is a bit unfair because he's proven time and time again that he *is* their best negotiator. He wishes he could have seen what his kids would turn out like before they were born – it would have saved him 'some nasty surprises'.

Everyone's Favourite Little Tralk: Chiana may be with D'Argo, but she's not averse to grinding herself up against an already distracted Crichton and telling him breathily that he needs to find someone who's fast with the body and slow with the soul.

Nosferatu in Rubber: Scorpius tries to talk calmly to D'Argo in the bar and is willing to be patient and play the political game until his opportunity comes. He offers D'Argo a deal: if Crichton surrenders he will let everyone else go and promises not to destroy Crichton's brain if he gives him access to the wormhole information.

A Ship, a Living Ship!: Leviathans were built by a people known only as The Builders. Moya worships them as gods, and they summoned her to them for reasons as yet unknown. Every StarBurst completely invalidates all previous navigational data. One of Moya's eight senses recognises the Builders' signal.

The Ballad of Aeryn and John: Aeryn is giving Crichton flying lessons in the WDP. She scents her hair to see if he will notice, willingly kisses him (Crichton: 'I was lips, you were tongue!'), and finally looks to have given in, until she bolts from the cockpit and shouts, 'No, I will not be a slave to your hormones!' Poor Crichton is 'standing to attention' but Aeryn bolts. Crichton tries to talk to her but she tells him to back off and give her some time, so he goes and hangs out with Chiana to try and make Aeryn jealous. Chiana advises Crichton to put less pressure on Aeryn, and she then gives Aeryn a hard time for not telling Crichton how she feels, and blames her for driving him away. When Aeryn finds out Crichton's getting married she refuses to attend the wedding. He tries to get her to talk one last time, but she just says goodbye, and walks out. Aeryn: 'There's never been anything we couldn't overcome together,' Crichton: 'Except each other.'

The Ballad of Chiana And D'Argo: D'Argo: 'My life has been one crushing disappointment after the next, but with this girl I have managed to find moments of pleasure.' They test themselves and find that they are not genetically compatible and cannot have children. That doesn't stop them having sex, though.

Worlds Apart: The breakaway Sebacean colonies declared independence and ran away from the Sebacean home system 1900 cycles ago. No one expected them to survive. They found a system with three habitable worlds, settled down, and have remained strictly neutral.

Alien Encounters: Scarrans are big, ugly creatures and are immensely strong – one of them demolishes Aeryn in hand-to-hand combat. They can shoot beams of heat from their hands, which immobilise their subject (it is implied that this effect also includes mind-reading, but see **211**, 'Look at the Princess II: I Do, I Think', when Janavian lies to Cargn while he's zapping her, so it is probably just pain used to coerce truth from the subject, rather than any form of telepathy). The Scarrans and the Peacekeepers form two power blocs, and are in some form of cold-war type political and military conflict that has not yet broken into outright war.

Hi, Harvey: Crichton tells Aeryn that Scorpius is 'in my head. He's in the back of my mind, the corner of my eye, he scares me, Aeryn, and I can't shake him.' This is the first hint that the vision of Scorpius in **204**, 'Crackers Don't Matter', was more than just light-induced madness. When he meets Scorpius, Crichton flashes back to his ordeal in the Aurora Chair and sees Scorpius wielding a long needle implement and saying 'something to remember me by', which is not something we saw in **119**, 'Nerve' or **120**, 'The Hidden Memory'.

Disney on Acid: Crichton bemoans that if he spends eighty cycles as a statue everyone he knows will be dead when he gets back to Earth, including Cameron Diaz and *Buffy The Vampire Slayer*. Hey, he's a *Buffy* fan!

Assuming he tested his WDP around the time **101**, 'Premiere' was broadcast, which was March 1999, then he'd have been halfway through Season Three of *Buffy* when he left and is probably annoyed as all hell that he never got to find out what happened with the Mayor and Faith.

Get Frelled: Crichton walks in on Chiana and D'Argo in *flagrante delicto*, not once but twice. The first time he's embarrassed and scurries away, the second time he's so preoccupied that he just sits down on the bed next to a bare-breasted Chi, waits for D'Argo to finish whatever he's doing, and spills his guts. From the looks of it, D'Argo and Chi are having regular, spectacular sex. Rygel starts groaning and gawping every time he sees anyone snogging – could he be a bit of a voyeur?

Stats: The breakaway colony has a chemical which two people drop on their tongues. If it tastes sweet when they kiss then they are genetically compatible and will have healthy children. Everyone wants to kiss Crichton, who loves it, and Aeryn, who hates it so much that she snogs Rygel to get everyone to go away and leave her alone. Planets can be protected by Automated PK Satellite Weaponry, which boast self-tracking pulse cannons and will fire at the first sign of attempted escape.

Logic Leaps: Why spend eighty cycles as a statue to learn the law – couldn't they just attend Law School for a while?

WHAT did you just say?: Crichton: 'Eighty cycles, that is roughly eighty years to you and me and over five hundred years to dogs!'

Guest Stars: Matt Day was Luke Ross on *A Country Practice*, and played the photographer Hurley in the TV film *Shackleton*. Tina Bursill was Sonia Stevens in *Prisoner: Cell Block H*, Hilary Scheppers in *Heartbreak High*, and Miss Crawford in *Home and Away*. Felix Williamson has appeared in such films as *Dirty Deeds* and *Babe: Pig In The City*. Felicity Price has appeared in the film *The Sugar Factory*. Aaron Cash can be briefly seen in *Titanic* and previously appeared as Pa'u Bitaal in **113**, 'Rhapsody In Blue'. Jonathan Hardy provides the voice of Rygel but has also appeared in *Mad Max*, *Moulin Rouge* and *Mr Reliable*. Francesca Buller, Ben Browder's wife, was M'Lee in **121**, 'Bone To Be Wild', and returned as Raxil in **313**, 'Scratch 'n' Sniff'.

Backstage: Was the little boy Crichton saw in the machine actually played by Ben Browder's kid? Who knows, he ain't saying (and fair enough). Originally written as a two-parter, the crew changed their minds once they looked at it. David Kemper told *Cult Times* that 'there was just so much really great material that would have been cut for timing.' So they shot new material, such as the space sequence with Crichton [in **211**, 'Look at the Princess II: I Do, I Think']. 'And we turned a blessing of riches into a bigger blessing.' The bulk of the extra stuff is in episode two, hence episodes one and three have the production numbers 10210 and 10211 but the middle episode is allocated a later production number, 10221.

The Verdict: Brilliant stuff as the Executive Producer, David Kemper, demonstrates just how well he knows the characters on his show. Both big relationships are seriously addressed; Scorpius crops up again, which always gives the show a lift; we are presented with a believably complex political situation that promises to become more complicated; and the episode looks gorgeous, with a stunning opening cityscape effect and lovely design work throughout. This opens up the world of *Farscape* – with the Scarran/PK conflict – and the relationships on Moya, and the show's ongoing narrative gets a huge boost.

211
Look at the Princess II: I Do, I Think

1st US Transmission Date: 28 July 2000
1st UK Transmission Date: 18 September 2000
1st Australian Transmission Date: 18 August 2001

Director: Andrew Prowse

Having saved Crichton from an assassination attempt, Prince Clavor's fiancée, Jenavian, reveals herself to be a PK operative whose mission is to kill Clavor if he ascends to the throne. Crichton allows her to believe that he is also a PK agent. He then slaps Clavor around a bit and tells him not to try and kill him again. However, Jenavian vaporised the assassins so there is no proof of the attempt.

The Empress begins to doubt Crichton's sanity and Princess Katrella slaps Crichton around a bit in turn for humiliating her – she refuses to believe her brother would kill anyone and thinks Crichton is lying. When a floating gas bomb nearly kills them both, she changes her mind (although it later appears the gas bomb was sent by Scorpius).

Rygel and the Empress conspire to send Crichton, along with ro-NA and a contingent of personal guards, to a cargo ship in orbit where he can hide until the wedding. Unfortunately ro-NA has sold Crichton out and Lt Braca is waiting for them. He kills the guards and contacts Scorpius. Crichton, realising that he is too valuable to be killed, counts on Braca not shooting him, and arms the ship's weapons systems, which attracts the attention of the weapons satellites, which open fire on the cargo ship. Ro-NA is killed, Braca abandons ship and Crichton is forced to jump across open space to the Transport Pod without a suit. When he returns to the planet he finds nothing has changed and the wedding still has to continue. He takes his vows and is turned into a statue . . .

Moya meets one of the Builders, who has decided to decommission her because she gave birth to a gunship. Moya accepts this and shuts herself down. Pilot is dying, and Zhaan is left alone on a ghost ship.

Buck Rogers Redux: 'I'm tired. What am I supposed to do . . . when there's no fight left . . . I'm not quitting, I just can't go on.' When he realises that Braca can't shoot him dead Crichton improvises madly, telling him that humans bleed out and die from a single wound, so he can't be shot in the arm or leg either. The insanity we saw in the first few episodes of the season finally flowers and he entirely loses his mind on the cargo ship, almost seeming to wish that Braca would kill him. Back on the planet he realises he still has no choice but to go ahead with the marriage and all the fight goes out of him. He's finally had enough, and being a statue for eighty cycles seems like a pretty good way out of things. Also, there's an air of self-sacrifice, going through with it to prevent Clavor starting wars and killing millions of people. He leaves messages for Zhaan, Aeryn and Pilot. Back home on Earth he had a collection of Charlie Parker CDs and a '62 T Bird.

You Can Be More: Aeryn tries to threaten Jenavian and Katralla that if they hurt Crichton she'll sort them out, but it's a futile gesture and only serves to demonstrate her own powerlessness. Aeryn tells Carzenonva to get lost but then, having walked out on Crichton again, takes him with her on an exploration to the Barren Lands outside the city.

Big Blue: 'I am so filled with uncharitable rage.' Despite her best efforts to convince the Builder, Zhaan is powerless and furious as Moya dies around her.

I was a Teenage Luxan: We get a good display of the friendship and rapport D'Argo has built up with Crichton when he tells him that whether he chooses to fight, run or marry he will back him up.

Buckwheat the Sixteenth: Rygel again proves his worth as a negotiator and his innate understanding of court intrigue and politics. He builds a nicely conspiratorial relationship with Empress Novia when planning to secrete Crichton on the cargo ship, and gleefully mutters, 'I smell power again' at the wedding ceremony. He's been teaching D'Argo the rules of politics.

Everyone's Favourite Little Tralk: Chiana again takes Aeryn to task over her treatment of Crichton: 'Look, Aeryn, all men are stupid, OK? Men equals Stupid. If you want them to know something, you have to tell them.' She uses her race's reputation to try and intimidate the Scarran into leaving Crichton alone. It's a ballsy move, but it's a bluff doomed to failure. Chi tells Crichton she loves him when she hugs him goodbye, but in a sisterly way.

In the Driving Seat: Pilot accepts his fate and tells Zhaan that he feels as fulfilled as Moya does and is ready to die.

Nosferatu in Rubber: 'Oh, to be there when the scales fall from John Crichton's eyes.' Scorpius plays a clever game.

With the gasbomb he gasses Crichton but ensures he doesn't die by having ro-NA save them. He knows this will flush Crichton out of protective custody and make him vulnerable. If only he hadn't made it so clear that Crichton was unique he'd have got away with it, too. Then again, he was so sure Crichton wouldn't be taken alive (**122**, 'Family Ties' and **201**, 'Mind the Baby'), he should have foreseen his suicidal tactics. Crichton requested before his wedding that Scorpius be forbidden from ever visiting the world again, and they granted his request. We get to see that freaky head thing he does again (**201**, 'Mind the Baby'), but we still don't know what it's for.

A Ship, a Living Ship!: The Builder allows Moya to speak so Zhaan can hear. Moya says it's OK that she's dying, she doesn't mind, and she feels fulfilled by her life. The Builders created Leviathans as emissaries of peace, and gave them souls.

The Ballad of Aeryn and John: Aeryn tells Crichton she's proud of him for fighting back and staying alive, but stops short of telling him how she feels, although he gives her another opportunity to do so. His defeatist attitude and acceptance of the marriage finally forces her to give up and leave. She does not attend the wedding.

Hi, Harvey: When the cargo ship is under fire and it looks like Crichton's for it, he hears Scorpius's voice in his head telling him he mustn't die yet.

Disney on Acid: When he sees the floating gas bomb Crichton remarks that Obi-Wan had one similar, but smaller. This was the floating gizmo he used to train Luke on the *Millennium Falcon* in *Star Wars*. In his mad moments on the cargo ship he also riffs on *Blazing Saddles*, *Ace Ventura* and *Apocalypse Now*.

Alien Encounters: The Peacekeepers have a unit called the Special Directorate who deploy spies to act as Disruptors. The Builders can manifest themselves as tendrils of smoke that can penetrate Moya's hull. Ro-NA is a Jekench, a species who do not believe in the acquisition of possessions.

Get Frelled: Crichton holds Braca's gun to his right hand and screams: 'My sex life . . . kill my sex life! Now, quick, shoot, just shoot!' The award for funniest moment on *Farscape* to date goes to D'Argo's farewell speech to Crichton just before he's frozen. D'Argo says he has both good and bad news: 'The bad news is that you're married and must endure as a statue for eighty cycles in a strange world.' When asked for the good news, he declares, 'Chiana and I are having *fantastic* sex.'

Indeed, Chiana screams so loudly that security guards storm their room at night.

Stats: The statue-freezing machine is only calibrated for Sebaceans and causes Crichton a lot of pain.

Logic Leaps: Would a human survive a space walk, sans suit, of that duration, or indeed of any duration?

The Verdict: The detour to the cargo pod doesn't move the story forward. Still, Ben Browder's mad Crichton is terrifying, Francesca Buller is marvellous as ro-NA and there are a lot of thrills and laughs on offer. It feels like a middle episode, in that we don't learn anything new, but it's still gripping stuff.

212
Look at the Princess III: The Maltese Crichton

1st US Transmission Date: 4 August 2000
1st UK Transmission Date: 25 September 2000
1st Australian Transmission Date: 25 August 2001

Director: Andrew Prowse & Tony Tilse

Prince Clavor and Cargn cut the head off the Crichton statue and drop it in acid. Scorpius fishes it out but is shot by Jenavian, who reconstitutes Crichton and takes him to a tent outside the city to recover. She realises he is not a PK but she senses he can still be a useful ally in stopping the Scarrans. Cargn kills Clavor because he dissolves their partnership. Cargn and Scorpius are both looking for Crichton and Cargn kidnaps Chiana to use as bait. D'Argo and Scorpius unite to attack Cargn.

Crichton and Jenavian return to the city where everyone is very glad to see him alive, because the Empress had been threatening to have all off-worlders executed in punishment for his disappearance and Clavor's death. Crichton kills Cargn, D'Argo rescues Chiana and Scorpius is left for Crichton to kill. But for some reason Crichton can't kill him, and walks away. Crichton is about to leave the planet when he discovers that Princess Katralla was impregnated with his DNA, and he insists he be refrozen for the sake of his child. Unfortunately his human physiology would not survive a second freezing, so he convinces the Empress to freeze Tyno instead – the public will never know there's been a switch, and Katralla and Tyno love each other. Crichton leaves knowing all is settled, but he will never see his daughter.

In the barren lands Aeryn and Carzenonva have a climbing accident and Aeryn has to haul the useless idiot back to the city despite her own broken leg.

On Moya, Zhaan takes revenge on the Builder by sucking him into the engine of the WDP. However, he reappears and reveals that Moya and Pilot are fine – they were only testing whether Zhaan was worthy of being Moya's protector. They conclude that she is and she, Pilot and Moya are all released.

Buck Rogers Redux: 'I do what I have to do.' It's a defining moment for Crichton's character when his decision to leave is instantly revoked the second he knows he's going to be a dad: 'A child deserves two parents. My child deserves a father. Make me a statue.' Could you ever imagine Jim Kirk saying that, or Buck Rogers? Crichton is a 21st-century hero. When the machine shows him the daughter he will never know his heartache is palpable, and it forges another bond between him and D'Argo – both separated from their only children. It's his idea to let Tyno be the regent, because he knows he's a good man and will be a good father to his child: 'You take care of my little girl.'

You Can Be More: Aeryn gets it all out of her system by climbing rocks, but when it all goes wrong and she breaks her leg it's hard not to conclude that it's exactly what she wanted – something extreme to take her mind off things. Carzenonva, like Chiana, reads Aeryn like a book and tells her: 'You're not trained to deal with emotions, so you're afraid of them.'

Big Blue: Zhaan's fury is something to behold, and though she instantly regrets her action, she ruthlessly sucks the Builder into the WDP's engines. When he reveals the true nature of his mission she is unforgiving and throws him off the ship immediately. She and Pilot never tell the others what happened with the Builders.

Buckwheat the Sixteenth: Rygel was initially intending to remain on the planet as an advisor to Crichton, which implies that, although he's already very old, eighty cycles is a drop in the ocean to him.

Nosferatu in Rubber: Scarrans love heat; Sebaceans are killed by it. Scorpius, as a Scarran-Sebacean hybrid, is a slave to heat. He wears a thermal regulator suit, and the rotating thing that comes out of his head contains cooling rods to maintain his body temperature. He hates Scarrans, and they consider him a 'biological mistake'. He again promises D'Argo that if given Crichton he will release him unharmed after he has extracted the wormhole information. He sampled Crichton's DNA when he was in the Aurora Chair and can use it to track him, even when he is a disembodied bronze head. D'Argo assures Scorpius that Crichton will never be taken alive, but Scorpius replies, cryptically: 'You underestimate the strength of a relationship, even your friend does not yet understand.' Crichton tries to throw Scorpius into acid but cannot, and after he's left, Scorpius runs his fingers through the liquid, indicating that it wouldn't have hurt him anyway – he was *very* in control of the situation.

A Ship, a Living Ship!: Moya could be used to breed an army of warships, but the Builders know that both she and Pilot are pure souls. They need to ensure that her crew will not misuse her, so they test Zhaan. Moya is given voice one last time and requests that Zhaan sing to her.

The Ballad of Aeryn and John: Back on Moya, Aeryn produces the compatibility chemical and she and Crichton share a kiss that will tell them whether they are compatible or not. Judging by the smiles on both their faces, they are. Of course any relationship they did embark on would be adulterous, because Crichton is now a married man.

The Ballad of Chiana and D'Argo: D'Argo dives across a vat of acid to save Chiana, and she tells him how proud she is of him, and gently mocks that he ever thought they weren't compatible. There's a genuinely tender edge to their scenes alone and they seem happy and on the same wavelength.

Alien Encounters: Scarrans are extremely hard to kill – Cargn takes numerous gun blasts and still remains standing. It takes an acid bath to finish him off. He again tries to force the truth out of someone using his heat projection powers, this time D'Argo, and again gets only lies.

Hi, Harvey: Why couldn't Crichton kill Scorpius? When he tries he has more flashes back to the Aurora Chair and this time we see Scorpius inserting the needle he brandished in the previous episode's flashback, and burying it in the back of Crichton's head.

Disney on Acid: D'Argo's acid-spanning leap makes Crichton shout, 'How Batman was that?'

Get Frelled: Crichton and Jenavian do the deed, so his sex life no longer consists solely of his right hand.

Seen it all Before: Crichton being frozen is very Han Solo.

Logic Leaps: The Empress and her cohorts want to know who beheaded Crichton, who reconstituted him and where he is now. Since they can communicate with the statue of Katralla using headsets, why don't they just ask her?

Bloopers: Just after D'Argo saves Chiana, look closely at his nose – it's all askew where it's come off Anthony Simcoe.

WHAT did you just say?: Jenavian's response to Crichton's life story: 'That's either the most pathetic fabrication I've ever heard, or the most pathetic life I could ever imagine. Either way . . .'

The Verdict: Were the Cargo Ship section of episode two, the un-engaging Barren Lands section of episode three, and the Builders subplot removed, this would have been a tight, focused, scorching two-parter. But it's nice that the show felt confident enough to do something epic and took its time with the story to allow the characters and the situation room to develop and deepen. Certain elements don't gel, but while the trilogy may not be the most watertight, economical piece of storytelling you'll ever see, it still has lots to recommend it, and the world of *Farscape* is a lot richer and more complex after it than it was before.

213
My Three Crichtons

1st US Transmission Date: 14 July 2000
1st UK Transmission Date: 2 October 2000
1st Australian Transmission Date: 1 September 2001

Writers: Gabrielle Stanton & Harry Werksman Jr
Teleplay: Grant McAloon
Director: Catherine Millar

An alien research vessel, which takes the form of a ball of glowing light, enters Moya and scans the crew. While it is scanning Crichton, Aeryn shoots it, causing a malfunction.

It expands into a huge, sealed globe, swallows Crichton, and eventually spits out three versions of him – the normal one, a hairy caveman version (Neandro), and a brainy, highly evolved model (Futuro). The globe then begins dragging Moya through a hole into another dimension. While Neandro is locked up and Chiana's making friends with him, Futuro and Crichton use the defence screen to counteract the globe and keep Moya in this dimension, but it is only a temporary solution. The globe transmits a message stating that the generation of the two Crichtons was a side effect of its scanning process and wouldn't have happened if it hadn't been shot. It needs to take one of them back with it for study within a few arns otherwise it will take every living thing within a metra. Despite trying to find another solution, normal Crichton eventually accepts Futuro's assertion that Neandro must be sacrificed. Chiana, however, has released Neandro because she thinks it's cruel to assume that he is the disposable one. Crichton finds Neandro but can't bring himself to condemn him. Futuro then tries to force Crichton, whom he sees as inferior, into the globe, not realising that Crichton intended to sacrifice himself anyway, to save Moya and his friends. Neandro kills Futuro in order to rescue Crichton and walks into the globe, knowing that this is not his place.

Buck Rogers Redux: When the Farscape project had its funding approved, Crichton went out for champagne with his dad, DK and Alex (**113**, 'Rhapsody In Blue'). Crichton and DK argued because DK thought things had gone too smoothly and was expecting something to go wrong. Crichton's willingness to sacrifice himself rather than condemn an innocent creature to death is big heroic stuff, but since Neandro is as much Crichton as Crichton himself, his act of self-sacrifice is both consistent with his character and not the cop-out it would otherwise be.

Chiana says that Neandro is warm and sensitive, 'everything I ever liked about you'. Futuro sees Crichton as a primitive and is willing to risk taking Moya through the dimensional hole rather than risk his own life. He is the epitomy of logical realpolitik, but Zhaan tells him, 'your logic may be firm, but it's cold'. Crichton also has little patience with Futuro's expediency and we get a statement of Crichton's greatest strength, and the thing that's kept him alive in the Uncharted Territories: 'I am *widening* my perspective. That is what I do, that's what makes me, *me*!'

After it's all over Crichton is left to ponder his initial decision to sacrifice Neandro, and the fact that the least evolved of him was the one that did the right thing – since he was willing to do the right thing as well he's not got anything to beat himself up about.

Neandro wears Crichton's flight suit from the Farscape test flight. Crichton abandoned this long ago in favour of PK black and leather, emphasising how far he's evolved since his arrival on Moya. Futuro wore the full PK captain's uniform from **120**, 'The Hidden Memory', indicating that Crichton is evolving into a more expedient and dangerous person and that he is halfway between the innocent who arrived on Moya and the ruthless killer he may need to be if he is to survive.

You Can Be More: Aeryn doesn't trust Futuro one bit, and is willing to throw him off the ship when it looks like it's a choice between him and Crichton. Uncharacteristically for her, however, she lets her guard down for a second and Futuro knocks her unconscious.

Buckwheat the Sixteenth: Rygel agrees with Futuro: 'Let's just give the sphere the hairy bastard and get it the frell out of here!' When Chiana lets Neandro go Rygel calls her a 'stupid bony-assed little bitch' and decides that the first Crichton he finds he will stun and throw to the globe – favouritism be damned, he just wants the situation resolved so he can go about his merry business.

Everyone's Favourite Little Tralk: Something about Neandro's vulnerability attracts Chiana and she forms a strong bond with him immediately, even though he initially throws her across the room in confusion and rage. She tells Crichton that she knew Neandro would be heroic, because he was Crichton as well, and she knows him.

In the Driving Seat: Catherine Millar – who hadn't directed *Farscape* before but who did return shoots Pilot in a new and interesting way – close up with a fish-eye lens effect – which works well. Unusually there is discord between Moya and Pilot – Moya is willing to sacrifice herself to save the crew but Pilot lacks Moya's fatalism.

A Ship, a Living Ship!: Rygel says he is underneath 'Maintenance Bay Two', which is a surprise because in dialogue the characters never refer to one or two but merely say 'I'll be in the Maintenance Bay'. Aeryn is fixing her Prowler with Moya parts taken from Crichton's modified WDP.

Alien Encounters: We don't know what race sent the survey vessel, but they live in another dimension and have encountered all the races on Moya before, except humans.

Disney on Acid: 'I'm in Bill and Ted land here, so I'm open to suggestions.' Crichton tries to formulate a strategy but happily resists the temptation to play air guitar and scream 'bodacious, dudes!'

Get Frelled: When Futuro emerges from the sphere he is naked (and give a hearty cheer because many prudish sci-fi shows would have had him clothed and never bothered to explain why). Aeryn gets a good look at his mivonks and finds them very amusing indeed: 'John has more hair . . . amongst other things. You going to blame that on feeling cold?'

Seen it all Before: *Star Trek* most notably – they split Kirk into two people in 'The Enemy Within', and it's been done hundreds of times since on numerous shows.

Backstage: Ben Browder on playing Neandro: 'I loved having the freedom to crawl around on the floor with Chiana.' The two Crichtons were named Neandro and Futuro on set.

The Verdict: Very *Star Trek* in many respects – alien menace enters ship, does something nasty to our hero and we get an examination of human nature capped with a final heroic act of self-sacrifice. Given its familiarity, then, it's surprising that this is such riveting stuff. Ben Browder is excellent as all three Crichtons, managing to make Neandro deeply sympathetic and Futuro sinister. It is a little disturbing to realise that we've evolved from hairy guys with big teeth, to middling folk with normal teeth, but will end up as Texans with huge teeth and speech impediments – obviously mankind's current incarnation is at the optimal stage of tooth evolution. Neandro was a disaster waiting to happen, so it's a credit to the make-up people that he is as credible as he is and doesn't inspire gales of laughter. Because each of the three Crichtons has Crichton's memories up to the point where the globe absorbed him, each at first believes himself to be the genuine article. Since the globe only wants to absorb one of him, it seems possible, for a while, that one will remain alongside our Crichton on Moya. That was not to be, and the status quo is restored at episode's end. But be realistic – there couldn't be two Crichtons running around, it would be daft and impractical and no show would ever take that kind of risk ... would it?

214
Beware of Dog

1st US Transmission Date: 11 August 2000
1st UK Transmission Date: 9 October 2000
1st Australian Transmission Date: 20 December 2001

Writer: Naren Shankar
Director: Tony Tilse
Guest Cast: Wayne Pygram (Scorpius)

Believing that they may have brought a deadly parasite aboard in a food shipment, D'Argo and Chiana buy a Vorc – a small predator that hunts and kills parasites – and release it on Moya. A large creature, which they believe to be the parasite, is seen on board and it attacks and poisons

D'Argo. They track it down but it's revealed to be the Vorc, which can change shape. They lock it up but Zhaan cannot find any trace of venom in it, so they conclude D'Argo was poisoned by something else, perhaps the parasite, and maybe the Vorc is doing its job after all. They release it again but it attacks Rygel, so they shoot it. However, as it lies wounded it shows them a cocoon, which it slits open to release an embalmed Rygel. The Rygel it attacked is a parasite copy, which Crichton and Aeryn kill. Unfortunately the Vorc dies from its wounds. D'Argo was poisoned by the parasite but his reaction was too severe for it to cocoon him. He eventually recovers.

Meanwhile, Crichton is tormented by visions of Scorpius, taunting him with threats of imminent capture.

Buck Rogers Redux: Crichton plays chess, presumably with a self-made set, and golf around the ship to try and take his mind off his visions of Scorpius. He's also playing with a ball that looks exactly like the one Scorpius was playing with in the last few episodes of Season One. He talks to the visions and even shoots at them, nearly shooting Aeryn at one point. He tells Aeryn, 'I'm not gonna lose my mind, it's all I've got left,' and explains that he couldn't kill Scorpius in **212**, 'Look at the Princess III: The Maltese Crichton' because 'something stopped me, something inside.'

You Can Be More: 'I know my translator microbes are working, because deranged as it always is, I do understand what you're saying.' Aeryn is making an effort to reach out to Crichton because she's certain there's something wrong with him now. She even leads Pilot to doubt Crichton by telling him of her suspicions. When Crichton assures her that he's not going mad she looks less than convinced. She comes within a hair's breadth of throwing the Vorc out of an airlock but she cries when it dies, guilty for killing an innocent creature.

Big Blue: Zhaan gets to do her healing bit again – she seems to be devolving into the ship's doctor but isn't getting that much to do recently, at least not with the rest of the crew. The Medbay now has a very complicated medical scanner installed.

Buckwheat the Sixteenth: When D'Argo is bitten by the Vorc, Rygel stays beside him willing him to live. This may seem uncharacteristic, until it's revealed that it was probably parasite Rygel worried about the other host. Also, though he's going to leave the ship it's not because Rygel's a coward, it's because the parasite knows it's being hunted. Finally, when he visits the sick D'Argo in the Medbay and is offended because they assume he's just after D'Argo's stuff when he dies, it's the parasite checking on its prey.

Everyone's Favourite Little Tralk: Chiana's a Nebari of action – when D'Argo's ill she can't bear just to sit beside his bed, she picks up a gun and goes to help catch the creature so the venom can be used to make an antidote. Only when told to go away by Crichton does she accept that her place is by D'Argo's bed.

In the Driving Seat: Pilot can understand the Vorc even though it can't speak. His bond with Moya means he's used to non-verbal communication. 'While I don't believe this creature has language in a true sense, it seems to be expressing itself in a mixture of simple concepts, sensations and instinctual reactions.'

A Ship, a Living Ship!: Moya has at least three cargo bays. Her neural clusters can be modified to fortify a person's immune system.

The Ballad of Chiana and D'Argo: D'Argo is quite short with Chiana at the start of the episode, but when he's ill she comforts him, and he even asks her for sex while he's lying, dying, on his sick bed.

Alien Encounters: The parasites killed an entire ship's crew of 200 people, leaving only husks behind them.

Hi, Harvey: 'You'll never see it coming, John. When the trap closes it'll be too late.' Phantom Scorpius tells

Crichton that he has already been beaten, he just doesn't know it yet.

Worlds Apart: The crew have bought a consignment of food from a system with three planets devoted to farming.

Disney on Acid: The madder Crichton gets the more references creep in. This week he references the Riddler in *Batman*, *E.T.*, Ewoks, *Caddyshack*, *Lassie* and *Invasion of the Body Snatchers*.

Get Frelled: The Vorc gets to have his wicked way with Aeryn's leg. Lucky critter.

What Does This Do?: Poor old D'Argo gets his best suit pissed on by the Vorc. Crichton and Aeryn realise the cocooned Rygel is the genuine article when he farts helium.

Seen it all Before: *Invasion of the Bodysnatchers* and its various rip-offs. The Vorc looks very like *E.T.*, and Crichton even references that at one point, imitating him when he says 'ouch'.

Logic Leaps: The crew gas the Vorc with grenades while they're standing right there – why don't they put respirators on? Are they immune to gas grenades?

The Verdict: Not as funny and cute as it wants to be, and laden down with the daftest puppet the show has yet seen, this episode plays with old ideas and doesn't come up with anything new. Still, there's a lot of fun to be had from the interaction between Aeryn and Crichton, and the Vorc puppet does have its moments – humping Aeryn's leg and sticking its fingers in her mouth (which, given that it's an animatronic, is no mean feat) – but it's so clearly being pulled along on wheels that it loses credibility instantly. The best aspect of the episode is the underlying tension caused by Crichton's flashes of Scorpius and the slowly growing conviction, both in Aeryn and viewers, that he is finally losing his mind.

215
Won't Get Fooled Again

1st US Transmission Date: 18 August 2000
1st UK Transmission Date: 30 October 2000
1st Australian Transmission Date: 21 December 2001

Writer: Richard Manning
Director: Rowan Woods
Guest Cast: Wayne Pygram (Scorpius), Kent McCord (Jack Crichton),
Murray Bartlett (DK), Thomas Holesgrove (Grath, the Scarran),
Lani Tupu (Capt. Bialar Crais), Carmen Duncan (Leslie Crichton)

Crichton wakes up back on Earth a week after crashing the
Farscape module during his test flight. He still has
memories of Moya and assumes, correctly, that everything
is an illusion a la **116**, 'A Human Reaction'. That his
psychiatrist is Zhaan, his new boss is Rygel and D'Argo is
a fellow astronaut, confirms that everything's a bit screwy.
Chiana crops up as an Astronaut groupie, Crais appears as
a dog-carrying, red high-heel wearing cop, and Pilot plays
bongos in a local club. Unlike **116**, 'A Human Reaction',
DK is present this time, as is Crichton's dead mother. One
person breaks the paradigm – Scorpius, of whom there are
two versions. The one that isn't a jazz drummer turns out
to be an unlikely ally. He reveals that Scorpius inserted a
neuro chip into Crichton's brain when he was in the
Aurora Chair (**119**, 'Nerve' and **120**, 'The Hidden Memory'). This chip contains a neural clone of Scorpius's
personality that lives in Crichton's subconscious and only
reveals itself when it has to. It tells Crichton that he has
been captured by a Scarran, who wants to find out why
Scorpius is after him (**210–213**, 'Look at the Princess'
trilogy and 'My Three Crichtons'). The Scarran's interrogation technique involves using a mind-control machine to
drive the subject insane. The Scorpius clone stops Crichton's brain function, convincing the Scarran that Crichton
is dead and releasing him from the machine. Crichton then
overloads his gun, rams it down the Scarran's throat and
blows its head off.

Buck Rogers Redux: 'Life sucks, nothing matters, let's *PARTY!*' Crichton's mother (who may or may not have been English or Australian, because her accent is all over the place) died of an unspecified illness five years ago (although it's unclear whether that's five years before the present or from the time of the test flight). His opinion of DK, hinted at in **213**, 'My Three Crichtons', is less than flattering given that he's supposed to be his best friend – he seems to think he's a bit of a whiner, play-it-safe kind of guy. Not for one second does he believe he's back on Earth. He checks the papers and the ladies' room, because they were what gave the game away in **116**, 'A Human Reaction'.

Once he's accepted that he's not going to play along he starts playing with reality: he throws his new boss (Rygel) off a car park, shoots everyone and drives into a truck. When this doesn't change things, and as the world gets more and more surreal, he comes very close to losing his mind, and the madness that's been creeping up on him all season becomes more extreme.

He's on a reconstruction of Earth and finds, to his surprise, that he's homesick for Moya. He does *not* boogie. His reaction to his mother's pleading for him to remain with her when she dies is horrible, and Ben Browder pulls out all the stops, turning in a shocking and powerful performance.

You Can Be More: 'I found new places to take your temperature.' Aeryn Sun *is* Doctor Bettina Fairchild (good name!) – nurse, wearer of amazing curlers, party girl extraordinaire, fancier of men with tentacles, and capable of doing the most amazing thing with her tongue!

Big Blue: 'Shared Unity. Interesting euphemism. No, Mr Crichton, you and I have never had sex. I'm sure I'd remember it if we had.' Pa'u Zotoh Zhaan *is* Doctor Kaminski – alien psychiatrist. She's blue but she's got a green card.

I was a Teenage Luxan: Would you participate 'with me in a little Luxan bonding ritual? . . . We need: some chains, my Qualta Blade, just a squirt of Lutra oil, and oooh, Chiana . . . she wants to watch!' Ka D'Argo *is* Gary Ragal – astronaut about town, hard drinkin', fast drivin', woman lovin', party dude who likes beer, bad cardigans and may, in fact, be gay.

Buckwheat the Sixteenth: 'This is for calling me Sparky! This is for calling me Fluffy! And this is for Buckwheat, whatever that means!' Dominar Rygel XVI *is* D Logan – disabled boss of the Farscape project with a taste for cigars, a motorised chair and an inability to fly.

Everyone's Favourite Little Tralk: 'You're an astronaut too? Oooh I *like* astronauts!' Chiana *is* Jessica – bisexual astronaut groupie.

The Insane Military Commander: 'I like your style, hombre.' Captain Bialar Crais *is* Officer Gordon – high-heel wearing, dog-carrying, gun-toting keeper of the peace.

Worlds Apart: Crichton is captured on an anonymous Commerce Planet.

Alien Encounters: The Scarrans are now after Crichton as well, although only to find out why Scorpius is after him. Their standard interrogation technique is to drive their prisoners insane.

Hi, Harvey: The needle we saw in **210–213** (the 'Look at the Princess' trilogy and 'My Three Crichtons') was a memory of Scorpius implanting a neuro chip, which explains why Crichton's been having flashes of Scorpius since the Aurora Chair, why he saw Scorpius in **205**, 'The Way We Weren't' heard him in **211**, 'Look at the Princess II: I Do, I Think', was unable to kill him in **212**, 'Look at the Princess III: The Maltese Crichton', and was hallucinating him in **214**, 'Beware of Dog'. It also explains the fairly regular moments of instability that began in **201**, 'Mind the Baby'. The neuro chip contains a neural clone of Scorpius's personality that can appear to Crichton and has the power to kill him at will. It is there to extract the wormhole information from his brain no matter how long it takes.

Crichton tries to decide if the neural clone is Clarence (the guardian Angel from the Jimmy Stewart film, *It's A Wonderful Life*) or Harvey (the invisible rabbit from Stewart's other great classic, *Harvey*). He eventually settles on Harvey. Having revealed itself in order to save him from the Scarran the neural clone then forces Crichton to forget he exists.

Disney on Acid: The references to *Wizard of Oz* begin immediately. Crichton says he feels as if he's been 'hit by a house'; he refers to the 'giant blue twister that sucks me down to Oz'; he quotes a song from the film, calling for people to come out 'and see the young man who fell from the star'; he accuses Scorpius of being 'the man behind the curtain'. Crais's dog is called Toto.

Get Frelled: Aeryn in a nurse's uniform, Chiana as a schoolgirl, Zhaan in black PVC and Oh ... My ... God ... Rygel in S&M gear. Sparky in leather with a whip is enough to give anyone nightmares.

Seen it all Before: In Season One, **116**, 'A Human Reaction', which is this episode's masterstroke.

WHAT did you just say?: Officer Gordon's version of the caution: 'You have the right to the remains of a silent attorney. If you cannot afford one, tough noogies! You can make one phone call. I recommend Trixie, 976-555-love.'

Guest Stars: Carmen Duncan has been a regular on a number of TV shows, most recently *Another World*.

Backstage: This episode was both loved by viewers who thought it was a brilliant bit of television and hated by those viewers who it offended. According to Ben Browder, 'There was very little in the middle ground ... it's basically Dennis Potter on acid. It's just fantastic. It's nuts. And it actually holds up as a story. I'm very proud of that.' (*TV Zone*)

Wayne Pygram is a drummer and has played professionally for twenty years.

The Verdict: An instant classic, demonstrating *Farscape*'s incredible nerve by taking a story that's already been done and doing it again, this time with the realisation that it's all a trick coming before the titles. By pre-empting the revelation, it becomes a surreal trip; outrageously funny, genuinely mysterious, allowing all the actors to let loose and play against type and yet still managing to further the ongoing storyline of Crichton's madness. It doesn't put a foot wrong and Ben Browder's performance is nothing short of astonishing. Many other sci-fi shows would, and have, done riffs similar to 116, 'A Human Reaction', but no other show except *Farscape* would dare try the same trick twice *and* pull it off with such panache. A masterclass in balls, and a clear demonstration of why this show is unique.

216
The Locket

1st US Transmission Date: 25 August 2000
1st UK Transmission Date: 6 November 2000
1st Australian Transmission Date: 8 September 2001

Writer: Justin Monjo
Director: Ian Watson
Guest Cast: Paul Goddard (Stark), Wayne Pygram (Scorpius),
Alyson Standen (Ennixx)

Moya hides in a stellar mist and Aeryn goes off to fly a reconnaissance flight. She returns one day later having aged 55 cycles. Moya is trapped in a Centre Halo, an area of time distortion which means that while the rest of the universe ages, time moves very slowly for Moya and crew. Aeryn leaves for a nearby planet and Crichton follows but he is unable to return to Moya as the mist vanishes and will not return for 55 cycles. He and Aeryn grow old on a lush planet, waiting for the next reappearance of the mist so they can rejoin Moya. Unfortunately Aeryn dies in the Transport Pod before they make it back.

Crichton theorises that if Moya leaves the mist at the exact point it entered, time will resume its natural course. Moya backs out of the mist, the great cosmic reset button is pressed, and everyone is back to normal. Only Zhaan and the recently returned Stark retain memories of what happened.

Buck Rogers Redux: 'I am too old for this shit!' Crichton grows old on the Favoured Planet but never lets go of his old life – he is a pilot and he belongs in the stars. Aeryn's company, and the hope that one day he will return to his previous life, is all that keeps him going. His southern accent gets stronger as he ages.

When he was young he and his dad use to go camping near a lake in Maine. He was about four when man landed on the moon in 1969, which makes him approximately 35 years old.

You Can Be More: Peacekeepers are born in space and have to 'die in space. I have spent most of my life with you, and it has been glorious, but when I die, I belong up there.' Aeryn lives to be approximately 240 cycles old. She marries and has three sons, all of whom die, but one of them leaves her a granddaughter, Ennixx. She adjusts to her life on the Favoured Planet and seems quite happy in her quiet rural life.

Big Blue: Zhaan is doing a lot of meditating on her own (the opening shot of her meditating nude is lifted from **101**, 'Premiere' – her make-up is a different colour). When she performs Unity with Stark she is worried that his mind will overwhelm hers. Delvians strive to achieve awareness of Time itself when they perform Unity, but she implies that she has never managed it before.

I was a Teenage Luxan: 'I do not want to live a life without a past. I want to see my son again.' Stark tells D'Argo that his son, Jothee, is being sold in a slave auction in a few solar days. Zhaan promises that they will find a way to rescue him.

Buckwheat the Sixteenth: Rygel and Chiana go rummaging in Aeryn's Transport Pod for things to steal, and he tells Pip, 'You're worse than me – I like that!'

Everyone's Favourite Little Tralk: Chiana has trashed Aeryn's Prowler and given her a stolen locket to apologise. Zhaan and Stark were not the only ones to sense danger in the mist, Chiana did too – another hint of her psychic abilities.

The Man in the Iron Mask: Stark is suddenly back, returning the Transport Pod that they lent him after they escaped from the Gammak base in **120**, 'The Hidden Memory' (spot the desperate attempt to explain away a previous goof). He uses his glowing face to soothe Aeryn, and performs Unity with Zhaan. Together he and she are strong enough to bring time to a halt, or to isolate a person from a time freeze (although Zhaan says it is only possible to do this for Crichton because she once shared Unity with him). He didn't want to tell D'Argo about Jothee until Zhaan was awake and could protect him from the Luxan's possible reaction.

In the Driving Seat: Pilot offers a prayer to Kahaynu the Builder (**211**, 'Look at the Princess II: I Do, I Think' and **212**, 'Look at the Princess III: The Maltese Crichton') before StarBursting free of the mist.

A Ship, a Living Ship!: Leviathans are not designed to perform reverse StarBursts, but Moya pulls it off.

The Ballad of Aeryn and John: Old Aeryn to young Crichton after 55 cycles separation: 'Look at you . . . I'd forgotten how beautiful you were.' Aeryn keeps Chiana's locket around her neck containing a picture of the one true love of her life. She tells Crichton it's her husband, but after she dies he opens it and it's him. He only tells her he loves her after she has died.

Back on Moya, in their normal timestream, both seem to have an inkling that something happened between them, but can't remember what it was. When they open the locket the picture inside has crumbled to dust.

The Ballad of Chiana and D'Argo: D'Argo shouts at Chiana for trying to steal from Aeryn. He tries to persuade her that she doesn't need to act that way because she's one of the crew now, but she insists she will never change, no matter how hard he tries. When they agree that D'Argo's 'pretty straight', Chiana's conclusion is, 'We're not gonna make it are we?'

Worlds Apart: The planet they glimpse through the mist is acidic and barren. We never learn how they travel to the Favoured Planet, which is lush and green – in fact, why bother with the acidic planet at all? There is a small colony on the Favoured Planet, presumably of Sebaceans, seeing that Ennixx is still young after 79 cycles. We do not discover why Aeryn's sons died so young, as war seems unlikely.

Hi, Harvey: Old Crichton still sees regular, persistent visions of Harvey.

Disney on Acid: Crichton sings a traditional sea shanty, 'The Maid Of Amsterdam'.

Stats: Zhaan gives Aeryn Zeccan leaf to chew as a remedy for headaches.

Seen it all Before: In *Star Trek: The Next Generation*'s masterpiece 'Inner Light' and, unusually, *Farscape* doesn't actually bring anything new to the table.

Logic Leaps: Where to begin? It's a technobabble episode, just go with the flow. In fact, when Pilot tells everyone that they can get out of the mist at the exact point they entered by just *going backwards*, it's hard not to conclude that Justin Monjo is poking fun at the ridiculousness of the idea and pointing out that it doesn't matter – it's the emotional heart not the scientific baggage that is the episode's *raison d'être*. Zhaan's comms inexplicably fail just at the exact moment they are needed to provide a dramatic race to save the day.

WHAT did you just say?: Crichton says 'shit' which was cut from the US broadcast but it's there for all the world to hear on the R2 DVD.

Guest Stars: Alyson Standen has appeared in *Summer Bay*, *Roar, Home and Away* and *Water Rats*.

Backstage: This episode was covered extensively in the fourth issue of the official *Farscape* Magazine. There is a short deleted scene, in which old Crichton flirts with Ennixx, on the R2 DVD.

The Verdict: There's no real tension to be had in this episode because not for one second do any of us actually believe that Crichton and Aeryn will remain old. It's clear from the first moment that there will have to be a reset button, and that when it comes it will be a huge cop-out. However, given that we know this from the off and if you can just accept that the time-field gubbins is a device necessary to tell a story, and enjoy the examination of old Crichton and Aeryn, there's a lot to like. Stark's reappearance is welcome, but too abrupt and a bit confusing – how did he find Moya when Scorpius can't? Old-age make-up is notoriously difficult but this episode's works well, and both Claudia Black and Ben Browder do a fine job as crotchety oldsters. Not the classic it wants to be, but it still has a romantic core that works well.

217
The Ugly Truth

1st US Transmission Date: 8 September 2000
1st UK Transmission Date: 13 November 2000
1st Australian Transmission Date: 15 September 2001

Writer: Gabrielle Stanton & Harry Werksman Jr
Director: Tony Tilse
Guest Cast: Paul Goddard (Stark), Lani Tupu (Capt. Bialar Crais),
Linda Cropper (Fento), Peter Carroll (Gahv)

Crais and Talyn contact Moya and ask for a meeting. While Moya's crew is aboard Talyn he fires on an approaching Plokavian vessel and destroys it. Crais throws Moya's crew off and StarBursts away. The Transport Pod containing D'Argo, Zhaan, Crichton, Aeryn and Stark is captured by a second Plokavian vessel. They each, in turn, are asked to give their version of events aboard Talyn.

Aeryn: In Aeryn's version of events D'Argo is violent, Zhaan is a total flake and Crichton wants to kill Crais. Stark tries to raise a defence screen but Aeryn stops him. Talyn's gun fires of its own accord – it must have been a malfunction.

Zhaan: Through Zhaan's eyes Crichton is stupid, indecisive and cowardly, and he agrees with everything everyone says. D'Argo loses his temper. Crichton tries to disarm the malfunctioning weapons console but Aeryn stops him in case he sets it off. Again Talyn's gun fires of its own accord.

Stark: Stark claims that Crais fired the cannon deliberately. According to him the others are lying to prevent the Plokavians going after Crais and perhaps killing Talyn in the process.

D'Argo: In D'Argo's tale he is the leader of the group and everyone defers to him. Stark is a total nutter, screaming and raving, who lunges at the weapons console and fires the gun.

Crichton: Crichton admits that they've been lying, but only because no one knows what happened. Stark did attempt to fire, but Crichton had already disarmed the weapons console, so he couldn't have been responsible.

The Plokavians decide to execute them all, so Stark takes responsibility and is dispersed. We subsequently discover that Talyn fired the gun himself.

Buck Rogers Redux: Crichton still distrusts Crais and it seems from most versions that he's quite happy to see him dead. Which is fair enough.

You Can Be More: Aeryn seems inclined to trust Crais, although whether that's just to give her a chance to undermine his captaincy of Talyn remains to be seen.

Big Blue: Zhaan and Stark are very touchy-feely now – sharing Unity in **216**, 'The Locket' has brought them closer together.

I was a Teenage Luxan: 'I've become so distrustful of people, even when they're trying to help me.' D'Argo blames Stark for what he's become and punches his mask off, which isn't exactly helpful. He later admits he misjudged him.

The Man in the Iron Mask: Stark distrusts Peacekeepers and hates Crais, as well as harbouring deep hatred for the Plokavians whose weapons helped subjugate his world. He has formed a deep attachment to Zhaan and is willing to risk death for the crew of Moya. If his mask is removed before he has had time to prepare himself he loses control of his 'energies'. When he removes the mask prior to dispersal his face does not glow, it is dark, indicating that he is fully in control of his energies. It is possible that he survived dispersion: 'my physical form is only part of my reality, much of me is energy that I can control and project . . . maybe . . . I can transfer enough of myself into another realm to survive.' Everyone thinks it unlikely that he did survive, and Zhaan is left holding his mask.

In the Driving Seat: Pilot uncharacteristically loses his temper with Chiana when she questions the wisdom of searching for Talyn.

The Insane Military Commander: Crais is having trouble controlling Talyn's aggressive urges and has decided to take drastic action. He requests Moya's help, and that of her crew, to persuade Talyn to allow them to anaesthetise him and replace his weapons with a Dampening Net, which will only disable, not destroy, enemy vessels. He can remove his Neural Transponder and thus sever his link with Talyn, but he has a spare.

A Ship, a Living Ship!: Moya tells Talyn that the Plokavian vessel is carrying Novatrin gas. She is torn between her concern for her crew and for Talyn and she chooses to search for Talyn rather than stand by the Plokavian ship in case she's needed. Chiana eventually manages to convince her and Pilot of the futility of the search and Moya returns to collect her crew after they are released by the Plokavians.

Big Baby: Talyn has grown and tells Moya he is healthy and happy. He is not under Crais's control – even though he trusts his Captain, he can act independently. He shoots the Plokavian vessel when he discovers it is carrying Novatrin gas because he believes it is the best way to protect Moya. Crais can activate Privacy Mode, which ensures Talyn cannot hear when the crew are talking about him. Talyn's capability to act freely can be manually overridden, but when his Weapons Console is shut down it restores his freedom of action.

The Ballad of Aeryn and John: When Crichton wants to conspire with Aeryn secretly he grabs her and whispers in her ear; her play-acting in response is risible. He seems suspicious of her motives and perhaps thinks she was not only protecting Talyn, but Crais as well.

Alien Encounters: The Plokavians are weapons dealers who may be ruthless savages or devoted to truth and justice, depending on who you listen to. The Dampening Net is the only non-lethal weapon they produce. They live ankle-deep in water and are covered in pustules which drip acidic pus.

Stats: Novatrin gas is one of the six cargos it is forbidden for any Leviathan to carry (one other is Clorium; **104**, 'I, E.T.').

Seen it all Before: In every sci-fi and cop show ever made, but they all stem from Akira Kurosawa's classic film *Rashomon*.

Logic Leaps: Stark found Moya with ease in **216**, 'The Locket'; now Talyn does the same. Given the size of the Uncharted Territories, and the fact that they're, um, uncharted, doesn't it seem a little odd that Moya's friends keep dropping by for a cup of tea and a chat while Scorpius is blundering around entirely failing to find them? We end with D'Argo looking at the picture of Jothee that Stark gave him in **216**, 'The Locket'. Given that he knows his son is about to be sold at auction, what on earth are they all doing messing around with Crais? Shouldn't they be making full speed to the rescue?

Guest Stars: Linda Cropper was Charlie Driscoll in *Water Rats* and returned to *Farscape* in Season Three in a crucial role (in **307**, 'Thanks for Sharing'). Peter Carroll has appeared in *Waking Ned* and in the miniseries *The Rainbow Warrior Conspiracy*.

The Verdict: The *Rashomon* rip-off is a TV standard but *Farscape* manages to make it fresh by filming four entirely different versions of the same scene, each time with subtly different dialogue, camera moves and relationships. It must have been very hard work to act and shoot. Cowardly Crichton is hilarious, as is D'Argo's image of himself as the leader, with everyone flanking him and deferring to his authority. Aeryn's vision of flaky Zhaan is fun too. It's nice to see Crais and Talyn again, and the fact that Crais considers Moya's crew potential allies and friends is an interesting indication of future events. The design work is sparse but effective, and the interrogation chair is nicely unique. The only drawback is that Stark hasn't been around long enough for us to become attached to him, so the played-for grief at his death doesn't quite feel earned, and Zhaan's sudden attachment to him seems like a ploy to make us feel more for him that we otherwise would.

218
A Clockwork Nebari

1st US Transmission Date: 15 September 2000
1st UK Transmission Date: 20 November 2000
1st Australian Transmission Date: 25 December 2001
Writer: Lily Taylor
Director: Rowan Woods
Guest Cast: Lani Tupu (Capt. Bialar Crais), Wayne Pygram (Scorpius), Malcolm Kennard (Meelak), Skye Wansey (Varla), Simon Bossell (Nerri)

Moya is boarded by two Nebari – Varla and Meelak – who have been hunting Chiana and intend to return her to Nebari space. They mentally cleanse everyone on board and put a collar on Pilot to prevent him initiating

StarBurst. Crichton is immune to the cleansing because of Harvey, and Rygel because of his fast metabolism. They plot to free Chiana, who is also not cleansed because the temporary drug-induced cleansing Varla is using does not work on Nebari. All sorts of interesting things about Nebari plans and Chiana's past are revealed (see **Alien Encounters** and **Everyone's Favourite Little Tralk**). Meelak is working undercover for the Nebari resistance, which is led by Chiana's brother, Nerri, who is still alive. Crichton, Rygel and Pilot stage a fake PK attack on Moya and in the confusion attempt to take down Varla, but fail. At the last moment Meelak decides to risk blowing his resistance cover and shoots Varla to save Chi. Meelak leaves for Nebari space carrying a secret message for Nerri while the rest of Moya's crew are locked up by Crichton until the mental cleansing drugs wear off.

Buck Rogers Redux: 'The Nebari are a bunch of geeks and their damn mind cleansing doesn't work on mother Crichton's baby boy – John Crichton, astronaut, Master of the Universe!' Crichton has named his pulse pistol 'Winona'. When he pretends to be mind cleansed he adopts full-on 'Bill and Ted' surf slacker speak and uses way more pop culture references than normal. However, when he's with Pilot and does not need to pretend he's still very nutty indeed; his madness continues to evolve. He's developing quite a fatalistic streak too: 'Since when do people like us get what we want?'

Big Blue: Zhaan is cleansed and does appear at the end of the episode, locked up with the others, but she's nowhere to be seen in between. Aeryn tends Varla's wounds rather than Zhaan, who would normally do so. Was Virginia Hey on holiday perhaps, or could the scriptwriters just think of nothing interesting to do with her character?

I was a Teenage Luxan: 'All the things I've done as a warrior, all the horrible thoughts I've had all the cycles of my life, even about you, I am *so* sorry!' Rygel, Crichton, Aeryn and Chiana go down to a planet to find information about the auction of D'Argo's son, Jothee, but D'Argo remains on Moya. Why? When he is cleansed he becomes a weeping, pathetic mess, a bit like the cowardly lion from *The Wizard of Oz*.

Buckwheat the Sixteenth: 'I'm *nobody's* puppet!' Rygel's metabolism is so fast that he processes the drug long before any of the others. He sells Crichton out to Meelak to convince the Nebari that he's still cleansed. Crichton later finds him hiding in a box in the Maintenance Bay and forces him to help save the ship. He enjoys locking up Aeryn, D'Argo and Zhaan.

Everyone's Favourite Little Tralk: Crichton: 'You can kick, kiss and cry your way out of any situation. I just wish you'd stop getting into them.' Chiana is three cycles younger than Nerri. It is never explained why her life disc stopped working (**203**, 'Taking the Stone') although it seems safe to assume that Nerri disabled it to help him elude capture by the Nebari establishment. He goes to great lengths to get a message to Chiana to let her know he's still alive, but he orders Meelak not to bring Chiana to him because it would be too dangerous. Chiana wants to join Nerri more than anything in the world. She did not tell her shipmates about the Nebari infection (see **Alien Encounters**) because she was afraid they wouldn't let her stay on board.

In the Driving Seat: 'Crichton, did that work for you? I thought it worked. Definitely.' Pilot's people are not susceptible to mental cleansing, presumably because of their much-vaunted multi-tasking abilities. He manages to stage a very convincing PK attack and exhibits just a hint of satisfied self-congratulation afterwards; I think he kind of enjoyed it.

A Ship, a Living Ship!: Moya is capable of causing explosions inside herself, as demonstrated when she and Pilot fake the PK attack.

The Ballad of Chiana and D'Argo: Crichton implies that Chiana was using her sexual allure to extract information about Jothee, and that D'Argo will not be best pleased when he finds out.

Alien Encounters: When they were very young Chi and Nerri were given exit visas by the Nebari Establishment, along with hundreds, maybe thousands of others. It took them two cycles to discover why they were allowed to leave. During their routine health inspections they were infected with a sexually transmitted disease which they very effectively helped spread to other races. At a certain specified time the infection will manifest itself and many worlds will be thrown into chaos, ready for Nebari invasion. This plan has been in operation for twenty cycles.

A figure high up in the Establishment gave Nerri a cure, and he and Chi are now both clean. Nerri and Chi split up to prevent their being captured and forced to reveal the traitor's identity. Nerri is now leading an active resistance movement.

Nebari bleed blue. The males have black hair and look like brooding members of 80s Goth bands. The ultra-calm Salis (**115**, 'Durka Returns') is not as typical of Nebari as we were led to believe – Varla is far from the mellow nasty he was, she's a full-blown sadistic nut job. Full mental cleansing, as applied to Durka (**115**, 'Durka Returns'), takes a hundred cycles. Their temporary mental cleansing, which is only used on aliens, involves attaching a metal gizmo to the exposed optic nerve which releases a drug into the system (see **Bloopers**).

Hi, Harvey: Crichton gets flashes of Harvey telling him to fight the mind-cleansing drugs, and it's implied that this is why he remains immune.

Disney on Acid: Crichton refers to Varla as Deborah Harry (of Blondie fame) and later says, 'she's gonna getcha, getcha, getcha, getcha', which is a quote from the Blondie song, 'One Way or Another'. He warns Rygel not to eat too much or he'll 'Belushi out', i.e. get big and fat like John Belushi of *Saturday Night Live*.

Logic Leaps: Although Nebari standard-class Host vessels are massively be-weaponed and easily destroyed the *Zelbinion* (**115**, 'Durka Returns'), their Star-Runner transport ships are capable of being overwhelmed by PK ships. A PK patrol attacked the Star-Runner carrying Varla and Meelak and killed all the other crew members, but we don't find out why – perhaps they are considered an enemy and are attacked on sight, or perhaps PK Command has discovered that it was the Nebari who destroyed the *Zelbinion*. If so, then why is Varla concerned that the Peacekeepers do not discover the infection? She seems to imply that the Peacekeepers would be a formidable enemy and would attack if they discovered the Nebari plan. If the Nebari are as powerful as we've been led to believe why are they worried? One of their bog-standard ships took out the PK flagship without breaking a sweat, surely there's no need for all this subterfuge. These are not *necessarily* problems, but we don't know enough about the PK/Nebari relationship to explain possible inconsistencies.

Bloopers: Lots of ophthalmologist *Farscape* fans complained loudly about the treatment Crichton's eyeballs receive and claimed it just wasn't realistic. Fair enough. It was marvellously, spectacularly, stomach-churningly gross though, which justifies it in my book. The Society Against Cruelty To Crichton (http://www.scaper.com/sacc/) were up in arms about it, naturally. Why does Crichton close the door when he's talking openly to Rygel to prevent being overheard, but not when he's talking to Pilot?

Guest Stars: Malcolm Kennard used to be a regular on *E-Street*. Skye Wansey appeared in *Chopper*. Simon Bossell was in *Better than Sex*.

Backstage: The name Winona came from Ben Browder and is a reference to Winona Ryder, a comic called 'Wynona Earp', or a homage to famous country singer, Wynnona, depending upon whom you believe. The episode title is a reference to the Anthony Burgess novel *A Clockwork Orange* in which a criminal is brainwashed to try and make him a better citizen.

The Verdict: The *Farscape* universe continues to deepen and the political situation between the races gets more complex. We've already got the Peacekeepers and the Scarrans after Moya, now the Nebari emerge as major players. Lots of fun for the cast as they once more play against type: Claudia Black's zombie Aeryn is scary, Anthony Simcoe's weepy act is marvellous, and Ben Browder's surfer dude is just unhinged. It's about time we got more background on Chiana, and it makes sense, giving Gigi Edgley more to play with. Finally, what other show except *Farscape* would have an alien race attempting to take over the universe using a venereal disease?

219
Liars, Guns and Money I: A Not So Simple Plan

1st US Transmission Date: 5 January 2001
1st UK Transmission Date: 4 December 2000
1st Australian Transmission Date: 27 December 2001

Writer: Grant McAloon
Director: Andrew Prowse
Guest Cast: Paul Goddard (Stark), Wayne Pygram (Scorpius),
Claudia Karvan (Natira), Nicholas Hope (Akkor),
Matt Newton (Jothee), David Franklin (Lt Braca), Adrian Brown (Gan),
Jennifer Fisher (PK Nurse)

Stark returns with blueprints to a Shadow Depository – a bank for criminals – and a daring heist plan to raise money to buy Jothee at the slave auction. Crichton refuses to go along with the plan but D'Argo and Stark act anyway, which results in D'Argo being arrested, forcing the others to get involved in order to save him.

Zhaan poses as a pirate with a deposit to make; Chiana, Crichton, Aeryn and D'Argo are her assistants. She convinces the Depository owner, Natira, that D'Argo was testing security on her instructions and he is released. Zhaan's deposit is a Hynerian statue containing Rygel.

Once sealed in her container he emerges, takes the ID tag for the deposit to another container, and when Zhaan makes a withdrawal she gets the content of the other box instead – a whole pile of ingots belonging to Scorpius. However, all does not go according to plan: Scorpius arrives to withdraw his goods, realises a heist is in progress and seals the depository. Zhaan, Chiana, Rygel and Aeryn escape but Crichton is caught by Scorpius. Luckily he earlier smeared one of Scorpius's coolant rods with explosive paste, which causes Scorpius all sorts of problems, and Crichton is able to make his exit, leaving the bad guy to die.

Moya departs for the auction with the money, but down in the cargo bay the ingots unfold and emerge as mechanical spiders . . .

Buck Rogers Redux: 'Die, you grotesque bastard! Even if it means I die, too.' Crichton's temper is getting shorter and he's becoming more unpredictable – he gets very rough with Stark very early on in the proceedings, and pulls a gun on him just for winding him up a bit. He wants Scorpius dead. For someone who's been spoiling for a fight recently it's surprising he doesn't immediately agree to help Stark and D'Argo who is, after all, his best friend.

Big Blue: Zhaan finally gets something to do outside of the Medbay – she gets to play pirate and puts on a black catsuit, an eye patch and adopts the name Aralla.

I was a Teenage Luxan: Natira: 'As a race, Luxans can be inartful at love, inadequate at war, and intrinsically inept. But this one is intelligent.' D'Argo condemns his crewmates as cowards when they will not help in Stark's plan to rob the Depository, and willingly sacrifices himself to capture and torture so as to force them to become involved. He takes quite some time to recover from Natira's attentions. He is slow to forgive Crichton for not helping from the off, but Chiana urges him to.

Buckwheat the Sixteenth: 'Ten per cent of this plan is lunacy; fifty per cent of these riches is not enough; one hundred per cent of dead is dead!' Rygel is quite intrepid, allowing himself to be sedated, smuggled into a sealed container inside a statue, and then clambering from one deposit container to another. He loses his robes while in the container and his orange undies are revealed – he's obviously reconsidered the awful Y-fronts he was wearing in **106**, 'Thank God it's Friday, Again'.

Everyone's Favourite Little Tralk: Chiana is immediately ready to endorse the heist scheme – any excuse for some larceny.

The Man in the Iron Mask: Stark has managed to reincorporate himself following his dispersal by the Plokavians (**217**, 'The Ugly Truth') because 'this body is only a molecular creation, which enables me to live in your realm. It's merely a vessel for my true, incorporeal self.' Immediately after his reintegration he located the plans for the Shadow Depository by helping its designer die; when asked if he killed him he replies 'not exactly'. He then stole a ship and sent word to Zhaan – he can transmit messages to his mask over huge distances using mental powers – to come and collect him. Being dispersed appears to have had an effect on his sanity: he is now almost as manic as he was in **120**, 'The Hidden Memory', not at all the more composed person he appeared when he stopped faking madness in **121**, 'Bone to be Wild', or when he returned in **216**, 'The Locket' and **217**, 'The Ugly Truth'. He even returns to his 'my side, your side' rant, which he delivered in his cell in the Gammak base. He is a capable hacker, gets into the Depository systems from orbit and, for a time, manipulates the systems well, but when it starts to go wrong he panics and begins smashing his equipment, forcing D'Argo to stun him and take over. When they escape D'Argo apologises for doubting him and says, 'you've proven yourself to be a worthy friend, and one not to be distrusted again'.

Nosferatu in Rubber: Scorpius is entirely dependent on the coolant rods established in **212**, 'Look at the Princess III: The Maltese Crichton', but seems unable to insert them himself, although heaven knows why. He apparently succumbs to heat exhaustion and dies in the Depository reaching for a coolant rod, but none of us believe he's dead, do we? Natira owes him greatly for unspecified reasons, and she appears to be his girlfriend, of a kind. He had some goods stored at the Depository but Natira sold them when she heard of his Gammak base's destruction and assumed he was dead. He intimidates her into reimbursing triple the value of the goods. He is strong enough to single-handedly open a security door that easily crushed a guard. Since the ingots that awake on Moya were intended for Scorpius, it appears Natira was attempting to double-cross him.

The Ballad of Aeryn and John: While under the influence of the chip, Crichton is afraid he's losing it for good and tries to tell Aeryn how he feels about her in case he goes mad or they don't escape the Depository. Back on Moya, he tells her again: 'I meant what I said . . . didn't say.' And she strokes his hair and tells her she knows.

Alien Encounters: We have no idea what race Natira is, but the Creature Shop design is stunning.

Hi, Harvey: 'A Neuro-Bio Tracer . . . A tiny chip, a tiny seed that's been growing in your brain and touching every aspect of your personality, your memory . . . and whispering advice.' The voices in Crichton's head get more insistent when Scorpius is around, and he hallucinates Scorpius at one point. He seems to be on the verge of a total breakdown, twitching and whispering to himself at the most inopportune moments. When he meets Scorpius in the flesh he finally finds out about the neuro chip (described as a Neuro-Bio-Tracer), which at least means he now knows he hasn't been imagining things. He is again restrained from killing Scorpius, or allowing him to die, but this time, unlike in **212**, 'Look at the Princess III: The Maltese Crichton', he is able to override the chip, although it's a hell of a struggle. He beats the chip by singing 'The Star Spangled Banner'.

Disney on Acid: Crichton tries to convince the Shadow Depository to store the eleven secret ingredients to KFC. He sees himself and Aeryn as Bonnie and Clyde, then recants when he remembers how that story ended – in a hail of bullets. When using the Depository video cameras, Crichton tells Aeryn he's looking for *Baywatch*.

Get Frelled: Looks like Scorpius and Natira got horizontal, or whatever it is they do. Scorpius tries to force Crichton to put in his coolant rod: 'Insert the rod, John!' but Crichton replies 'You're really not my type.'

Stats: We get to see Moya's Docking Web being deployed for the first time. Borinium is a valuable metal pressed into ingots and used as currency. Zhaan creates Jelifan paste for Crichton to smear on Scorpius's cooling rods – it reacts explosively to heat. She develops a mixture called Melar gas, which suspends body activity long enough for a living person to register as inanimate when scanned. They use this to smuggle Rygel into the Depository. A simple pill immunises someone from the gas's effects.

Logic Leaps: Stark insists that the computer connection into the Depository's systems could only be made once, at the instant they changed their codes. But later, when he freaks out and severs the connection, D'Argo is able to break into the systems again almost immediately. How does Rygel know which container belongs to Scorpius?

WHAT did you just say?: Crichton is trying to explain what Aeryn should do if Scorpius gets him: 'I know, shoot you,' she says. 'No, no no no, shoot *him!*'

Guest Stars: Claudia Karvan is thus far best known for her role in the excellent Aussie drama *The Secret Life of Us*, but she also appears as Sola Naberrie in *Star Wars: Episode II – Attack of the Clones*. Nicholas Hope returned to *Farscape* as Kreetago in **303**, 'Self Inflicted Wounds I: Could'a, Would'a, Should'a' and **304**, 'Self Inflicted Wounds II: Wait for the Wheel'. Matt Newton, who plays Jothee, used to study acting under Anthony Simcoe and stars alongside Claudia Black in *Queen of the Damned*.

Backstage: In an online chat, Wayne Pygram stated that the final four episodes of Season Two were filmed simultaneously. This is the first time episodes were filmed in blocks since the very beginning of Season One.

The Verdict: The biggest sets, the best CGI and the funkiest creature yet seen on the show give this a cinematic feel. Ben Browder's performance in his final scene with Scorpius is staggering. The return of Stark is welcome but a little strange as he now appears to be an almost entirely different character. Rygel climbs up a ladder, a deceptively simple effect but it must have been hell to do with a puppet – bravo. Even Zhaan finally gets a proactive role for the first time in ages. All this and the return of Scorpius too. Excellent.

220
Liars, Guns and Money II: With Friends Like These . . .

1st US Transmission Date: 12 January 2001
1st UK Transmission Date: 11 December 2000
1st Australian Transmission Date: 28 December 2001

Writer: Naren Shankar
Director: Catherine Millar
Guest Cast: Paul Goddard (Stark), Wayne Pygram (Scorpius),
Claudia Karvan (Natira), Nicholas Hope (Akkor),
Matt Newton (Jothee), David Franklin (Lt Braca),
John Adam (Bekesh), Jeremy Sims (Rorf), Jo Kerrigan (Rorg), David
Wheeler (Durka), Lionel Haft (Zelkin), David Bowers (Kurz), Thomas
Holesgrove (Teurac)

Scorpius traced Stark's computer hack during the heist in **219**, 'Liars, Guns and Money I: A Not So Simple Plan' and extracted information from his terminal revealing the location of Jothee. When Moya arrives to buy the slaves they discover that Scorpius has bought them all and will kill Jothee unless Crichton gives himself up. Jothee and the slaves are being transported to Scorpius at the Shadow Depository, which gives them three days to devise a plan. Crichton decides they need Vorcarian Bloodtrackers (**111**,

'Till the Blood Runs Clear') to locate Jothee, a Sheyang (**107**, 'PK Tech Girl') to help them get through any doors, a Tavloid . . . sorry, a Tav*lek* (**102**, 'Throne For a Loss') for close quarters combat, and the Flax (**112**, 'The Flax') to help in their escape. Crichton recruits Bekesh (from **102**, 'Throne For a Loss') who has turned to religion but is persuaded to help with the offer of money; D'Argo recruits Rorf and Rorg (from **111**, 'Till the Blood Runs Clear') by killing a PK patrol that is hunting them; Aeryn recruits a wounded Sheyang Captain who turns out to be Teurac from **107**, 'PK Tech Girl'; and Rygel goes to find the Zenetan Pirates and ask for the Flax. Rygel discovers that the Pirates are now being led by Durka (**115**, 'Durka Returns'), whose ship got caught in the Flax. Rygel kills Durka and cuts off his head, which impresses the Pirates into joining up as well. This motley crew is assembled on Moya, but the ingots they were going to be paid with have turned into a horde of Karack Metalites spiders and eaten a portion of Moya.

In order to save the ship Zhaan and Pilot have had to start a huge fire to kill the creatures, severely wounding Moya and destroying all their money. Knowing that the recruits will now leave because there's no money with which to pay them, Crichton flies to the Depository and surrenders. Jothee is released and flies to Moya, where he is reunited with D'Argo. But Crichton is in Scorpius's hands at last . . .

Buck Rogers Redux: 'You want the wormhole technology, I want your implant out of my head. . . . the rift between us is not so great. You do what you got to do. You win.' Crichton's the one who comes up with the *Seven Samurai*-style plan, intending to go into the Depository hard and fight their way to Jothee. He doesn't believe that Bekesh has changed, but waits the guy out until his need for the stimulant in his Gauntlet forces him to accede. The second it looks as if his plan has failed he doesn't hesitate in doing the honourable thing and surrendering to save Jothee.

Big Blue: Zhaan takes as much of Pilot and Moya's pain as she can when they burn out the infestation, and it leaves her very fragile indeed.

I was a Teenage Luxan: D'Argo not only finds some Bloodtrackers, he actually finds the very two who tortured him in **111**, 'Till the Blood Runs Clear', although we never find out how. For one moment he considers dragging Crichton to Scorpius in exchange for Jothee, but later he is ashamed of the impulse. He does, however, blame their situation on Crichton's initial reluctance to help with the heist. He sees a vision of his son that is so accurate it even predicts what clothes he would be wearing when they met (oops, bad continuity there, methinks). He is overwhelmed at being reunited with Jothee: 'Everything you've been through, so many cycles. I'm sorry ... I *never* stopped thinking about you, trying to find you, I almost lost hope ... My son. My son!' He last saw Jothee on the night of Lo'laan's murder.

Buckwheat the Sixteenth: Rygel confronts Durka, his great nemesis, and instantly kills him and chops off his head. After the shock of seeing the bad guy return the audience was all set for a big showdown, but it was short, anticlimactic, and downright hilarious.

Everyone's Favourite Little Tralk: Rygel: 'Every time I think that there's more to you than a pair of pushed-up lumers in a corset, you disappoint me.' Chiana tells Stark that if his actions lead to Jothee's death she will kill him – already acting the protective stepmother. She and Rygel both decide to steal some of the ingots before anyone else does, but have no joy.

The Man in the Iron Mask: Stark is a Stykera, a special form of Banik attuned to energy and death, which Scorpius found useful. Even in Moya, across huge distances, he senses when the Banik slaves that were part of Jothee's lot at the slave auction are slaughtered by Scorpius. He helps Zhaan take some of Moya's pain during the burning. When Scorpius demands to talk to Crichton, Stark steps forward and tells Scorpius to kill Jothee because he will never surrender. Zhaan and Chi are shocked but Stark claims it was a ploy to distract Scorpius and prevent him realising Moya was weakened by the Metalites.

Nosferatu in Rubber: Scorpius and Natira go way back – she took him in when he was a young hot-head, he saved her from the Peacekeepers. He is not surprised that Natira tried to destroy his Marauder with Metalites, and she claims he wouldn't have respected her if she hadn't tried to kill him. His cooling system has greatly advanced since he had the initial surgery. He has a burning hatred of Scarrans. Anything else is not worthy of his hatred.

A Ship, a Living Ship!: Moya is afraid of fire and burns one ninth of herself so badly that she cannot StarBurst for some time and may never fully heal.

Alien Encounters: Natira's head is encased in prehensile tentacles. Sheyangs bleed green. The Voracarian female, Rorg, is pregnant. Zelkin now rules the Zenetan Pirates; Kcrackic was presumably killed by Durka. There are, according to Braca, more inter-species hybrids every year, despite PK Command's best efforts to keep the race pure.

Hi, Harvey: Crichton is able to initiate a conversation with the Neural Clone in his head, which shouldn't be possible. He now believes that the link goes both ways: Scorpius may be inside his head, but Crichton is able to understand how Scorpius thinks.

Disney on Acid: Crichton thinks *The Texas Chainsaw Massacre* is a classic.

Get Frelled: Scorpius and Natira have a bizarre sex life, and when Scorpius climaxes he pops his coolant rods, not his cookies.

Seen it all Before: In *The Seven Samurai*, *The Magnificent Seven*, *The Dirty Dozen* etc.

Logic Leaps: Why is Scorpius still at the Shadow Depository? Surely he would have left for his Command Carrier.

It's hard not to conclude that the only reason he's still there is that the spectacular set needed to be used for three episodes to justify the cost. The Flax and the Tavlek planet are within a day's pod travel of Moya and the Shadow Depository. That's a bit of a stretch isn't it? Plus, they find both places easily, so Moya and Pilot must have been compiling navigational charts during their travels. So the territory's not so uncharted any more . . .

WHAT did you just say?: Lumers = breasts.

The Verdict: Continuity runs rampant as we get loads of characters from Season One. They, and a liberal dose of flashbacks, tie this episode strongly to the show's history so far and provide a familiar riff on the classic 'misfits go to war' story. The perfunctory despatching of Durka is an excellent comic moment, Natira continues to impress, and we have a great cliffhanger. Definitely the middle episode of a trilogy, so little is resolved, but a lot is set up. Roll on part three.

221
Liars, Guns and Money III: Plan B

1st US Transmission Date: 19 January 2001
1st UK Transmission Date: 18 December 2000
1st Australian Transmission Date: 29 December 2001

Writer: Justin Monjo
Director: Tony Tilse
Guest Cast: Paul Goddard (Stark), Wayne Pygram (Scorpius),
Lani Tupu (Capt. Bialar Crais), Claudia Karvan (Natira),
Nicholas Hope (Akkor), Matt Newton (Jothee),
John Adam (Bekesh), Jeremy Sims (Rorf), Lionel Haft (Zelkin),
David Bowers (Kurz), Thomas Holesgrove (Teurac)

Aeryn and Stark persuade the mercenaries to help rescue Crichton by reminding them that the Depository is full of currency they can steal. Talyn responds to a distress call from Moya and performs a transfusion to heal her burn damage. Aeryn asks Crais to help in the rescue but he refuses to use Talyn for violent ends.

Rorf goes to the Depository first and locates Crichton but is captured and tortured by Scorpius and Natira, who eats one of his eyes. He reveals the rescue plan in full. Aeryn, D'Argo and Bekesh storm the Depository main entrance while Zhaan, Stark and Teurac go to blow up the generator. However Teurac is unable to breathe fire and destroy the generator, so they are captured by Scorpius. Teurac shoots himself and explodes, destroying the generator, killing the lights and allowing Zhaan and Stark to escape. Aeryn, D'Argo and Bekesh manage to kill the PK troops defending the main entrance using night goggles so they can see in the sudden darkness. Meanwhile, Crichton has persuaded Natira that Scorpius is going to kill her, so she releases him and they, together with Rorf, try to escape. They meet up with Aeryn, D'Argo and Bekesh, but are pinned down in a corridor by PK troops. Rorf sacrifices himself to save Crichton; Natira runs off on her own. Rygel and Jothee take a Transport Pod to collect Zhaan and Stark but Zelkin betrays them to Scorpius and deploys the Flax, trapping the pod and Moya. Talyn responds to Moya's call for help and destroys the Zenetan ship, while Chiana kills Zelkin. Zhaan and Stark are collected by the pod. Aeryn tells Crais to use Talyn to demolish the Depository. She, Bekesh, Crichton and D'Argo lock themselves in one of the Depository containers and survive the destruction. They leave on Moya, loaded with wealth.

Buck Rogers Redux: The chip now controls Crichton so much that he wants to go to Scorpius. He believes the removal of the chip will kill him and since he doesn't want to live as a madman he figures surrendering and getting it over with is the only thing to do. However, Natira tells him that it can be removed safely – there is no need for him to die. In his mind he still wears his IASA uniform. After being rescued forcibly by Aeryn he is a shattered, gibbering wreck, unable to silence the voice of Scorpius in his mind. He tries to get the white king on his chessboard to stand up but can't; next to the board is his gun, Winona, but it seems likely the chip prevents him from killing himself. Eventually he begs D'Argo to kill him.

You Can Be More: Aeryn plays a dangerous game, convincing the mercenaries to follow through on the plan using risky reverse psychology. She offers Crais anything at all if he will help them save Crichton, and when he asks if she is offering herself to him she remains deadpan. If Crichton is insane and can't be rescued she resolves to kill him herself to put him out of his misery.

I was a Teenage Luxan: D'Argo's Qualta Blade runs out of power during the battle and he uses it as a sword instead. He is at first surprised when Jothee doesn't want to help rescue Crichton, although he tries to hide his disappointment. When the boy changes his mind he is proud but keeps him out of harm's way on the Transport Pod with Rygel. The eventual plan of attack is D'Argo's – a two-pronged attack with himself leading a frontal assault – typically Luxan. Now that he is reunited with Jothee his quest is over, but there are some unresolved issues to deal with. Jothee has had to do some terrible things to stay alive and his first instinct is to look after himself, whatever the cost. He tries to change that, and accepts that his father's fights are his fights too. He tells D'Argo: 'In a way, you've done everything that ever happened to me . . . [but] I'm not angry with you.'

Buckwheat the Sixteenth: 'Mine, mine, mine! Can I have this? Can this be mine? We can all have anything we want now, right? Any food, any female, anything! Right?' Rygel's quite a dab hand at flying a Transport Pod. He keeps Durka's head with him, on a spike, because he likes the fact that his one-time torturer can't answer back. He is ecstatic at finally being rich again.

The Man in the Iron Mask: Stark's madness is again to the fore, but it's his berserker bravery that convinces Rorf to go ahead with the rescue. His initial plan is so complicated that none of the mercenaries can follow it.

The Insane Military Commander: Crais has changed, and he gives Aeryn quite a lecture: 'Is this violence more acceptable because it's for you? There's always a reason for violence, Aeryn. Thousands of people die for the most virtuous causes.' What a turnaround, from the murderous nutter of Season One to a wannabe Buddhist who insists there should be no violence at any time unless in defence. He is amused at the thought of Aeryn offering herself to him in return for his help but he must have refused, because it is only Moya's distress at being caught in the Flax that brings Talyn back.

Nosferatu in Rubber: 'You overestimate me, John. I have no desire to dominate the universe.' Scorpius doesn't need to kill Crichton to remove the chip, but he intends to kill him afterwards anyway. His Command Carrier is in battle, we don't know who with, and that is why Peacekeepers are not at the Depository in massive force. He does not want the wormhole information in order to further his own ambition, he wants it so he can sway the balance of power, presumably with the Scarrans. Given that he is still in the Depository when it is demolished by Talyn he must be dead . . . right?

A Ship, a Living Ship!: Moya may never heal from the burning, but Talyn's transfusion will help. Eight tiers were destroyed by the fire, and her immune system suffered serious damage. She performs a low-level flypast of the Depository as a diversion, shattering all its windows, allowing the rescue mission to begin. She has the ability to flood the Maintenance Bay with poison gas.

Big Baby: Talyn decided to return and fight. He acted alone and Crais did not command it: 'As much as any of us would want, he has the instincts of a warrior and does exactly as he pleases.'

Alien Encounters: Natira has a taste for eyeballs – lovely. Bloodtracker males are not as good at hunting by scent as females. Sheyangs can be injected with Taakar serum to stimulate the production of fireballs. If you shoot a Sheyang he explodes (although the one in **107**, 'PK Tech Girl' didn't).

Hi, Harvey: Harvey has reached the wormhole information in Crichton's brain and tells Scorpius that the chip is ready to be removed. He also tells Natira that Scorpius plans to kill her – the first time he acts contrary to his real-world self's best interests. Harvey believes that Crichton's not conscious of the wormhole knowledge.

Disney on Acid: Crichton makes a couple of references to the Mel Brooks film, *Young Frankenstein*, calling Scorpius Fronkensteen, and Natira Frau Blücher.

Get Frelled: Natira tickles Crichton's prostate. Yowch!

Seen it all Before: In every heist movie ever, plus there are nods to *Butch Cassidy and the Sundance Kid*, *The Magnificent Seven*, and more.

The Verdict: This is a logistical triumph. The superb CGI; the stunning battle scenes; the sequence where D'Argo, Bekesh and Aeryn take on insurmountable odds seen through Aeryn's malfunctioning eyepiece; Ben Browder's performance as a man losing his mind and desperate to remain sane; and above all, lots of groovy ray guns. Has sci-fi TV ever felt this epic? There are a few clichés scattered here and there – of *course* some of the mercenaries were going to die heroically, and someone would turn out to be a traitor, but we'd have almost felt cheated had the script not delivered these things.

Dramatic and exciting, as well as managing to move the characters of Crais, Aeryn, D'Argo, Scorpius and Crichton along considerably, this juggles a lot of elements and for the most part pulls it off with aplomb (although the inability of PK troops to hit a sitting duck at point-blank range is unintentionally hilarious).

222
Die Me, Dichotomy

1st US Transmission Date: 26 January 2001
1st UK Transmission Date: 19 December 2000
1st Australian Transmission Date: 30 December 2001

Writer: David Kemper
Director: Rowan Woods
Guest Cast: Wayne Pygram (Scorpius), Lani Tupu (Capt. Bialar Crais),
David Franklin (Lt Braca), Thomas Holesgrove (Diagnosian Tocot),
Hugh Keays-Burne (Grunchlk)

'The goddess ... [holds] a special place for those who
travel this life as a journey. Aeryn Sun will surely harvest
favour ... she sought a balance of lasting inner peace.'

A Diagnosian doctor, Tocot, and his assistant,
Grunchlk, agree to help heal Moya and try to remove
Crichton's neuro chip. Their surgical facility contains a
cavern filled with cryogenic chambers housing accident
victims frozen at the moment of death and available for
use as donors. At first Tocot believes Crichton's chip is
impossible to remove, but he finds a compatible donor
whose brain can be used to repair any damage inflicted
during the chip's removal.

Harvey takes complete control of Crichton. He knocks
Aeryn unconscious, signals Scorpius to come and get him,
and takes off in the WDP. Aeryn gives pursuit in her
Prowler and, under the influence of Harvey, Crichton
forces her to eject over a frozen lake. She is trapped in her
chair and sinks, drowning. Aeryn's body is frozen in one
of the cryo chambers.

Tocot removes the chip, which destroys Crichton's
power of speech. Before he can restore Crichton, Scorpius
and Braca arrive. Scorpius kills the Diagnosian, takes the
chip, and walks away leaving Crichton lying on the
operating table, unable to speak, with a huge hole in his
brain, and the only person who can save him lying dead on
the floor ...

Buck Rogers Redux: Zhaan: 'He is no more. His body now shelters some horrific evil. Crichton's gone!' Crichton loses the battle with Harvey and sees himself as Scorpius, adopting his speech, mannerisms and behaviour. Real Crichton does not want anyone to die in order for him to be saved, not even any of the Diagnosian's specimens, but he agrees when he discovers they would die anyway. The neuro chip has created black tendrils encircling his brain which Tocot has to remove before taking out the chip. These tendrils appear to have burrowed into and absorbed some of Crichton's memories – removing them means losing some of his past. He loses his memory of US politics from Nixon to Clinton, tries to keep his memories of his dogs, but we don't know if he keeps or loses his memories of Aeryn. He takes a lock of hair from Aeryn's body.

You Can Be More: Aeryn is willing to shoot Crichton down to prevent him being claimed by Scorpius. She tells Crichton that he was the one who brought hope to Moya and her crew. The harness on her ejector seat is stuck, so when she lands on the ice she goes down with her Prowler seat . . . her last word is 'Crichton'. Her Prowler crashes and blows up.

Big Blue: Zhaan is horrified that the Diagnosian keeps his specimens alive in a moment before death, not allowing them to die and thus interfering with the natural course of events. She plans to remain on Moya even if the others leave. She turns on Rygel for discussing money when things look so bleak, but apologises for misjudging him when he points out that they're only taking a few things each, and the rest is going to pay for Tocot's services.

I was a Teenage Luxan: D'Argo's temper is very short, especially with Chiana, but that's just his nervousness about proposing and his confusion about Jothee. When he finds out that Jothee cut off his own tenkas, he is horrified that his son hates his Luxan heritage so much, but Jothee assures him it doesn't hurt any more, implying he's got over it. D'Argo buries Aeryn with his ancestral Qualta

Blade. He plans to use his share of the money from the Depository to buy a farm and grow Prowsa fruit. Jothee can sting with his tongue the same as D'Argo. When Aeryn is pursuing Crichton in her Prowler D'Argo tells her not to hesitate to shoot, because in her place he would.

Buckwheat the Sixteenth: Rygel gives Grunchlk a number of jewels to procure him a ship of his own so he can leave. The ship is on its way, so will he go? Rygel buries Aeryn with his seal of office, which he reclaimed in **107**, 'PK Tech Girl'.

The Man in the Iron Mask: Stark seems to have calmed down from the manic excesses of the previous three episodes. He tries to negotiate with Grunchlk, but fails miserably. He tells Zhaan: 'If you are in agreement, Pa'u Zotoh Zhaan, it would be an honour and a pleasure to share the future with you.'

In the Driving Seat: The anaesthetic that Tocot gives Moya leaves Pilot high as a kite.

The Insane Military Commander: Crais is now one of the gang. He comes down to visit Crichton in the surgery as a gesture of support, and prevents Talyn shooting the WDP down when Harvey/Crichton is flying it. Aeryn appears to trust him completely. He tells Aeryn: 'Unlike your institutional upbringing, my parents were compassionate, moral, emotional. I value those traits. They're beginning to emerge in you.' Crais values compassion, emotion and morality? He really *has* changed!

Nosferatu in Rubber: 'You've cost me much, and I do not suffer disappointment well. I condemn you, John Crichton, to live, so that your thirst for unfulfilled revenge will consume you. Goodbye.' Scorpius now has the neuro chip containing the wormhole information – his interest in Crichton is at an end. He hums the Star Spangled Banner when walking to the surgery. Tocot installed his coolant rod system.

A Ship, a Living Ship!: The Diagnosian helps heal Moya with an anaesthetic and a gel. She will not be able to StarBurst for a while.

Big Baby: Crais: 'This emotional ship needs guidance. Talyn has chosen you, and I agree with his choice. There is much that you can learn that will surprise you.' It is Talyn and Crais who locate the Diagnosian to help Moya. They want Aeryn to join them but agree it must be her choice and they cannot coerce or blackmail her into it. Crais has a chip containing information he believes would have made Aeryn very happy. When talking to her Crais almost touches Aeryn's arm – his body language hints that he continues to find her attractive. He is distraught at her death.

The Ballad of Aeryn and John: Harvey/Crichton tells Aeryn he loves her and she responds that she loves him too and moves to kiss him, finally breaking down the barriers that have kept her distant all this time. Unfortunately, because it's Harvey she's talking to, she gets knocked out and the real Crichton doesn't remember what happened. When she's plummeting towards the lake she tells Crichton she meant what she said. When she's in her coffin the real Crichton finally tells her he loves her, but it's way too late.

The Ballad of Chiana and D'Argo: D'Argo has been using the DRDs to rehearse a proposal of marriage to Chiana. When a spaced-out Pilot shows her the recording and gives the secret away she looks less than thrilled at the prospect.

Chiana shares Jothee's desire to live loud and fast, unlike D'Argo's longing for the quiet life. She and Jothee nearly kiss but are interrupted.

Alien Encounters: The Diagnosian detects infection using its sense of smell. Its olfactory system is so sensitive that the merest whiff of untreated air in both its mouth and nose at the same time would kill it instantly. Scorpius removes Tocot's protective mask and breathes on him, causing Tocot to collapse, apparently dead. There are millions of bodies in the Diagnosian's cold-storage facility, including five thousand different species. One species, the Interions, of which he has three specimens, are sufficiently similar to humans to be compatible (this implies that there are either no Sebaceans in their storage room, or that they are less genetically similar than we have so far been led to believe). Interions may even be a branch of the same genetic stock, which implies that Earth is in the area.

Guest Stars: You can see Hugh Keays-Burne in TV versions of *Journey to the Centre of the Earth* and *Moby Dick*.

Backstage: Claudia Black had mixed feelings about the end of Season Two. On finding out that Aeryn was going to die and then return, she said, 'I remember feeling this over-whelming, incredible sensation of relief because I knew then I'd get some rest ... I was happy either way. I was happy to leave and I was happy to stay.' To *SFX* she confided that David Kemper had told her that Aeryn's death was a gift for all Black's hard work during the season. 'He gave the nod ... and then they dumped me in a tank full of water, chained to a weighted seat. I now get a little traumatised when people say they have a present for me.'

The Verdict: Wow. Aeryn dead, Crichton speechless, everyone planning to leave Moya, Scorpius triumphant ... top that. An object lesson in how a cliffhanger should be done.

*'If I make it back will they follow? . . . Earth is
unprepared . . . for the nightmares I've seen . . .
Should I stay? But then you'll never know the
wonders I have seen.'*

Season Three

Regular Cast
Ben Browder (Commander John Crichton)
Claudia Black (Aeryn Sun)
Virginia Hey (Pa'u Zotoh Zhaan)
Anthony Simcoe (Ka D'Argo)
Gigi Edgley (Chiana)
Lani Tupu (Capt. Bialar Crais and voice of Pilot)
Wayne Pygram (Scorpius)
Jonathan Hardy (Voice of Dominar Rygel XVI)
Tim Mieville (Head puppeteer for Rygel)

301
Season of Death

1st US Transmission Date: 16 March 2001
1st UK Transmission Date: 27 August 2001

Writer: Richard Manning
Director: Ian Watson
Guest Cast: Matt Newton (Jothee), David Franklin (Lt Braca), Thomas
Holesgrove (Diagnosian Tocot/Plonek),
Aaron Catalan (Officer Kobrin)

Tocot survives, with help from Rygel and Zhaan. Zhaan
performs Unity with Crichton and discovers that Harvey
is still present and that Crichton wants to die. She tries to
kill him but Stark stops her and D'Argo banishes Stark
and Zhaan from the operating room.

Scorpius and Braca, who had paid Grunchlk to alert
them if Crichton arrived, and who flew in undetected while

Crichton and Aeryn were dogfighting, are trapped in the medical complex due to the Command Carrier being delayed in battle. With no diversion available to cover their escape, Grunchlk hides them in a safe room. Scorpius takes control of Grunchlk's body and mind and uses him to convince the others that Scorpius has left.

Tocot restores Crichton's speech using an Interion donor. One of the cryo-storage pods activates, waking a Scarran – they discovered this was where Scorpius had his cooling system fitted and the Scarran is a spy that was sent to await his return. The spy kills Tocot. Grunchlk froze the Scarran intending to turn him over to Scorpius. However, when Scorpius arrived Grunchlk set the pod to auto-activate in three arns just in case Scorpius refused to honour his deal. Scorpius, again controlling Grunchlk, tells the Scarran that Scorpius is not here, but Crichton, Scorpius's prey, is. The Scarran freezes Grunchlk and goes to get Crichton. Crichton and D'Argo run outside into the snow and the Scarran pursues them . . .

Zhaan and Stark have found Aeryn's cryo-pod and discover that, although they had been told she was dead, her body is being kept alive so that Grunchlk can use her as a donor. Zhaan uses some of Stark's energy and performs Unity with Aeryn's buried soul, transferring spiritual energy which revives her. Aeryn uses the Qualta Blade she was buried with to help Crichton and D'Argo kill the Scarran. Scorpius sends his Marauder pilot up to the newly arrived Command Carrier, knowing Talyn will shoot it down. He talks to Crais on the intercom during the pursuit so that when the Marauder is destroyed everyone believes Scorpius was on board and is now dead. Moya and Talyn leave, and Scorpius takes the neuro chip and heads for a new Gammak base so he can begin developing wormhole technology.

And back on Moya Chiana and Jothee get to know each other more intimately.

Buck Rogers Redux: 'Can I get a "Hell yeah"?' Crichton's initially beaten and wants to die rather than live with

Harvey and without Aeryn. He doesn't want any donors to be used to restore him, but D'Argo insists. Crichton in turn demands that the two remaining Interions be taken up to Moya in their cryo-storage pods in the hope that one day they can be revived.

You Can Be More: 'I shouldn't be here.' During Unity, Aeryn realises that her revival will kill Zhaan and she refuses to allow it. However, she can't stop it, and is revived anyway.

Big Blue: Zhaan is willing to kill Crichton to end his pain. She knows Stark is likely to prevent her from saving Aeryn so she knocks him out and uses energy from his mask to help her. She gives Aeryn so much spiritual energy that it ensures Zhaan's eventual death. She loves Aeryn, but she did it more importantly, because Crichton does.

I was a Teenage Luxan: 'Do *not* make me tongue you!' D'Argo takes control, threatens to tongue Crichton in order to force him to accept the donor tissue, and takes a Scarran on in single combat, losing badly. He recharged his Qualta Blade before burying it with Aeryn.

Buckwheat the Sixteenth: Rygel performs CPR on Tocot, but is glad when he's told Grunchlk is dead because he paid for a ship that Grunchlk never delivered.

The Man in the Iron Mask: Stark can hear the anguished souls of the frozen donors crying out to be released to death. He even goes so far as to kill one in order to free it. He cannot sense anything from Aeryn, however, which indicates how deeply buried her spirit is when she's frozen.

The Insane Military Commander: Crais hangs around intending to give Aeryn a burial in space. He shoots down the Marauder, believes he has killed Scorpius, and is glad to have avenged Aeryn's death.

Nosferatu in Rubber: Scorpius eats the remaining brain tissue off Crichton's neuro chip, and just when you think that's the grossest thing you've ever see he goes and makes Grunchlk bite his own finger off. Yeuch! His Command Carrier has again been in battle; it won but it's not clear who it was fighting. He has a new Gammak base ready and waiting.

Hi, Harvey: 'Death is the only sensible course, John.' The chip is gone but Harvey remains. He tries to drive Crichton to suicide in order to free himself but Crichton, at Stark's urging, beats him into submission. Crichton can now recall the role played by Harvey in **215**, 'Won't Get Fooled Again'. Harvey is now just 'an impotent wraith'.

The Ballad of Aeryn and John: When Crichton first sees the revived Aeryn he's greatly distressed, thinking it a cruel trick of the mind. But when he realises she's real he holds on to her for dear life. On Moya he tells her he loves her, really this time, and she repeats that she loves him too. A proper kiss at last, and then Aeryn drops a bombshell – she says they shouldn't act on it because, when soldiers have emotional attachments, it distorts their thinking in battle. 'I will not be the cause of any more deaths, because my judgment was faulty. I will not permit anyone else to sacrifice their life for mine.'

The Ballad of Chiana and D'Argo: So Chiana is having sex with D'Argo's son Jothee, even though she just found out D'Argo wants to marry her. What *are* they thinking? Nonetheless, it's true that Chi has more in common with Jothee – they seem the same age and they're both survivors who like to live in the fast lane.

Alien Encounters: Luxans hate the cold and prolonged exposure takes away their sense of smell. Scarran skin is tough enough to break a knife. However, it can be penetrated by repeated Qualta Blade blasts. Cold inhibits Scarrans' ability to project heat energy. The Scarrans are after Scorpius, and also want to find Crichton to discover why Scorpius is so interested in him.

Get Frelled: Jothee and Chiana have sex in the kitchen, which has to be the most ill-advised coupling in TV history. Jothee is surely right when he says D'Argo will kill them if he finds out.

Logic Leaps: In **222**, 'Die Me, Dichotomy' it was stated that Tocot would die if anyone even sneezed near him, so when Scorpius breathed full in his face he should have died instantly. But with him dead Crichton couldn't be restored, so he miraculously survives and there's no explanation given.

The Verdict: A new opening sequence heralding a change of direction, Lani Tupu as Crais and Wayne Pygram as Scorpius in the title sequence, and a new theme tune, mark a new year. The episode title, 'Season of Death', is a herald of what we can expect from it. As with all two-parters the conclusion is a slight disappointment after the cliffhanger and it does cop out: Aeryn was only *nearly* dead, implying she was dragged out of the water reasonably quickly; Tocot wasn't dead at all. Aeryn's resurrection could have been corny and annoying, no matter how much we all wanted her back, but that's avoided somewhat by ensuring that Zhaan will likely die as a result. Some lovely direction in the possession scene between Grunchlk and Scorpius, a nice twist in leaving Harvey alive, and the promise of domestic strife on Moya, all combine to offset the unavoidable second-part slump, and this is a confident, stylish opener.

302
Suns and Lovers

1st US Transmission Date: 23 March 2001
1st UK Transmission Date: 3 September 2001

Writer: Justin Monjo
Director: Andrew Prowse
Guest Cast: Matt Newton (Jothee), Leanna Walsmann (Borlik),
Thomas Holesgrove (Moordil), Jessica Fallico (Alien Girl),
David Lucas (Cryoman)

Moya docks at a trading station near the twin suns of Qell. The station is severely damaged by a storm, and Moya is trapped by cables. The station is in an area considered holy by a fanatical religious cult, and it is discovered that the storm was attracted to the station by a flux broadcast coming from inside the body of the security officer, Borlik. She magnetises herself to a cooling pipe and taunts everyone that they will be cleansed by the wrath of her god, Gezma, when the next storm arrives.

On Moya the storm has cracked open one of the cryo-tubes (**301**, 'Season of Death') and released an Interion, who almost immediately dies. Crichton uses the cryo-tube to attract Borlik off the pipe, seals her inside and takes her to Moya, intending to draw the storm away. Borlik manages to escape and magnetises herself to the wall of the storage bay. Happily, the wall is detachable – Crichton flushes her out into space and the storm destroys her.

Chiana and Jothee are having sex on Moya when the storm hits. D'Argo discovers their betrayal. He confronts them and then, drunk and heartbroken, he goes outside the ship to try and release Moya from the cables. He attempts suicide by shorting two power cables, but he survives. Jothee leaves the ship.

Aeryn treks through miles of waste pipes on the station and manages to rescue children trapped in the station's nursery.

Buck Rogers Redux: Crichton is drowning his sorrows in aviation fuel and moaning to the bartender about Harvey. He's getting quite a reputation in the Uncharted Territories, although his shipmates are relegated to bit-part players in the legends. Borlik has heard about the Gammak base destruction (**122**, 'Family Ties') and the Shadow Depository raid (**221**, 'Liars, Guns and Money III: Plan B'); she has also heard that he destroyed an entire Nebari battalion and that he likes to do a bit of raping, pillaging and eyeball popping in his spare time: 'Where do they get these stories? Let's set the facts straight. First off: there was no raping, very little pillaging, and Frau Blücher popped all the eyeballs!'

You Can Be More: Aeryn has traded in a pulse pistol for some Tarnek Deployers, which she uses to blast open the nursery door.

Big Blue: Because of her revival of Aeryn, Zhaan is deteriorating faster than she and Stark predicted and has sores all over her head. The crew are searching for a planet that has the right soil and climate to help her recover.

I was a Teenage Luxan: D'Argo finds a ship drifting among the station wreckage; he gets Moya to bring it aboard but cannot enter because its defence screen remains active. (From now I shall refer to this ship as the D'Argomobile.)

Buckwheat the Sixteenth: Rygel is a pervert – he's rigged a portable viewer so he can stroke his eyebrows and watch Chi and Jothee having sex. Nonetheless the deluded little slug thinks that he still has the moral authority to call Chi a slut and tell her to keep her legs together. When Borlik is stuck to the coolant pipe Rygel wants to kill her, and tries ramming her to death with his Thronesled.

The Man in the Iron Mask: Stark screams at Zhaan when she is reluctant to show him her sores, and he's horrified by her decay. He tips the servants hugely out of sympathy. He has charts that he hopes will enable them to find a planet where Zhaan can heal.

In the Driving Seat: Pilot gives out a huge, gleeful laugh when Borlik is ejected into space; who knew he was capable of such *Schadenfreude?*

A Ship, a Living Ship!: Moya's elastic skin prevents her being too seriously damaged by her collision with the station, but three tiers are ruptured. The cables that hold her appear to have been deliberately attached, which implies that she was taking on power and perhaps nutrients from the station, much like a car takes on fuel. She can produce an 'Inertial Field' which allows people to walk on her skin outside the ship; it can't stop them drifting off if forcefully dislodged, however.

The Ballad of Aeryn and John: 'I don't need your emotions, but we can have sex if you want.' The tension is getting to Aeryn and she proposes an emotion-free lowering of fluid levels; she goes so far as to start undressing in a cooling pipe while on a rescue mission, so eager is she to jump Crichton's bones. Crichton interprets her offer as pity and tells her: 'I got two hands, I can alternate, I can release all the tension I want.' For once it's Aeryn asking Crichton what he's afraid of rather than the other way around. Later, Crichton seems about to take her up on the offer but she pre-empts him by agreeing that they should do nothing about it, even though it will lead to a backlog of body fluids.

The Ballad of Chiana and D'Argo: Chiana was freaked out by learning of D'Argo's marriage plans (**222**, 'Die Me, Dichotomy') and knew he wouldn't take no for an answer. She decided she had to do something he would never forgive – have sex with his son. She makes a pretence of trying to keep it secret, but it's hopeless and she effectively gives the game away by being obvious and nervous.

D'Argo bought her Luxan Union Tattoos, 'a Luxan symbol of courage, honour and loyalty' which are burned into the skin of a couple; he instead brands Jothee with one and destroys the other. D'Argo will not listen to anything either of them have to say ever again and is utterly betrayed. Even when Chiana, distraught that she may have driven him to suicide, tries to comfort him, he tells them to get lost. He overhears them talking afterwards; Jothee realises he's been used by Chiana and decides to leave, but tells her to tell his father that one day he will return to make amends to both of them.

Alien Encounters: The Interion who is released from the cryo-tube was part of an expedition to find the 'Dimordis Tomb in the Berger Nebula'. He and his colleague Stanis (whose brain was used to heal Crichton in **301**, 'Season of Death') fell sick and were found by someone called Jool, who is presumably the sole remaining frozen Interion in the Cargo bay. Given that Tocot froze his specimens just before death when they could not be saved, it's no surprise that the Interion vomits and dies very quickly. Crichton still thinks they may be related to humans, as Grunchlk implied in **222** 'Die Me, Dichotomy'.

Disney on Acid: When trying to find the signal device that attracts the storms Crichton says it's 'Scooby-Doo time'; but does that make him Shaggy or Fred?

Get Frelled: Jothee and Chi with an appreciative Hynerian audience. Crichton and Aeryn almost, and at least negotiations have been opened . . .

Stats: There were three stations in the area but the first was destroyed by an asteroid, and the second by fire. The DRD that Crichton fixed way back in **101**, 'Premiere' returns and has been nicknamed 'one-eye' by the crew.

WHAT did you just say?: Manin = fiancée or partner.

Backstage: UK viewers missed Rygel's voyeuristic activities and most of the scene where Crichton and Aeryn discuss sex, when this episode was shown on BBC2.

The Verdict: This is a good tale, with lots of tension, escalating threat and it seems about a hundred things happen at once. It might have been expected that the Chiana/Jothee/D'Argo triangle would play out over a few episodes, but that would have been traditional and safe; instead it is dealt with quickly and efficiently in an action-packed episode so as to avoid the show getting mired in soap opera (although D'Argo overhearing Jothee and Chiana is a bit soapy). Crichton telling Borlik that the wall is detachable is laugh-out-loud funny, but on the whole the tone of the episode is bleak, as Zhaan continues to decline and D'Argo's left so broken-hearted that he tries to end it all.

303
Self Inflicted Wounds I: Could'a, Would'a, Should'a

1st US Transmission Date: 30 March 2001
1st UK Transmission Date: 10 September 2001

Writer: David Kemper
Director: Tony Tilse
Guest Cast: Tammy MacIntosh (Jool), Victoria Longley (Neeyala),
Nicholas Hope (Kreetago), Dwayne Fernandez (Cresto),
Kerith Atkinson (Shreena), Brian Carbee (Lastren)

Moya collides with a vessel as it emerges from a wormhole.
The two ships are fused together and are trapped, looping
through a series of wormholes. Moya reacts badly to the
collision and her systems break down, Pilot passes out, and
the ship begins to die. In order to escape, the two ships
must be separated, which means one will be flung through
the wormhole wall and destroyed. Pathfinder Neeyala, of
the alien vessel, asks Crichton to take a trip in the WDP
and collect data to help them escape safely; he uses a device
she gives him to gather images from the worlds he passes
on his circuit of the wormhole cluster. Rygel, who he's
taken along for the ride, tries to force the ship to freedom,
but Crichton punches Sparky, breaking his nose, and
heads back to Moya with the image data. Neeyala sends
one of her subordinates on a secret suicide mission into
Moya . . .

Rygel accidentally opens the final cryo-tube and the
Interion, Joolushko Tunai Fenta Hovalis, emerges. Rygel,
in revenge for Crichton punching him, tells her that her
cousin was used to restore Crichton's brain (**301**, 'Season
of Death'). She tries to kill Crichton so she is tied up and
gagged.

A huge serpent creature that lives in wormholes boards
Moya and the final decision is taken, after much soul
searching, to abandon Moya and go in the alien craft.
Crichton is alone in Pilot's Den and notices that one of the

images he collected on his wormhole trip is of the Three Stooges. He is attacked by the serpent ...

Buck Rogers Redux: Moya is only an arn away from a planet that could save Zhaan when they pass the wormhole. Crichton diverts the ship to take readings, putting his own interests first, and causing all sorts of trouble. Aeryn thinks he is blinded by wormholes and that where they are concerned his judgment is not sound. Crichton believes that Scorpius is still alive, so he wants to get wormhole knowledge first because it could be used as a weapon (it's not clear how, though). He is the first to decide to abandon Moya and escape with the aliens, a decision roundly condemned by all his crewmates, although they all eventually come to the same conclusion. He wants the Interion who died in **302,** 'Suns and Lovers' to be buried, and still clings to the hope that they are related to humans; the first thing he asks Jool when she awakens is if she knows of Earth or humans. She doesn't.

You Can Be More: Aeryn doesn't trust the aliens at all, acts as the voice of reason, and tries to rein in Crichton's enthusiasm for wormhole knowledge with little success.

Big Blue: Zhaan's head is turning red as she nears death. She believes the serpent is a harbinger of her death and asks Stark to remain on Moya and take her place ministering to the ship and crew. She believes that she has failed in her job – keeping Moya and her crew safe. She ministers to Stark, Rygel and Chiana at different points, reinforcing her role as the counsellor of the crew.

I was a Teenage Luxan: The D'Argomobile is accidentally shot by Jool, which reveals a hole in the defence screen. He uses this as a key to shut it down.

Buckwheat the Sixteenth: Rygel reverts to his sneaky, self-serving nastiest when he tries to hijack Crichton's WDP and run out on his shipmates. He then considers killing Crichton until Zhaan talks him out of it. He claims to appreciate her counsel, but later he calls her mad for wanting to try and save Moya. Telling Jool about her cousin is an act of sheer spite, and he's free with the disparaging remarks about Chi's behaviour too.

Everyone's Favourite Little Tralk: Chiana takes an instant dislike to Jool (but then so does everyone), and calls her 'hairdo' because of her big orange barnet. She feels guilty about wanting to leave Moya because she loves Pilot and the ship; unlike Rygel who has reverted to type, she has grown to think of Moya as home and it seems unlikely that she'd try to run away again, as she did so often during Season Two, unless given no choice.

The Man in the Iron Mask: Stark tells Zhaan: 'I have a darkness which frightens lovers away.' Each time he helps the dying, he absorbs a tiny amount of their existence. 'Over the cycles, the endless parade of death, I've accumulated a vast reservoir of evil.' He cannot bear to lose Zhaan; he tells her he loves her and is reluctant to bear her burden of being Moya's spiritual centre. At one point he is downright menacing and scary: he leans in to Aeryn, glares at her and tells her that she's very pretty. For a moment it looks like he's going to do something truly psychopathic and, although Aeryn diverts him, he shows a disturbing glimpse of the evil he warned Zhaan about.

Jool in the Crown: Jool has been in the cryo-tube for 22 cycles and is an aristocratic woman of the intellectual elite who considers everyone on Moya inferior and below her station. The two Interions who died in **301**, 'Season of Death' and **302**, 'Suns and Lovers' were her cousins. She does not die when released from stasis, although since she was reportedly frozen a second before death, and her cousin died when awoken, it is a mystery why not; her cousin did state that only he and his companion were ill and that Jool found them, so perhaps she was never infected, but if not how did she end up in the cryo-tube? Her scream can melt metal; her hair can change from orange to red; she has translator microbes and recognises Sebaceans.

In the Driving Seat: Pilot vomits thick green gunk, and lots of it, before passing out.

Hi, Harvey: Crichton can call Harvey up and talk to him inside his head whenever he wants. He discusses strategy and options, and when Harvey's unco-operative he threatens him with the dumpster he placed him in (**301**, 'Season of Death'). Harvey resents the intrusion, and longs for the dumpster.

A Ship, a Living Ship!: The crash trashes tier six and plunges tier three into darkness. Moya's systems begin to burn out, her amnexus system backs up and Pilot is unconscious. She is on the verge of death, which, given she's been skewered by another ship and is floating about a wormhole like a Leviathan kebab, isn't surprising.

The Ballad Of Aeryn and Crichton: D'Argo asks Aeryn if she can ever trust Crichton again, but why has she reason to distrust him? What's he done wrong? (Well, except for killing her, I suppose.)

The Ballad of Chiana And D'Argo: Chi wants D'Argo to forgive her but he's having none of it. He does, however, say that although he can't let her into his heart again he will not abandon her when she's hurting, so perhaps there's a chance they can stay on the same ship without killing each other. Chiana admits that she acted badly but pleads that when she's cornered she doesn't think clearly.

Alien Encounters: The fish-head aliens (there's no race name given and they look like fish) have flaps on their heads which can shoot poisonous spines. Their ship is a huge repository of knowledge and if it does not return home safely the families of those on board will die, though it's unclear whether from reprisals or some catastrophe only the ship can avert. Most of the crew are killed by the crash. Like the PKs they have strict rules about exposure to aliens – this is borne out by the fact that they do not have translator microbes.

Disney on Acid: Crichton calls Kreetago 'Col Klink', a reference to *Hogan's Heroes*; he calls Rygel 'F Lee', referring to the famous lawyer F Lee Bailey.

Seen it all Before: Two ships fused together in the *Doctor Who* adventure 'Nightmare of Eden'.

WHAT did you just say?: Jool hasn't got the hang of *Farscape* swearing yet: she says 'crap' not 'dren', and calls Chiana a 'whore', not a 'tralk'.

Guest Stars: Victoria Longley was a regular on *Wildside*; Nicholas Hope played Akkor in Season Two's 'Liars, Guns and Money' trilogy. Tammy MacIntosh, who used to share a flat with Anthony Simcoe, was also a regular on *Wildside*, as well as *The Flying Doctors* and *Police Rescue*.

The Verdict: This episode is just drowning in technobabble. I've seen it three times and I'm still not sure I have a handle on what's actually going on with the wormhole walls and clusters, and phaztillon generators, and non-thermal dimensional forces, and phasic restin ions, and . . . argh my head hurts! The effects are superb, especially the terrified face in the window of the alien ship as it collides with Moya; Victoria Longley is marvellously arch and very English as Neeyala; Jool makes a stunning entrance, instantly winds everyone up and tries to kill the hero; and there's a sense of doom about Zhaan that's really worrying. Confusing as hell, but lots of fun.

304
Self Inflicted Wounds II: Wait for the Wheel

1st US Transmission Date: 6 April 2001
1st UK Transmission Date: 17 September 2001

Writer: David Kemper
Director: Tony Tilse
Guest Cast: see 303, 'Self Inflicted Wounds I: Could'a, Would'a, Should'a'

'I feared physical demise because my spiritual essence was suspect. But now I know ... the transgressions have melted from my soul ... I shall meet my goddess and be accepted to her bosom.'

The aliens have been using their Phaztillon Generator to turn themselves invisible so they can sabotage Moya – the ship is not as badly damaged as it appears. The Generator reaches critical phase and Neeyala sets a countdown to automatic: in one arn the ships will separate. However, if Moya StarBursts after separation they can spin free of the wormholes and the alien ship will be destroyed. Crichton uses the D'Argomobile's defence shield to kill the serpent, and Neeyala dies when she tries to kill Crichton and ensure her ship's survival. Unfortunately someone has to remain on the alien ship to trigger the Generator, and that person will die. Zhaan makes the sacrifice, Moya is saved and the alien ship disintegrates.

Buck Rogers Redux: 'My grandmother used to say that life is a great wheel. Sometimes it grinds you down into the mud, and other times it lifts you up into the light.' Crichton blames himself for their situation and tries to sacrifice himself on the alien ship to make amends. He's lost the trust of D'Argo and Aeryn, who believe his judgment is seriously clouded and are concerned that he still speaks to Harvey.

He used to own a green Chevy and hitchhiked to Lauderdale to see strippers during spring break from college.

You Can Be More: Aeryn thinks Crichton's plans never work. She tells Zhaan that she will only ever be a soldier and that Zhaan's sacrifice is a bad choice. Zhaan tells her, as she has been told so many times before, that she underestimates herself and can be more. Aeryn, uncharacteristically, lets her emotions show as she cries and tries to prevent Zhaan from sacrificing herself.

Big Blue: Zhaan continues her counselling round, this time talking to D'Argo and Aeryn. At one point she loses

control, her eyes turn red (**113**, 'Rhapsody In Blue') and
she makes to kill Neeyala, but is prevented by Aeryn. She
offers prayers for Moya's survival and refers to them all as
a family. She visited Pilot while he was unconscious and
spoke to him telepathically, too. At the moment of her
death she bonds telepathically with Stark, so that he can
share her death. As we see the ship explode she appears to
emerge as a glowing chiaroscuro of orange light which
leaves the wormhole. Could she have survived in some
way?

I was a Teenage Luxan: D'Argo likes playing with his new
ship and pressing random buttons just to see what they do.
Its shield is so powerful that when the serpent rams it, it
dies. He says it feels familiar to him but he doesn't know
why. Could it be a Luxan vessel?

Buckwheat the Sixteenth: According to Stark, Pilot likes
Rygel and told Stark so. Rygel is hugely impressed by this
and takes to stroking Pilot lovingly and telling him how
much he likes him, which disconcerts poor Pilot no end. He
calls Zhaan a 'big, beautiful, blue bitch'. Charming.

Everyone's Favourite Little Tralk: Chiana is shot by one of
the aliens' spines but Zhaan heals her. She considers Zhaan
one of her 'very, very best friends'.

The Man in the Iron Mask: Stark's dark side emerges again
when he really lets Jool have it: 'Your list is short, and
unworthy of entry to this ship of horror . . . You want to
cry, young creature? I will show you something that will
make you cry, forever!' Luckily he's interrupted before he
can do whatever it was he was going to do. Aeryn thinks
he's a cold fish and should be more upset by Zhaan's
death, but he's helped fifteen thousand souls die and none
has ever been so at peace as Zhaan. He will try to honour
her by carrying on with hope but knows it will be difficult
at times.

Jool in the Crown: 'Everything I have seen so far is
despicable!' Jool knows a lot of physics and Crichton trusts

her to watch the Generator countdown, but she's still selfish and annoying and even Zhaan has a go at her. She took a multi-civilization tour for her birthday, met her cousins and then remembered nothing else until waking up. Crichton speculates that she was never ill and that perhaps she was included as a freebie within a job lot with her two ill cousins to be used for body parts. Her hair turns red when she's under extreme stress. She sheds her hair and it ends up everywhere, normally in people's mouths. Yeuch. Her scream melts the tips of Neeyala's poison bristles and handcuffs, too. Crichton refers to her as 'ballast'.

Hi, Harvey: 'John Crichton was riveting in the role of cheerleader, rallying his comrades in the aid of the stricken ship he had earlier betrayed.' Harvey flexes his muscles and leaves the dumpster, demanding autonomy. He demonstrates that he can instigate conversations with Crichton now. He's absorbing some of Crichton's sense of drama and humour, dressing in a tux because he wants to look good, yeah! He calls a truce and warns Crichton about Neeyala's treachery. It now seems that they are uneasy allies.

In the Driving Seat: Pilot cries when Zhaan dies.

A Ship, a Living Ship!: We see the manual control for flying Moya for the first time since **103**, 'Back and Back and Back to the Future'. Neeyala implants a beacon in Moya's hull that signals to her race's High Command. That's another bunch of bad guys after Moya, then. Crichton believes the crew feel as if Moya raised them.

Worlds Apart: The Three Stooges image confirms that Earth is at most forty light years from some part of the wormhole, which confirms to Crichton that it is possible for him to get home one day.

Alien Encounters: The families of the aliens will be killed by the authorities if the ship does not return, which explains why Neeyala is so desperate to sacrifice Moya. The aliens have encountered no race as knowledgeable as Crichton is about physics, which fits, given that they have no translator microbes. Instead of being a research vessel that uses wormholes to travel, as it first appeared, it seems their mission was specifically to gather wormhole information – information that is now lost.

Disney on Acid: Aeryn remembers Crichton's reference to Yoda back in **104**, 'I, E.T.'. He warns the others that the serpent is now dangerous by saying 'One-Adam-Twelve, guys', which was the call sign of the cops from the show *Adam-12* which used to star Kent McCord, who plays Crichton's dad.

Get Frelled: Spoiled little rich girl moans about her shoes to Chiana: 'Do you know how much these shoes cost, young whore?' Chiana: 'For me, three sex acts. Probably double that for you.'

Stats: DRDs can project green lasers, which'll be handy if they ever decide to have a rave in the Maintenance Bay.

Logic Leaps: It's hard to follow the technobabble but Neeyala implies she set the Generator on automatic. Then it transpires that it needs someone to activate it. Is this a mistake or was Neeyala lying? And, if she was lying, why?

Bloopers: When Aeryn is walking through a section of Moya that is decompressed there is a sparking junction box behind her. How is it burning when there's no atmosphere?

WHAT did you just say?: Crichton welcomes Jool to the crew: 'Welcome, to the Federation Starship SS *Buttcrack*.'

Backstage: Virginia Hey was contracted for more seasons but the combination of having to shave off all her hair and the make-up regimen was too much, so she asked to be released. Her original idea was that she would leave Moya but could return for about six episodes a year and play the part with a bald cap, allowing her to grow back her hair. The decision to kill Zhaan perhaps indicates that this was a vain hope.

The Verdict: The Season of Death claims its first victim as Zhaan dies and we are left with a very different crew that now includes Jool and Stark. As awash in technobabble as **303**, 'Self Inflicted Wounds I: Could'a, Would'a, Should'a', it's still hard to follow exactly what's happening at times, but David Kemper again demonstrates his total understanding of Moya's crew, and there's a lot of really good character development and exploration here. Especially good is the scene where the gang are split into two groups – Crichton, Chi and Rygel in one, everyone else in the other – yet their thought processes and conclusions are shown to be exactly the same. By the end Crichton is isolated from the rest; blaming himself for Zhaan's death, taunted by visions of Earth but unable to get home, forced to share his head with Harvey, and distrusted by all his shipmates. The introduction of Jool and Stark, one of them deeply unsympathetic and irritating, the other dangerously unstable and potentially violent, increases the levels of tension on board – already high following Chi's affair and Zhaan's death – to near breaking point. This promises oodles of tension, suspicion and conflict.

305
... Different Destinations

1st US Transmission Date: 13 April 2001
1st UK Transmission Date: 24 September 2001

Writer: Steve Worland
Director: Peter Andrikidis
Guest Cast: Tammy MacIntosh (Jool), Lucy Bell (Nurse Kelsa), Basia A'hern (Cyntrina), Marshall Napier (General Grynes), Dan Spielman (Sub-officer Dacon), Terry Serio (Colonel Lennok), Alan Cinis (Officer Tarn)

While he is visiting a shrine to a historic peace accord, Stark's energy interfaces with a tear in time and whisks him, Jool, D'Argo, Crichton and Aeryn back in time to a monastery under siege by a Venek horde. Before they can get their bearings they are attacked and are forced to defend themselves; unfortunately this changes history. The monastery is full of Jocacean nurses and children who are being protected by a five-man PK squad. In the original history all but one of the Peacekeepers were killed in the fight and the remaining man, Sub-officer Dacon, is shot and killed sending a ceasefire plan (which was accepted) to the enemy General Grynes. Although Dacon is still the only remaining PK officer, General Grynes is captured as a result of the time travellers' interference. They locate the time tear and push Jool through but Stark realises that the future has changed and that unless they set it right billions will die. Crichton assures Grynes that they will leave the monastery if he returns to his men and persuades them to enter the monastery peacefully. Crichton is seen smuggling Grynes out of the monastery and Nurse Kelsa kills the General, believing Crichton to be betraying them to the enemy. The Veneks find the General's body and declare that they will attack at dawn. The time tear disappears entirely and on Moya, back in the future, the world below them becomes a barren radioactive rock.

Crichton convinces Aeryn that Dacon must die to set history right, so they let Dacon send his ceasefire offer and he dies, as he did in the original history. This does not fix things – in the future Moya sees the world disappear entirely.

Crichton accepts Aeryn's demand that they stay and fight, so they repel the dawn attack and find that the tear reappears and history is restored. Crichton promises the nurses that they will be safe and that the Veneks will offer peace when they return if he and the others have left.

They return to the future and discover that one detail is different – the nurses and children were massacred by the Veneks; what was a memorial to a historic peace is now a memorial of a massacre. The nurses died with Crichton's name on their lips.

Buck Rogers Redux: 'I'm in a hell of a slump here. Everything I do just makes things worse.' Crichton gets it all wrong, again. Why didn't he tell everyone he was going to smuggle the General out? By keeping it a secret he blew it and cost the women and children their lives. When he's tied up Aeryn is reluctant to let him go, and you can understand why – he's becoming a liability. After the events of **303** and **304**, 'Self Inflicted Wounds' I and II, which were his fault, and this little debacle, his sense of self is taking a hell of a beating.

You Can Be More: 'This is what Peacekeepers are meant to do – help the defenceless.' You'd think Aeryn would have realised by now that the things she was taught in PK school were suspect. The last PK hero she met was Durka, but she's still surprised when the hero of the monastery, the fabled Sub-officer Dacon, turns out to be a cook. She wants to keep him alive, even tries to take the fall for him, and then tells him how brave he is just before he dies. She fits back into the PK world very easily, and seems wistful for the days when the Peacekeepers really did stand for justice and peace.

I was a Teenage Luxan: 'I'm not going to kill anyone. Oh, but I might kill this guy.' D'Argo gets to meet a child he's good with at last, and what does he do? He teaches her how to graffiti. What a role model. He couldn't care less when it looks as if Jool may have been cast adrift in time, and he even seems to enjoy throwing her against a wall a couple of times. Can't blame him, really.

Everyone's Favourite Little Tralk: Chiana ignores everything Jool has to say and then deliberately punches her wounded arm to make her scream. She bumps into Rygel in Zhaan's quarters but neither of them have the stomach actually to steal any of Zhaan's stuff.

The Man in the Iron Mask: 'Fear is good, keep that. But travel light, forget hate.' Stark is trying to fill Zhaan's place, even going so far as to do impressions of her. Somehow the energy from under his mask throws them through time, and he is able to both sense the location of the time tear and hold it in one place. When looking through to the future he can feel the accumulated deaths in the time between then and now. He is wearing new clothes that Zhaan bought for him.

Jool in the Crown: 'Mud! You threw me in mud! Bastards! They shoot me, they punch me, they make me drink piss.' Jool sheds so badly that she leaves piles of hair on Moya's consoles. She drinks by reverse gargling into a glass and making a weird sound. When she is shot through the arm with an arrow the nurses give her fellip urine to dull the pain. She has encountered Peacekeepers before and has a very low opinion of them indeed.

Hi, Harvey: Harvey wears cowboy boots and plays 'Home on the Range' on the harmonica for Crichton, because he knows the situation reminds Crichton of old Western movies. Crichton summons him to ask for help but Harvey refuses to make suggestions because he doesn't want to carry the can if everything goes wrong.

A Ship, a Living Ship!: Moya is recovering from her ordeal in **302**, 'Suns and Lovers' and **303**, 'Self Inflicted Wounds: Could'a, Would'a, Should'a' and repairs are still underway.

Alien Encounters: The Venek horde are almost impossible to control when they are in the grip of bloodlust, although a skilful general can just about keep them in check. They are attacking the monastery to get to a water source that will save them from drought.

Jocaceans can live up to seven hundred cycles. Once upon a time the Peacekeepers were truly a police force for hire; Kelsa says they 'uphold all that is good'.

Disney on Acid: Harvey's cowboy boots have ANDY written on the soles, complete with reverse N – this is a lovely reference to *Toy Story*. Crichton sees the situation as like *The Alamo*. Crichton calls Stark 'Astroboy', which means he reads Manga comics. He shoots a Venek and cries 'Tony Montana!' which refers to Brian DePalma's remake of *Scarface*.

Seen it all Before: Time alteration stories are a staple of *Star Trek* and this episode has a lot in common with *Deep Space Nine*'s excellent two-parter, 'Past Tense'.

Logic Leaps: Why would Stark's energy throw them back in time? Any explanation we were given would only be technobabble to excuse a story idea, so it's fine they don't even bother to try explaining it. Were this *Star Trek* we'd have been given a pointless five-paragraph dissertation on decaying Chronon particles and phase loop quasar pulses. Or something.

Guest Stars: Lucy Bell was Detective Tessa Vance on *Murder Call*. Marshall Napier has appeared in many TV shows and films, including *The Navigator: A Mediaeval Odyssey* and *Flirting*. Terry Serio was Captain Sam Phillips on *Ocean Girl*.

The Verdict: How many shows are willing to have their hero screw up to this degree and not provide a cop-out loophole? Crichton is responsible for the deaths of the nurses and children – he knows it, we know it, and there's no getting away from it. Compare this episode to one of the stand-alones from this point in Season Two – **203** 'Taking the Stone' or **202** 'Vitas Mortis' – and it's clear that the show continues to improve in leaps and bounds.

306
Eat Me

1st US Transmission Date: 20 April 2001
1st UK Transmission Date: 1 October 2001

Writer: Matt Ford
Director: Ian Watson
Guest Cast: Tammy MacIntosh (Jool), Shane Briant (Kaarvok),
Lisa Griffiths (Belima), Sean Masterson (Voice of *Rovhu*'s pilot)

After a Transport Pod accident Crichton, D'Argo, Chiana and Jool are forced to seek refuge on a diseased PK

Leviathan that still has its control collar. The ship is full of zombies – the degraded remains of its crew – who are eating the ship, the pilot, and each other. The Leviathan, *Rovhu*, was a prison for the criminally insane and was transporting its sole prisoner, Kaarvok, when it was ambushed by Scarrans and left to drift. Kaarvok is loose and he sucks something out of D'Argo's brain, killing D'Argo, and injects it into his own in front of a horrified Crichton and Chiana; they burn D'Argo's body. Kaarvok next attacks Chiana and doubles her, producing two equal and opposite copies of her, one of which he kills and brain-sucks. It transpires that D'Argo was doubled too and Kaarvok chains up the remaining Luxan and tries to make him breed with one of the PK zombies, which are the product of degradation caused by too many doublings. The surviving Chiana rescues him.

Crichton, believing both his friends to be dead, tries to repair the pilot's connections with the ship, but Kaarvok kills the pilot before Crichton is finished. Instead Crichton sets the ship to StarBurst, knowing it is so damaged it will explode. Kaarvok tries to stop him and in the struggle Crichton is doubled. Everyone escapes on the Transport Pod, the ship is destroyed and the zombies and Kaarvok are killed. *But we are left with two John Crichtons.*

Moya finds Talyn dead in space, severely damaged, with Crais unconscious. They take Talyn in tow and bring Crais aboard for medical treatment.

Buck Rogers Redux: 'I don't think so, brain-sucker. I can arrange my own death!' When D'Argo won't agree to his plan Crichton just walks away and goes to do it himself. The independence that caused so much trouble in **305**, '. . . Different Destinations' is still there and he hasn't learned his lesson; he later blames his stubbornness for D'Argo's death. He is able to reconnect *Rovhu*'s pilot to the ship, and knows the control sequence to initiate StarBurst. He's willing to die if it means he takes Kaarvok with him. When he leaves Chiana with Jool in the Maintenance Bay, Chi warns him that she'll kill Jool and he murmurs 'whatever';

when he returns he's surprised to find Jool still alive. Does she annoy him so much he was willing to let Chi kill her, perhaps even hoping she would? The two Crichtons play Rock/Scissors/Paper and both choose the same thing every time.

I was a Teenage Luxan: Crichton's plan – find the pilot, get things sorted out – makes perfect sense, but D'Argo is so freaked out by being on a PK ship that he refuses to endorse it and just wants to grab the stuff they need and run, even though the chances of making it without the pilot's help are slim. The surviving D'Argo does not seem hugely bothered by being doubled and even speculates that he may be a copy.

Buckwheat the Sixteenth: Rygel rips out Crais's neural transponder and tries to persuade Aeryn to leave Talyn in case whatever shot him up returns to finish the job and decides to attack Moya as well. When Aeryn goes to collect Crichton and the others Rygel threatens that, if she's not back in three hundred microts, he will cut Talyn loose and StarBurst away.

Everyone's Favourite Little Tralk: Chiana is horrified by D'Argo's apparent death and burns his body to stop him being eaten. When she is doubled she callously leaves her other self to be eaten by Kaarvok, even though the doomed one begs for help. She is so traumatised and guilty at her actions that she refuses to accept that the doubling creates two equal copies and tries to convince herself that she is the original and the dead one was a clone. Chi punches Jool a couple of times until she punches her back. This is ostensibly to teach Jool how to behave violently, but more likely it was because she just felt like it.

Jool in the Crown: 'I shouldn't be here. I'm a civilised being. There's got to be someone here who recognises that. I just need to find them.' Jool grabs the control of the Transport Pod for no adequately explained reason, and manages to cause critical systems breakdowns; she would, had they not stumbled across *Rovhu*, have been the cause of all their deaths. It's a miracle that a few punches from

Chiana is the worst treatment she receives. She is left to guard the Transport Pod but is so scared that she tries to shoot herself in the head with a pulse rifle; Chiana's disappointed that she can't even get that right.

Jool's world has no violence or war. Her parents were very supportive of her when she was young.

In the Driving Seat: *Rovhu*'s pilot's arms are cut off and eaten every time they regenerate.

The Insane Military Commander: Crais may not recover from his wounds. Removing his neural transponder causes Talyn to shut down.

A Ship, a Living Ship!: Since Leviathans are living beings, parts of them are edible. They can survive for a long time while being eaten from the inside out. They ooze puss when they are diseased.

Big Baby: Rygel: 'Listen, you bartantic bitch, Talyn's supposedly the meanest, deadliest, all-time yave-of-the-yuvo fighter ship. But somebody, something, beat the yotz out of him.' Talyn has been seriously damaged by persons unknown and is unable to communicate with Moya, but he will recover.

Alien Encounters: Although the Scarrans and the Peace-keepers are not openly at war, Scarrans will ambush PK convoys. Kaarvok can patch himself directly into *Rovhu*'s controls using his own Biomechanoid parts.

Disney on Acid: Crichton calls himself and D'Argo 'Abbot and Costello in the House of Horrors', again referring to the 30s comedy double act he likes so much. He refers to Kaarvok as a 'sick, Hammer Horror son of a bitch', which is good since the actor, Shane Briant, starred in a number of Hammer Horror films.

Get Frelled: Kaarvok wants fresh food, so he ties up D'Argo and chains Belima to him hoping that they will breed. When Chi finds them D'Argo is receiving all kinds of attentions and he claims not to be enjoying it at all. So why didn't he tongue her unconscious then?

Seen it all Before: As Crichton points out, this is all very *Night of the Living Dead*, even down to the fact that Kaarvok sucks something out of his victims' brains.

Stats: Crichton and D'Argo go in search of Narium Coil and 3K wire with which to repair the Transport Pod. D'Argo's Qualta Blade and Winona are not doubled – Chiana finds them in a locker near the chained D'Argo.

Logic Leaps: It's a little hard to believe that Jool simply grabbing the controls could so catastrophically damage a Transport Pod. The doubling process also duplicates clothing.

Guest Stars: Shane Briant has appeared in many TV series and films, most notably *Lady Chatterley's Lover*, *The Naked Civil Servant* and *Frankenstein and the Monster from Hell*. Sean Masterson, normally a voiceless puppeteer, gets to voice *Rovhu*'s pilot.

Backstage: David Kemper talked to *DreamWatch* about the decision to create two John Crichtons. 'I knew I wanted to do it, because the whole idea made me nervous – anything that's good makes us nervous.' However, he wouldn't have gone ahead if Rockne S O'Bannon or Ben Browder had been against the idea. 'But Rock and Ben were like "Let's do it!" And that was essentially it.'

The Verdict: Pure horror movie, with a great score from Guy Gross, excellent camera work and lighting, scary zombies, brain-sucking, gruesome deaths and lots and lots of pus. Definitely the scariest *Farscape* so far and chock-full of atmosphere. And then the ending, which is a stroke of genius and will dominate the rest of the season, takes a similar premise to **213** 'My Three Crichtons' and actually runs with it, which is something no other show has ever had the mivonks to do. Should be interesting . . .

307
Thanks for Sharing

1st US Transmission Date: 15 June 2001
1st UK Transmission Date: 8 October 2001

Writer: Clayvon C. Harris
Director: Ian Barry
Guest Cast: Tammy MacIntosh (Jool), Rebecca Gibney (Sarova), Robert
Brunning (Pralanoth), Sandy Winton (Tolven),
Linda Cropper (Xhalax Sun), Julianne Newbould (Felor),
Hunter Perske (Bloy)

Note: *There are now two John Crichtons, equal and original.
Aeryn gives one a green T-shirt and the other a black T-shirt
so she can tell them apart. Since they are in effect two
characters they now get their own names and sections.*

Moya and Talyn hide in the dense atmosphere of the
planet Kanvia while negotiating for the Chromextin they
need to heal Talyn, who was attacked by a PK Retrieval
Squad led by Aeryn's mother. Kanvia is ruled by
Pralanoth, who has two children – a son, Tolven, and a
daughter, Sarova. Tolven gets into a bar fight with D'Argo
after trying to force himself on Chiana. He gives them an
arn to get off the planet and when they remain, he fires on
Moya and Talyn, forcing them to descend and train
Talyn's guns on the main government building. Black T
Crichton goes to see Pralanoth whereupon a lie-detecting
creature called a strannat is attached to his head, and it is
established that he is genuinely trying to negotiate for
Chromextin and not take power on the planet, as Tolven
suspected. Sarova calls Black T to a secret meeting and
tries to warn him that Tolven will sabotage the shipment
of Chromextin. A bomb explodes, Sarova and Black T are
injured; Black T is smuggled back to Moya by D'Argo and
Chi. Sarova is killed and replaced by a disguised PK
Retrieval agent.

Green T Crichton saves his doppelgänger with a blood
transfusion. Some Chromextin is delivered but it has been
poisoned with Clorium. Tolven has reports of Crichton

being taken, injured, from the bomb site, so Green T goes down, puts the strannat on his head and tells Tolven the truth: *he* wasn't at a secret meeting with Sarova and wasn't plotting with her. He then turns the tables, strannats Tolven and finds, to his surprise, that Tolven did not plant the bomb or poison the Chromextin (it must have been the disguised PK agent). However, Tolven lies about being loyal to his father and the strannat kills him. Moya filters out the Clorium and gives the Chromextin to Talyn who is partly healed. The PK Agent kills Pralanoth and fires on the Leviathans, forcing them to separate and escape. Upon leaving the atmosphere, they find the Retrieval Squad waiting for them and both ships StarBurst away – Green T, D'Argo, Jool and Chiana on Moya; Aeryn, Black T, Rygel, Stark and Crais on Talyn. To lessen the chances of the Retrieval Squad capturing Moya and using her to force Talyn's surrender, there will be no contact between the two ships until the Squad has been dealt with.

Buck Rogers Redux: Jool does genetic tests to compare both Crichtons with samples Zhaan took back when there was only one of him. She establishes that they are both identical, there is no discernible difference between them and the single Crichton they were doubled from. It is therefore impossible to call either of them clones or copies – they are both John Crichton.

Green T: 'Cross my heart, smack me dead, stick a lobster on my head.' He wants to establish that he's the original and thinks Black T is 'an ugly loudmouthed son-of-a-bitch' but gives him blood because he refuses to let him die. He is furious that Black T gets to leave on Talyn with Aeryn and has taken the notebook and Winona, although he admits he'd probably have done the same thing had the opportunity presented itself.

Black T: Nice going Black T, he's got himself exactly where he wants to be – alone on a ship with Aeryn, far away from his irritating other half.

You Can Be More: Crais shows Aeryn footage of her mother, Xhalax, visiting her as a child (this is the chip referred to in **222**, 'Die Me, Dichotomy' and the footage portrays an incident Aeryn related to Crichton in **122**, 'Family Ties'). Although Crais could find no information at all about her father, Talyn, Xhalax has been promoted to an elite battle group and is now heading the squad sent to retrieve Talyn; Aeryn does not think her appointment to that post was an accident. Aeryn chooses to stay with Talyn because Crais thinks her presence may help sway her mother's loyalties if the squad captures them. Aeryn swears she will kill her mother if that is what is required.

I was a Teenage Luxan: 'I'm your daddy!' D'Argo is your daddy, and don't you forget it.

Buckwheat the Sixteenth: Rygel's negotiation skills again come to the fore and, had Tolven not started trouble, Rygel would no doubt have secured the Chromextin. He is not at all happy at being stuck on Talyn and is even less pleased at having to share quarters with Stark.

Everyone's Favourite Little Tralk: Chi tries not to start trouble on Kanvia, but her very presence is enough to provoke Torven. D'Argo comes running to her defence, as always, but doesn't blame her, for a change.

Jool in the Crown: Jool has a sweet tooth and T ratings in Genetics, Neuro science and Xenobiology. She's filling Zhaan's role as ship's doctor and making a pretty good fist of it: she patches up Black T and Crais pretty well, and performs complex genetic tests. Finally, she's earning her keep.

The Insane Military Commander: Neither Crichton trusts new improved Crais even though, as Aeryn points out, he's saved their lives more than once. Crais is stunned to see Aeryn alive and again tries to persuade her to join him on Talyn, although this time ostensibly because of her mother. He's really annoyed when he sees she's brought Black T along with her.

Nosferatu in Rubber: Aeryn still believes Scorpius to be dead.

A Ship, A Living Ship!: Moya can filter Clorium out of Chromextin provided there is not too much of it. She repays Talyn's transfusion after her fire damage in **221**, 'Liars, Guns and Money III: Plan B' by transfusing him to help him heal.

Big Baby: Talyn is near fatally injured and has not received enough Chromextin so, although he can StarBurst, just, he will be weak for some time to come. Talyn was designed with 'intelligence-gathering facilities' and Crais and he have 'been able to tap into high-level Peacekeeper comm channels, accessing their central database', which is where they found the footage of Aeryn's mother. His passenger sections have not yet fully grown, but he has started producing DRDs.

Worlds Apart: Kanvia was a world at war until Pralanoth united the various countries and established peace.

Alien Encounters: The strannat is a lobster of truth that, when placed on the head, detects lies and kills anyone who tells one. The PK agent who disguises himself as Sarova is a shape-shifter and is surprised not to be killed for failing to secure Talyn's capture (**310**, 'Relativity' names his race Colartas). The Retrieval Squad is using a Pantak Class vigilante ship with an Immobiliser Pulse. The reputations of Moya's crew again precedes them and Torven wants them thrown off Kanvia for being dangerous criminals.

Disney on Acid: Crichton refers back to **213**, 'My Three Crichtons' and says at least having another of him isn't as bad as having the 'Cro-Magnon copy or the *Alien Nation* reject'; Rockne S O'Bannon created *Alien Nation*. Crichton asks Crais if the Skeksis are after him, surely a reference to the fact that the Halosians in **209**, 'Out of Their Minds', looked like the Skeksis from the Henson film *The Dark Crystal*. Crichton introduces himself to Pralanoth as the

Wizard of Oz. He nearly quotes Jack Nicholson from the film *A Few Good Men* when he shouts, 'you can't handle . . . ah, let's cut the crap'. 'Who's Your Daddy?' comes from the film *Scum*.

Seen it all Before: The alien shape-shifter looks uncannily like the justly famous Ergon (often described as the Chicken of Doom) from the *Doctor Who* adventure 'Arc Of Infinity'. The political set-up on the planet – strong ruler with two heirs jostling for power, one male, one female – is very reminiscent of the 'Look At The Princess' trilogy (**210–212**).

Stats: Chromextin helps to heal Talyn but can also be used to power weapons. Clorium (**104**, 'I, E.T.') numbs Leviathans.

Logic Leaps: We know Peacekeepers are nasty paranoid types but they video their children asleep and then append that film to their personnel records? That's a bit of a stretch, surely.

WHAT did you just say?: When D'Argo says, 'Crack a smile, will you? At least he's out of your nose,' Green T corrects him, saying, 'Hair.' D'Argo: 'That's what I meant, at least he's out of your nosehair.'

Guest Stars: Rebecca Gibney is extremely well known as *Halifax f.p.* Sandy Winton has guested on *Xena: Warrior Princess* and *The Secret Life of Us*. Linda Cropper was one of the Plokavians in **217**, 'The Ugly Truth'.

The Verdict: Another good episode that sets us up for a split ship season. It uses the two Crichtons superbly and Jool is becoming amusing rather than irritating, which is a relief. As ever the sets and the CGI are excellent and everything comes together well, even though there are echoes of previous episodes. Not a classic but a damn good 45 minutes of sci-fi.

308
Green-eyed Monster

1st US Transmission Date: 22 June 2001
1st UK Transmission Date: 22 October 2001

Writer: Ben Browder
Director: Tony Tilse

NOTE: *This episode features the crew of Talyn.*

While Rygel and Stark are on recon in a Transport Pod, Talyn is swallowed by a live Budong (**207**, 'Home on the Remains'). Crichton and Aeryn manage to anchor the ship inside the gullet and prevent it being digested, their plan being to fly through the stomach and intestines, exiting through its arse. Aeryn takes a neural transponder and links herself to Talyn and Crais. Crichton finds a PK vid-chip with footage of Crais and Aeryn having sex. Talyn panics and tries to disengage the anchoring cables, and when this fails he reverses his transponder and takes control of Crais. Crichton is able to stop Crais releasing the cable but he discovers that Talyn's personality is so strong he can torture Crais, who's covered in lesions and welts as a result. Stark and Rygel return in their Transport Pod and contact Talyn to warn them that a Budong's stomach is a furnace and Talyn would be destroyed. Stark realises they have to make the Budong vomit Talyn free. They use the Pod to lure the Budong along a planetary ring, forcing it to swallow ice; Talyn dumps some fuel, which reacts with the ice, and Crichton uses a warhead to ignite it, freeing the ship.

During the escape Talyn tries to kill Crichton by locking him out of the ship; Aeryn saves him by sharing her love for Crichton with Talyn and ripping out the transponder. The vid-chip turns out to be a fabrication, left by Talyn to drive Crichton away because he distrusts him.

Black T: 'Open the door, you soulless, tinheaded, adolescent pig!' Crichton refuses to trust Crais, despite all his claims that he's changed, but he still doesn't shoot him to stop him releasing the cables when he's possessed by Talyn.

With Talyn bonded to Crais and Aeryn, his gun missing, the doors not opening for him, and DRDs keeping him awake all the time, Crichton's feeling isolated, useless and cranky. But he still tries to keep control, do what's best for the crew, and not let his emotions cloud his judgment or dictate his actions. Understandably, he blames all of this on Crais, especially after seeing the footage of Crais and Aeryn 'recreating'. However, when he's stuck outside the ship he realises that his persecutor is Talyn because Crais wouldn't risk alienating Aeryn by killing him.

He keeps star charts and always uses one star as his point of reference. This star he calls Aeryn.

You Can Be More: 'My life has been filled with doing what others think is right. For me, for now, this is right.' Aeryn thinks Talyn is 'beyond beautiful' and she learns how to interface with him very quickly, possibly because she has got some of Pilot's multi-tasking abilities (**109**, 'DNA Mad Scientist'). At one point she calls Crais 'sir', dropping effortlessly back into her PK role.

Buckwheat the Sixteenth: Rygel reverts to cowardly, self-serving type and swallows the Transport Pod Comms Relay Circuit to prevent Stark contacting Talyn and embarking on the kind of dangerous rescue plan he eventually does embark on.

The Man in the Iron Mask: Stark spent five years on a Budong mining colony and saw endless miners disappear into the innards of the space whales; he is something of an expert on the creatures. He's still manic as all hell, and he joins the illustrious line of characters who've given Rygel the punching he so thoroughly deserves. He saves the day and is the hero of the piece, which is a nice change for a character who's so far been more often a liability than an asset. He now has the dubious distinction of having been puked on by two characters: Pilot and Rygel.

The Insane Military Commander: Crais tries to persuade Talyn that Crichton is not a threat; he calls him an honourable man, but Aeryn blames Crais for Talyn's distrust of Crichton because the ship learned everything he knows from Crais. Crais suffers extreme pain and lesions as a result of Cybernetic Bleedback from Talyn; the pain is so severe he begs Crichton to kill him to release him from it. His tactic for stealing Aeryn's affections from Crichton is to get her to bond with the ship and thus with him. No wonder he's so annoyed when she removes the link. It's unclear whether Crais was complicit in Talyn's attempts to kill Crichton; he remains a character of ambiguous loyalty and suspect motives.

Big Baby: Talyn does not trust Crichton because he's non-Sebacean and not a PK. He hides his gun, hassles him with DRDs, fakes a vid-chip to cause tension and eventually locks Crichton outside to try and kill him. His first reaction to any situation is to start firing, and his insistence on focusing on weapons rather than propulsion contributes to his being swallowed. When anchored he wants to rip free and escape, acting against his best interests and forcing Aeryn to short him out and knock him unconscious; he even deploys his weapons against her. In short he is impulsive, hard to control, violent and willing to kill his crew.

He has a docking web. His DRDs are a different design to Moya's. In extreme circumstances he can use the neural transponder to take physical control of Crais. He still responds well to Aeryn's guidance and she is able to calm him down and teach him control when he's panicking. Had she been in control of Talyn from the start he'd probably be a far more balanced individual.

The Ballad of Aeryn and John: Aeryn liked her life before, she liked the rules that were there to follow. 'Then you come along and you frell everything up. This strange human, with arrogance, stubbornness. You are like a plague, John Crichton ... And yet, I just keep coming back.' Crichton tells Aeryn that he is not her boyfriend or her husband and she can do what she likes, but there's real bitterness when he tells her 'it's always about what you want'. The vid-chip Talyn created to force Crichton away actually manages to bring them closer, forcing Aeryn to explain her feelings for Crichton. He tells her she is his reference point, his one constant, and they kiss, not for the first time but this time it looks as if the relationship might stick.

Alien Encounters: Live Budongs are extremely rare. Their stomachs are furnaces burning at five thousand *klanches*, which is hot enough to melt everything. They home in on and eat things that generate electromagnetic energy fields.

Disney on Acid: Crichton names three stars Huey, Louie and Dewey, after Donald Duck's nephews. He refers to Mintaka Three, which was a planet from the *Star Trek: The Next Generation* episode 'Who Watches the Watchers?', which was written by Richard Manning, who now writes for *Farscape*.

Get Frelled: Aeryn tries to defuse Crichton and Crais's feud by asking Talyn, whose seen them both naked: 'Perhaps you can tell us who's bigger.'

Seen it all Before: In the Bible: Jonah and the Whale.

What Does This Do?: Rygel can vomit massively at will; his puke is clear.

Logic Leaps: Why were Crais's lesions not discovered when Jool examined him in **307**, 'Thanks for Sharing'? If Talyn is anchored above the Budong's stomach, why does the ice being swallowed by the creature not smash Talyn to bits on its way down?

WHAT did you just say?: Ben Browder's familiarity with English vernacular shows when Crichton says that Talyn's mooring control is 'totally buggered'.

Backstage: It was Rockne S O'Bannon and David Kemper's idea to get Ben Browder to write an episode, and it was agreed as far back as the end of Season One. He's obviously a natural. The thing Browder most loves about writing is that 'you are alone with your thoughts and you are totally responsible for the story at that point, as opposed to being a part of it . . . whereas in acting you are

. . . interpreting.' Claudia Black also took pleasure in this episode: 'Tony Tilse [the director] really loved the episode and he rose to the occasion as only he can. It was such an action-packed and beautifully shot episode, and I really enjoyed it.'

The Verdict: In an age when so many TV stars have a chance to direct written into their contract, it's rare indeed to find an actor choosing instead to *write* for the show they act in. Inevitably there are worries that such a script will be a vanity piece, sanctioned as a way of keeping the star happy. Happily no such situation appends here – Browder's script is tight, cogent, funny and demonstrates a firm grasp of character, structure and mood. On the basis of this performance it's no surprise that he will be writing for *Farscape* at least once during Season Four. The episode's great strength is to take the traditional love triangle story and spin it by having the environment, the ship itself, be a part of the relationship too: it muddies things up, allowing all sorts of conflict and emotional re-examinations. Parts of the episode are straightforward character drama that wouldn't be out of place on a soap opera, but the involvement of Talyn means that, despite its familiar themes, this is a story that could only be told on *Farscape*.

309
Losing Time

1st US Transmission Date: 29 July 2001
1st UK Transmission Date: 29 October 2001

Writer: Justin Monjo
Director: Catherine Millar
Guest Cast: Tammy Macintosh (Jool), David Franklin (Lt Braca),
Jo Kerrigan (Linfer), Danny Adcock (Co-Kura Strappa),
Ian Bliss (PK Scientist Drillic), Tux Akindoyeni (PK Pilot Rinon)

Note: *This episode features the crew of Moya.*
While passing through an energy cluster, Moya is boarded by two Energy Riders, beings that inhabit and

possess host bodies. One hides inside a crew member while the other, Tallip, takes over Pilot. Tallip informs the crew that the Energy Rider he is chasing is young and diseased and will harm the host if it remains inside too long. They try to identify which person the Rider is in but Tallip has to 'taste' them in turn to be sure. When he tastes Jool it's inconclusive and nearly kills her. Moya leads Crichton to her StarBurst chamber, which contains no sensors and is thus hidden from Pilot/Tallip. He discovers that Chiana is the host. The Energy Rider protests that Tallip wants to kill it, that it is not diseased, and that Tallip is dangerous. Crichton and D'Argo tell Tallip that if he takes Moya back to the cluster they will give him Chiana and the two Riders can leave and sort out their differences. Tallip rejects this plan and tastes D'Argo.

Jool fetches Chi from the StarBurst chamber at gunpoint, revealing the Energy Rider to Tallip, who absorbs it and kills it. Tallip refuses to leave Pilot, intending to remain in control of Moya. Crichton convinces him that Pilot is dying and Tallip leaves Pilot, intending to inhabit Moya. As he leaves Chiana triggers a StarBurst pulse, which kills the creature.

On the Command Carrier, Scorpius has found a wormhole. Unmanned Prowlers can enter and exit easily but when they are manned the PK pilot is liquidised upon exit.

Green T: Crichton has been dragging Moya around in search of wormholes for ten solar days and finally his shipmates have had enough. When he is tasted by the Energy Rider he bleeds, a lot, but it's never explained why none of the others do. Pilot suggests it may be because of his doubling (**306**, 'Eat Me'), and Crichton worries that he is the copy and Black T is the original; Jool posits that it's because he's 'an irritating and inferior species'.

Crichton had a dog called Hubble.

I was a Teenage Luxan: 'Actually, now that you mention it, I've been feeling a little angry.' D'Argo is played for laughs as he fails to interrogate Chiana sensibly, bemoans the hopelessness of their plans and generally looks pissed off and resigned to weirdness. It's a trend that will continue, especially in **313**, 'Scratch 'n' Sniff', and it makes him an even better foil for the increasingly frustrated Green T Crichton.

Everyone's Favourite Little Tralk: Chi isn't Chi for the majority of the episode. She survives being possessed but at the end she is aware of D'Argo's presence before he enters the room, the implication being that her possession has left her with some form of psychic power, or has improved the abilities already hinted at. The crew still don't know if Chi killed Salis (**115**, 'Durka Returns').The Energy Rider implies that Chiana fancies Crichton, but how trustworthy is a space parasite?

Jool in the Crown: 'I feel like I had a spiritual enema.' Nice new costume, very Arabian Nights. Jool reveals that she found a Noatian Gem Mine and was captured by the guards and sold to Grunchlk; her cousins were waiting for her in a village, got sick, and were similarly sold. This is not the tale Jool originally told everyone, but it would explain why she didn't die as soon as she was defrosted. She takes matters into her own hands for the first time and instead of cowering and crying she grabs a gun and takes the Energy Rider in Chiana hostage. When the creature leaves Chi stunned, Jool's surprisingly tender with her – heart of gold under there?

In the Driving Seat: You take a pilot's pulse behind the neck, between the vertebrae.

Nosferatu in Rubber: Scorpius is plugging a strange device into his head and having nightmares where Crichton taunts him for not solving the wormhole problem. His medical regime expands, as we see him inject himself in the throat. Finally we get an explanation of why he wants the wormhole technology so badly, and it makes perfect sense both in terms of the wider political scene and his own personal issues. The Scarrans were preparing to attack PK space, but they held back because PK Command convinced them that they have wormhole weapons. The

Scarrans are beginning to realise they've been duped and are massing an army to invade; they outnumber PK soldiers ten to one and without a wormhole weapon the Sebaceans and the Peacekeepers will be defeated. Scorpius worries that a Scarran victory may already be impossible to avert.

A Ship, a Living Ship!: Crichton talks to Moya through a DRD and Moya talks back by blinking its eye lights once for yes and twice for no. She has a chamber beneath Pilot's Den in which the StarBurst energy is gathered; there are no sensors in this room. The energy for StarBurst can be directed through Pilot's Den.

Alien Encounters: Energy Riders live in clusters. Their first law, according to Tallip, is never to harm their host body. They get stronger as they age, and only a child could easily possess a lower life form like Chiana without killing it; adults need something as complex as Pilot to host them. The longer a host is inhabited the more psychological damage is done until eventually all that is left is desire and despair.

Disney on Acid: Crichton tells the DRD that they'll communicate the *Star Trek* way and calls it DRD Pike. This refers to the *Star Trek* two-parter, 'Menagerie' when the Enterprise's crippled first captain, Christopher Pike, gives evidence at a trial from a wheelchair with lights that blink, allowing him to answer questions. Poor old DRD Pike gets fried in the StarBurst blast. 'If I'm Linda Blair why am I telling you guys anything?'; Crichton riffs on *The Exorcist*. Crichton calls Tallip 'Casper', after the friendly ghost.

Get Frelled: D'Argo lost his virginity when he was seven. Crichton restates that he lost his to Karen Shaw in the back of a truck (**108**, 'That Old Black Magic'). The Energy Rider in Chi can zap Crichton with a huge sexual buzz that leaves him gasping and amazed.

Seen it all Before: This episode has a similar premise to **118**, 'A Bug's Life'.

What Does This Do?: When forced to watch Crichton for signs of bleeding Chiana bluntly demands to know what happens if she wants to piss. D'Argo replies they will all 'urinate together', and Chiana responds: 'You promise?' I could say that Jool's familiarity with the concept of an enema tells us stuff about her biology, but I don't want to go there.

Logic Leaps: It's implied that Scorpius and co. just found the wormhole they are experimenting on, and in **311**, 'Incubator' Linfer will confirm that it was discovered and not created. This is a bit of a leap given that Furlow said no one had ever found one before (**111**, 'Till the Blood Runs Clear'). They cannot stabilise it.

Guest Stars: Ian Bliss was in *Scary Movie* and *AntiTrust* prior to which he played Mr Bell on *Heartbreak High*. Danny Adcock played T'raltixx in **204**, 'Crackers Don't Matter'.

The Verdict: Not original enough to be truly memorable, this episode is mostly distinguished by Gigi Edgley's work as possessed Chiana and the interplay between the characters. Jool is becoming more likeable, D'Argo is funnier and Green T is getting more and more grumpy. It's interesting that Scorpius is a sufficiently important character to get his own storyline, albeit one that we know started with, and will end with, Crichton.

310
Relativity

1st US Transmission Date: 6 July 2001
1st UK Transmission Date: 5 November 2001

Writer: Rockne S O'Bannon
Director: Peter Andrikidis
Guest Cast: Linda Cropper (Xhalax Sun), Thomas Holesgrove (Vek), Dominique Sweeney (Thek and Kek)

Note: *This episode features the crew of Talyn.*

Talyn is healing on a planet that has heavy gravity and restorative plant life when the Retrieval Squad lands nearby. Xhalax, along with two Colartas, begins hunting for the ship but Crichton, Crais and Aeryn act as decoys and lead them away. There is a fierce firefight in which Xhalax is wounded in the leg and captured by Aeryn who takes her to Talyn. Crais is also wounded but he and Crichton evade the Colartas and run deeper into the jungle. Crichton stakes out Crais and when the Colartas come for Crais Crichton ambushes and kills them.

On Talyn, Xhalax breaks free of her bonds and stabs Rygel, who Stark sews up with restorative plants. She severs Talyn's higher functions and leaves Stark and Aeryn tied up as she goes to hunt for Crais. Rygel revives and releases Aeryn and Stark. Aeryn, Crichton, Crais, Xhalax and one of the Colartas who survived Crichton's ambush, meet in the jungle and there is another firefight. The Colartas is killed and Aeryn insists Xhalax must die also; Crais remains behind to kill her, and the shots are heard. Crais revives Talyn by splicing his consciousness with the ship's, and they fly free.

Black T: Crichton's distrust of Crais comes to the fore when he realises he's been lying to them about his motives, and when he stakes the Captain out to die it really looks as if he'll leave him there. When he reveals it was a ploy, and has killed the Colartas, he makes as if to walk away and leave Crais but as Crais points out, it's in Crichton's own best interests to keep him alive. Although he says there's been too much killing, Crichton doesn't protest too strongly against Xhalax being killed – though he won't let Aeryn shoot her own mother. The Crichton who let Crais live in **108**, 'That Old Black Magic', is gone and has been replaced by a desperate man of expedience who is more willing to let people die.

His first girlfriend was called Julie and mazes used to get her hot; he hates them.

You Can Be More: It seems that Xhalax didn't know she was hunting Aeryn, although she seems to recognise her at first. When she visited Aeryn as a child she was caught and punished for breaking PK rules; she redeemed herself by killing Aeryn's father, Talyn, who was older and less valuable as a soldier. Aeryn tries to reach Xhalax, to convince her that she is a rebel because her mother made her that way: 'she grew up wanting to be exactly like 'a woman I'd only seen once . . . I am the part of you that wanted to be a rebel, the part of you that knew deep down inside what was right.' Xhalax is having none of it and calls Aeryn an aberration whose corruption is too far advanced for redemption. Aeryn knows Xhalax must die to ensure Talyn's safety but she's distraught at her mother's death, understandably. With Xhalax dead Aeryn tells Crichton she 'was my last connection to the Peacekeepers. All my ties to them are now completely severed.'

Big Blue: When Stark bonded with Rygel to bring him back from death Stark says he encountered Zhaan. She seemed contented and said a prayer of Guardianship.

Buckwheat the Sixteenth: Rygel does indeed have three stomachs, and a tiny heart. He can wink. As ever he's planning to run out on his shipmates at the first opportunity, but doesn't get the chance. Even accounting for the restorative plants and Stark's help, he must be remarkably resilient to survive so severe a stabbing for any amount of time. He actually died for a few microts but was brought back by Stark.

The Man in the Iron Mask: Stark hums when he's nervous. He sews Rygel up very badly indeed – he actually stitches Rygel's robes into the wound. He's absolutely hopeless in a fight and his tactic for dealing with Xhalax seems to consist of running at her screaming and hoping she flinches.

The Insane Military Commander: Crais knew that a PK Squad would pursue him when he went rogue in **122**, 'Family Ties', so he stole Talyn and bonded himself to the ship in part to force the assistance of Crichton and the others. He knew they'd never raise a finger to help him but they would do anything for Talyn; as he puts it, 'I used all my assets to stay alive, and those assets were you.' When Crais protests that this is not the only reason he had for helping Crichton and company, it's hard not to conclude that his other motive was his plan to get into Aeryn's leather pants.

Hi, Harvey: Crichton's subconscious can summon Harvey without Crichton knowing he's doing it. It's Harvey who alerts Crichton to Crais's muddy motivations.

Big Baby: Sleeping in heavy gravity helps Talyn recuperate. With his higher functions severed he is powerless to act, so Crais splices his own neural engrams with Talyn's, allowing him self-will again. Unfortunately this means that a large part of Crais's personality now rests in Talyn.

Alien Encounters: Colartas have two hearts and can track by scent and body heat. They act as mercenaries and after nine successful missions they can buy their freedom; one failed mission and the counter resets to zero. Peacekeepers carry a drug for use in combat that can enhance strength and dull pain.

Get Frelled: Aeryn: 'You were louder than that, believe it or not.' Black T Crichton and Aeryn are at it and they're LOUD. Rygel is disgusted that Crichton, who is loudest, sounds like he's exerting himself, so we can assume the skill of Hynerian nookie is to appear effortless. Crichton enjoys banging the wall and faking too, just to torment the Dominar. Stark likes to listen so, like Rygel, he's a bit of a perv.

Stats: Some of the gasses on the planet interfere with PK weapons. Oarusk fruits are acidic and Crichton uses some of their juice to cauterise Crais's wound.

Logic Leaps: This episode appears to wrap up the Retrieval Squad threat so Talyn can contact Moya again. Given the ease with which Talyn's located Moya in the past it's a bit of a leap that they are not together in the next episode.

The Retrieval Squad, which boasts Prowlers and a ship strong enough nearly to destroy Talyn, consists solely of

Xhalax Sun and three mercenaries? Surely the planet would have been swarming with PK troops.

Bloopers: Crichton uses the Colartas's tracking device to lead him back to Talyn, but earlier the Colartas didn't use it to find the ship.

The Verdict: The evolution of Aeryn continues and Claudia Black acts her socks off in an episode that goes right to the heart of the character and shows just how far she's come, and how far back her rebellious streak goes. The ending is a cop-out, though, as no one believes for a moment that Xhalax is actually dead. If Crais had really shot her it would have been shown on screen, so he spared her, but why? Studio-set forests are always difficult to realise but this one is very good indeed. It's great to see Black T Crichton and Aeryn together and so obviously happy – how long can it last; when's the other shoe going to drop?

311
Incubator

1st US Transmission Date: 13 July 2001
1st UK Transmission Date: 12 November 2001

Writer: Richard Manning
Director: Ian Watson
Guest Cast: Tammy MacIntosh (Jool), David Franklin (Lt Braca), Amy Salas (Tauza), Evan Sheaves (Young Scorpius), Stephanie Jacobsen (Nurse Froy), Paul Shedlowich (Plint), Jo Kerrigan (Linfer), Danny Adcock (Co-Kura Strappa), Thomas Holesgrove (Wolesh), Sam Healy (Rylani Jeema Dellos), Nicholas Bishop (Ghebb Dellos), William Zappa (Captain Molayne)

Note: *This episode features the crew of Moya.*

On the Command Carrier Scorpius discovers that some of the equations extracted from Crichton's neuro chip are so strongly encrypted that they cannot be accessed. He inserts the chip into his own head and makes contact with a neural clone of Crichton contained within it. He tells this version of Crichton his life story, explains his motivations, and tries to persuade him to unlock the encrypted equations. The neural clone refuses and the chip is destroyed, but not before Scorpius extracts a few of the equations.

Linfer, one of the scientists helping Scorpius research wormholes, is so convinced that she has cracked the liquefaction problem (**309**, 'Losing Time') that she pilots a test herself. She takes some of Scorpius's data, flies through a nexus of wormholes and defects to Moya. She offers to give Crichton all her research if he will give her Moya. Crichton wants to accept the deal, telling his shipmates he can use wormholes to get them all home. Unfortunately Linfer's solution is not as good as she thought – she has only delayed the onset of liquefaction, not prevented it. She leaves Moya in her Prowler and blows herself up.

Green T: 'You ever think we've been on this boat way too long?' Separated from Aeryn, stuck on Moya, Crichton is becoming obsessed with wormholes and he's driving everyone else up the wall. He's had them flying around for fifteen days looking for a wormhole that he thinks is out there. Pilot and D'Argo conspire to get him to sleep for twelve arns because he's spending all his time pacing on the bridge running scans. When Linfer makes her offer he tries to persuade the others to go for it, and he's angry when they allow Linfer to leave and kill herself. D'Argo turns on him and accuses him of contributing to Zhaan's death with his selfishness (and he's right, of course), and later Jool has a go as well, pointing out that he only supports Pilot when Pilot agrees with him. D'Argo none too subtly hints that it's sexual frustration that's really getting to Crichton, and Crichton doesn't disagree. He's concerned that Scorpius is ahead in the race for wormhole technology, and he's worried that if Linfer found Moya, Scorpius can too.

I was a Teenage Luxan: D'Argo and Crichton are bickering a lot, but D'Argo doesn't sustain the argument, whereas during the first season he would have tongued everyone unconscious and asserted his command.

Jool in the Crown: Jool takes action, allowing Linfer to leave without telling Crichton, and then giving Crichton a telling off. She also grabs a gun without a hint of complaint and stands with D'Argo and Chiana when Linfer comes aboard. She's definitely one of the crew now.

In the Driving Seat: Pilot would never abandon his crew, but he and Moya both long to voyage into truly uncharted deep space on a mission of pure exploration. If given a free choice he would probably have chosen to travel with Linfer and leave his current crew behind.

Nosferatu in Rubber: Crichton: 'Scorpy the teenage hero outwits the Scarrans, makes it look easy. You going for pity or applause?' This is essentially Scorpius's episode and we learn the story of his life. A group of Sebacean colonists were travelling in a Leviathan when Scarrans attacked it. Only one couple escaped and made planetfall on Montok 4 in a Transport Pod. They were located, whereupon a Scarran killed the male and kidnapped the female, Rylani, who was raped as part of a programme to determine whether Sebacean genetics could be useful to Scarrans. She died giving birth to the only one of ninety such experimental offspring to survive – Scorpius (although this is the name he chose for himself after his escape). Born with Sebacean heat delirium, Scorpius was a weak and feeble child whose first twelve cycles were a blur of pain. He was raised on a Dreadnought by a female Scarran named Tauza who tortured and humiliated him in an attempt to make him strong. She told him he was the product of a Sebacean breeding programme, but his ability to detect people's energy signatures told him she was lying. He escaped and went looking for information about his parents. During this time Tocet fitted him with a cooling system which he carried on his back and plugged into his head; also this is presumably the period in which he first met Natira (the 'Liars, Guns and Money' trilogy 219– 221).

Eventually he surrendered to a PK ship and gave them all his knowledge of the Scarrans in return for information about his parents. This led him to his mother's abandoned Transport Pod where Tauza had laid a trap. He was recaptured and tortured, but he managed to kill Tauza and escape. He then joined the Peacekeepers and rose through the ranks until he was given permission to begin his wormhole experiments. He does not want power, he wants revenge, and only by developing a superior weapon to prevent the Scarrans overrunning the universe can he get it. He sees his actions in pursuit of this goal as necessary and unavoidable: he is a man with a mission and will not be diverted from it.

This backstory completely changes our view of Scorpius; his motivations are clear, easy to understand and not hard to sympathise with, and he makes a genuine attempt to win neural clone Crichton over to his side simply by telling him the truth.

He can detect the energy signatures of creatures, and these signatures are different for every species (which finally explains how he knew Crichton was an impostor way back in **119**, 'Nerve'); they also change when people are lying (which tells us how he knew Crichton was being less than truthful in the same episode). He is surprisingly sentimental – he keeps a flower from Montok 4 in his quarters and strokes it with a wistful smile on his face. Who'd have thought it, the great softie?

A Ship, a Living Ship!: Moya is enjoying scanning for wormholes because it gives her a chance to fly free in space.

Worlds Apart: Rylani was born on New Heather and her Transport Pod landed on Montok 4.

Alien Encounters: Linfer is a Ralgarian, a peaceful race of explorers who travel into deep space on Leviathans. Pilot and Moya trust them implicitly. Once the Scarrans discovered that Sebacean genetics were no use to them they decided to destroy Sebaceans for ever. Scorpius claims that they will destroy all races, including humans, until they are the only remaining sentient life form. Female Scarrans have different-shaped heads to males and like wearing skin-tight black PVC, so we can see where Scorpius got his fetish for cute PVC-wearing nurses from. According to Scorpius the Scarran's main weakness is hubris. Peacekeepers have Purity Regulations to ensure that no one not of pure Sebacean blood is allowed to join. However, Scorpius demonstrates such loyalty that they waive these laws for him.

Disney on Acid: 'What am I . . . Holodeck Crichton?' neural clone Crichton riffs on *Star Trek: The Next Generation*.

Stats: A Flibisk is a small ten-legged creature that's good to eat but becomes ratty if prevented from mating. Scorpius tells Crichton that a PK Command Carrier destroyed a Scarran Dreadnought, even though in **314**, 'Infinite Possibilities I: Daedalus Demands', it becomes clear that Dreadnoughts are twice their size. Most wormholes are unstable and contain Rantath Flux variation, which is what is liquidising the PK pilots. Linfer has developed a system of Phase Negative Shield Deployment which, when programmed with the right Phase Progression, should protect against this, but it doesn't work. She claims the wormhole that brought Crichton from Earth was unusual in that it was stable and therefore didn't liquefy him – this implies that the wormholes in **303** and **304**, 'Self Inflicted Wounds' I & II were also unusually stable. The wormhole Scorpius is studying is part of a nexus of wormholes, one of which exits near Moya – so Crichton was right, there was a wormhole nearby.

Guest Stars: Sam Healy was on *All Saints* and now plays the demon Iara on *Beastmaster*. Nicholas Bishop is a regular on *Above the Law*. William Zappa was a regular on *The Sullivans*, *One Summer Again* and *House Rules*, as well as appearing in films such as *Mad Max II*, *Quigley Down Under* and *Mr Reliable*.

The Verdict: It's daring to run the risk of making Scorpius sympathetic, but his story is believable and very well realised – the look of young Scorpius, and the pre-PK young man with his coolant backpack, are especially nicely done. His motivations are entirely explained and nagging questions about his abilities are answered. Green T Crichton, meanwhile, is irritable, restless, now knows for certain that Scorpius is alive and in danger of beating him to wormhole technology, and is far and away less sympathetic than Scorpius. What other show would dare build up the villain and undercut the good guy's likeability to such an extent? It's a difficult balancing act they're attempting, but it's lots of fun to watch. There is also a lot of implied and unsettling horror in this episode which is not directly shown, except Tauza's marvellously grotesque death, which we get to see in all its gruesomeness.

312
Meltdown

1st US Transmission Date: 14 July 2001
1st UK Transmission Date: 19 November 2001

Writer: Matt Ford
Director: Ian Barry
Guest Cast: Susan Lyons (Sierjna), Mark Mitchell (Mu-Quillus),
Linda Cropper (Xhalax)

Note: *This episode features the crew of Talyn.*

The crew believes another Retrieval Squad will be dispatched; nonetheless they are trying, and failing, to contact Moya. Talyn is lured into a sun by radiation pulses generated by a being called Mu-Quillus. Talyn manages to resist, but only just, and the heat causes him to ooze Drexim mist which affects the crew's judgment. A woman called Sierjna manifests to Stark and he realises she is caught between life and death, held in limbo by Mu-Quillus. He bonds himself to Talyn in a vestigial pilot's Den in order to save the ship. Crichton and Aeryn locate Mu-Quillus's power source and destroy it with Talyn's cannon, killing Mu-Quillus and releasing Sierjna so that Stark can help her cross over to death.

Black T: 'Man, do I hate godlike aliens! I'll trade a critter for a godlike alien, any day.' Yeah, Crichton, you and me both. Crichton thinks that Crais betrayed them, let Xhalax live (**310**, 'Relativity') and promised to deliver her the crews of Talyn and Moya in return for PK reinstatement and Aeryn. Crais denies this, of course.

You Can Be More: Aeryn's technical expertise is coming on in leaps and bounds and she is now proficient at fixing Talyn's systems.

Buckwheat the Sixteenth: Rygel's response to the mist is to find and eat everything on the ship until he's dangerously huge, can't stop farting and begs to be shot just to end the gorging. He would rather bite a chunk out of Crais than take orders from him.

The Man in the Iron Mask: 'I am now Talyn's pilot, and we are flying back into the sun!' Stark saves the girl and the ship, but everyone just thinks he's a madman and a liability. When threatened by Crichton and Aeryn he sends a DRD after them, again showing that he can go from friend to foe in an instant. He believes he is a failure, having failed both Zhaan and Crichton, and it is only by calling on Zhaan's memory that he is brought back to the moment and restores his self-control. He now has knowledge that Crais finds threatening.

The Insane Military Commander: The Drexim mist heightens Crais's aggression and paranoia, leading him to assert his authority as ship's captain and shoot at things. Unfortunately no one seems to take him terribly seriously as an authority figure – Rygel bites his ear, Crichton ignores him and Aeryn just laughs in his face. He threatens to kill Stark if he tells anyone what he learned about Talyn's relationship with Crais when he was bonded to the ship.

Big Baby: Talyn is not yet fully healed from the PK Retrieval Squad attack and his electrical systems are fragile. He has shields and has grown a vestigial, but functional, pilot's Den even though he has no need of a pilot. A substance called Drexim improves Talyn's response time and reflexes in times of crisis. However, it can become acidic, burn the seals on the pipes and seep into the ship as a mist. It is not lethal but can act as a stimulant on the crew.

When Talyn accepts Stark as his pilot is it a conscious decision or is it an autonomic response triggered by the presence of a being in the pilot's space? While Stark is in place as pilot, Crais's neural transponder is inactive. Crais physically cuts Stark free of Talyn – is this because Talyn couldn't or wouldn't release him? Stark claims that he now knows how Talyn feels about Crais, and he implies that the relationship between ship and Captain is not as friendly as Crais wants his shipmates to believe.

Crais believes Talyn will grow to be as big as Moya.

The Ballad of Aeryn and John: Crichton tells Stark that Aeryn is his Zhaan, his soulmate, he loves her and would die for her.

Alien Encounters: If we believe Sierjna then Mu-Quillus was hired by the Pratikrah, a race of shipbuilders, to destroy Leviathans and thus increase demand for alternative ships. Mu-Quillus can manifest aboard Talyn at will and lives in the corona of the sun; he can change between matter and energy; he has no weapons and cannot act against Talyn's crew; he uses a power source in the sun's corona to transmit a pulse that lures Leviathans (83 so far) to their deaths; he keeps Sierjna trapped between life and death for reasons unknown. Sierjna is from Delfarion and was travelling in a Leviathan when she was captured by Mu-Quillus.

Disney on Acid: Crichton to Crais on his chances of becoming a PK again: 'Never say never again, 007', and if you don't know what film series that's a reference to then shame on you. 'All right, Phantom, new tune for the opera,' – Crichton referring to Stark's half mask as being like the Phantom's from Gaston Leroux's novel.

Get Frelled: Crichton and Aeryn react to the Drexim by going into a frenzy of sexual tension, hardly able to keep their hands off each other long enough to get anything done. It's hilarious to see, and when the gas has dispersed they christen Talyn's bridge.

Seen it all Before: How many times now have people in this show been driven nuts by external factors? It feels a bit tired this time around.

Logic Leaps: Mu-Quillus can live in the corona of a star, he can change from matter to energy, he can materialise inside a ship, he can suspend people between life and death, but he can't stop two people firing a cannon when he's *in the same room*? That's just daft. And why does he die when his power source is destroyed?

WHAT did you just say?: Zylimbron = a person who is trapped between life and death.

Guest Stars: Susan Lyons is a regular on *Dog's Head Bay*. Mark Mitchell appeared in *A Cry in the Dark* and *Inspector Gadget 2* and is a regular in *The Genie from Down Under*.

The Verdict: Paul Goddard is great, Aeryn and Crichton are hilarious, and Crais comes on like Officer Gordon from 215, 'Won't Get Fooled Again', but good performances and some funny bits do not a strong episode make. This is a weak instalment that doesn't go anywhere terribly interesting or stay long in the memory after it's gone; this is fast food compared to the three-course meal *Farscape* usually serves.

313
Scratch 'n' Sniff

1st US Transmission Date: 20 July 2001
1st UK Transmission Date: 24 November 2001

Writer: Lily Taylor
Director: Tony Tilse

Guest Cast: Tammy MacIntosh (Jool), Francesca Buller (Raxil),
Tamblyn Lord (Fe'Tor), Laura Keneally (Theiadh),
Anthony Martin (Mitols), Milan Keyser (Sarl), Jaye Paul (Heska Tinaco),
Julia Trappe (Blue Girl), Rachel Sheriff (Green Girl),
Richard Carter (Voice of Kabaah)

Note: *This episode features the crew of Moya. It takes the
form of a tale being told by Crichton to Pilot and as such
may or may not be a complete lie on Crichton's part.*

Pilot throws Crichton and D'Argo off the ship because
they bicker constantly. They and the girls then head to a
pleasure planet, LoMo. At a bar Crichton and D'Argo are
picked up by two girls who spike their drinks and steal
their money. Jool and Chiana leave with local hotshot
Fe'Tor. The next morning, heavy with hangovers, Crichton
and D'Argo meet Raxil, a female alien who was at the
bar the previous night. She claims that Fe'Tor is big
trouble, and takes them to a creature who can show them
pictures of what happened in the bar last night. They see
Fe'Tor giving Chi a hit of some smelly drug called
Freslin. D'Argo goes to Fe'Tor's house and breaks in
but finds Chi and Jool drugged up, blissed out and
unwilling to leave. Fe'Tor's guards throw D'Argo out.
Raxil reveals that Freslin is a drug milked from the glands
of people. Fe'Tor is the local producer and sometimes he
milks people till they die. Back at the house Fe'Tor hooks
Jool up to the milking machine and begins to extract
Freslin.

It turns out that Raxil paid the two girls at the bar to
distract Crichton and D'Argo so that Fe'Tor could capture
Jool and Chi. Raxil's heard of their exploits and is hoping
that when they rescue their shipmates they will rescue her
mate, who is also being held captive in Fe'Tor's house.

Fe'Tor calls an auction to sell Chiana, whose Freslin is
particularly high quality. Crichton and a disguised D'Argo
enter the auction but Crichton is outbid. Crichton shoots
out the lights and rescues Chi while D'Argo and Raxil
storm the milking room and disconnect Jool. Raxil's mate
is there and he is dead, but she has one more trick up her
sleeve: her mate stole the milking machine from her and

she was really using Crichton and D'Argo to get in there so she could remove the program chip from the machine and set up in Freslin production herself. She runs off with the chip, happy that her convoluted plan has worked. Fe'Tor fights Crichton but Chiana douses him in Freslin and then pours it down his throat, killing him. Back on Moya, Crichton explains that he and D'Argo can't return to LoMo because they'd be arrested, but Pilot refuses to believe Crichton's tale, takes them to an industrial planet, and throws them off the ship for another eight days.

Green T: 'It's a weird universe out there, man.' Is Crichton just making it all up? Who knows, chances are it's partly true. He and D'Argo bicker almost constantly, like children in a schoolyard. His first worry when he wakes up after being ripped off is that he's lost his pulse pistol – he's come to rely on it so much that he feels naked without it. We get to see Crichton in thigh-high stockings, causing women all across the world to swoon, and producers to add Ben Browder to their list of possible actors to play Frank N. Furter in their next production of *The Rocky Horror Picture Show*.

I was a Teenage Luxan: D'Argo tells the ladies that he is full-blooded Luxan and that he has a lot of cash. So 'the three of us will be out of here on our hands and knees come sunrise tomorrow morning. I've been arrested for saying exactly the same thing on four different planets.' It was D'Argo's idea to go to LoMo, implying that he finally persuaded Crichton to accept the need to wind down. When he's on Freslin he dances like crazy and does the funky chicken.

Everyone's Favourite Little Tralk: Chiana can twirl fireballs on chains so fast that she can render a viewer unconscious. She's become quite protective of Jool, promising to take her back to Moya if she passes out, and anxiously trying to find her when she suspects something is wrong at Fe'Tor's house. Her visions of the future are becoming more specific – she removes Crichton's night-vision goggles

just before he is punched in the face, but she knew his neck
would be fine. She produces particularly fine Freslin. Once
again she proves ruthless and vengeful – she kills Fe'Tor
and enjoys doing it.

Jool in the Crown: Jool can do acrobatics, likes to drink
effervescent alcohol, can get drunk, likes to dance (especially with Chiana), enjoys bubble baths, and is only in
the bar for a short time before she's been pegged by fellow
drinkers as 'annoying'. Her com badge is melted around
the edges from when she screams.

In the Driving Seat: Pilot is so sick and tired of Crichton
and D'Argo arguing that he throws them off the ship,
refuses to believe Crichton's explanation of events on
LoMo, and then dumps them on an industrial planet as
punishment. Crichton asks how long they've known each
other and Pilot replies 'approximately two and a half
loooooong cycles', but he concedes that Crichton has never
lied to him before.

Hi, Harvey: When D'Argo and Crichton are using the
Hangi to scope out the auction room, Harvey is able to
meet and interact with D'Argo. He asks the Luxan to give
him five, hands out very useful information indeed on the
layout of the complex (how did he know this?) and camps
it up for all he's worth. Crichton calls him a Pooka, which
is the type of spirit in the original film *Harvey*.

A Ship, a Living Ship!: Pilot isn't the only one sick of
Crichton and D'Argo's bickering – Moya too wants a few
days' peace and quiet.

The Ballad of Chiana and D'Argo: Although D'Argo and
Chi aren't together any more – a point she raises when
telling him to leave her alone at Fe'Tor's house – he gets
very jealous indeed when Crichton manhandles Chi on the
auction stage.

Worlds Apart: LoMo is renowned as a pleasure planet and
it boasts lovely beaches. Officially no weapons are allowed

on the planet, although Fe'Tor's men have guns. It is close to an industrial world that has accommodation for visitors.

Alien Encounters: Hangis have removable eyes that continue to send signals back to them which they can record. Stick a Hangi's tentacle into your eye and you can experience the recording as 3D visions with surround sound.

Disney on Acid: Crichton calls D'Argo Lassie and refers to Raxil and the Hangi as Ren and Stimpy.

Get Frelled: You've got to reckon that Jool and Chiana got up to all sorts of mischief during their drugged-up night at Fe'Tor's. We don't how far Crichton and D'Argo got with the feathered girls but D'Argo claims there were 'breasts; blue breasts, green breasts, I don't know'. Chi and Jool dancing together was not a little suggestive.

What Does This Do?: The senal gland of most sentient creatures produces a chemical called Freslin which is a powerful aphrodisiac, attractant and, um, disguise!

Stats: Brandar tiles are acceptable currency on LoMo. Crichton and D'Argo have plenty of them, presumably from the Shadow Depository raid (**221**, 'Liars, Guns and Money III: Plan B').

Seen it all Before: This episode riffs on the movie *Swingers* and stylistically it owes a lot to the marvellous and criminally short-lived series *Good vs Evil*. Fe'Tor is reputed to have the finest nose around, and he tells Chi that she 'smells exotic'; shades of Patrick Susskind's book *Perfume*.

Logic Leaps: Cunningly, any things which may appear to defy logic are accounted for by the script and in some cases are even specifically mentioned – to wit the amount of liquid drained from Jool, the daft idea that Freslin can also be used to disguise a person etc. Pilot even says, 'I don't believe you . . . too many inconsistencies, too much obfuscation.' One leap that isn't addressed though is the way the Hangi's eyes work: Raxil says its optic nerves record images and transmit them back to the body, but when Crichton and D'Argo see the recording they hear sound as well, so the Hangi can *see* sound?

Bloopers: When Jool screams we can see Tammy MacIntosh's fillings.

WHAT did you just say?: Raxil on Crichton: 'You're not very smart, are you? Now he [D'Argo], he's got a brain. But you, you're a bit of an idiot.'

Guest Stars: Welcome back Francesca Buller, for the third time (she previously appeared in **121**, 'Bone to be Wild' and **210** and **211**, 'Look at the Princess' I & II). Tamblyn Lord was a regular on *The Law of the Land*. Laura Keneally appeared in *Dark City*. Richard Carter has appeared in *Babe: Pig in the City*, and *Muriel's Wedding* among other film and TV appearances.

Backstage: The BBC in the UK realised that if they were to cut this episode to fit the normal *Farscape* 6.45 p.m. time-slot there'd be nothing left to broadcast, so they showed it at 11.20 p.m. instead. When Raxil shouts at the guys for bringing 'two little weapons that wouldn't kill a Negnec' there is a split-second flash of a squeaking, blobby creature with an eye. This is a shot of the Boolite taken from **318**, 'Fractures'.

Gigi Edgley did her own fire twirling. She is also sporting a new wig in this episode. Despite the fact that it is cut in such a way that it looks like a stunt double, Tammy Macintosh did actually perform Jool's acrobatic back flips herself. Anthony Simcoe told *DreamWatch* that 'Scratch 'n' Sniff' was his favourite episode of Season Three because it was crazy. 'I love *Farscape* when it's left of centre; when it takes really bizarre and weird and odd choices. Tony Tilse took us right out on the edge and it was really fun to play.'

The Verdict: Amazing – it just doesn't get much better than this. The jump cuts, the insane editing, the music, the colour, the SM costumes, the drugs, the drink, the sex, the gun fight – this episode oozes style, confidence, class and wit from every pore. All this, plus Fran Buller's hilarious turn as Raxil, makes this episode as close to perfect as TV gets.

314
Infinite Possibilities I: Daedalus Demands

1st US Transmission Date: 27 July 2001
1st UK Transmission Date: 26 November 2001

Writer: Carleton Eastlake
Director: Peter Andrikidis
Guest Cast: Kent McCord (Jack Crichton), Magda Szubanski (Furlow),
Patrick Ward (Zylar)

Note: *This two-parter features the crew of Talyn.*

The Ancients have found a new homeworld (116, 'A Human Reaction'), but on their way there they encounter a copy of Crichton's module flying through an unstable wormhole. The Ancient who appeared to Crichton as his father, Jack, remains behind to find out who is using wormholes and stop them. He summons Crichton and Talyn and they establish that Furlow (111, 'Till the Blood Runs Clear') is the most likely suspect, so they go to Dam-Ba-Da. The planet is ravaged by solar flares and has been carpet-bombed.

They find that Furlow has built a copy of Crichton's module and equipped it with a Phase Stabiliser which allows her to travel through unstable wormholes. She recruited a race, the Charrids, to help but they tied her up, took over the depot and summoned their allies, the Scarrans. Crichton and Aeryn rescue Furlow, seize the depot from the Charrids and prepare to destroy the wormhole technology. They discover that a Scarran Dreadnought is five arns away and has hacked into Furlow's computers and uploaded all the wormhole data. Jack says he can unlock the hidden wormhole knowledge in Crichton's head and together they can modify the Phase Stabiliser into a weapon which will destroy the Dreadnought.

Crichton tells Jack about Harvey and they agree that Harvey must be expelled before the knowledge is unlocked. But when Jack tries to expel the neural clone mentally he is knocked unconscious. It appears that Harvey is now in permanent control of Crichton . . .

Talyn is caught in a solar flare and is blinded and severely damaged (again!). Crais is also blinded and he and Stark return to Talyn to try and help with repairs.

Rygel mans an automated gun turret outside the depot to help repel the Charrids. He is caught in a mortar blast and badly wounded (again!).

Black T: When Jack placed the wormhole knowledge in Crichton's mind he left a residual link between them, which he uses to summon Crichton. Crichton's resentment at the Ancient's placing the wormhole knowledge in his brain shows, but he doesn't want to tell Jack about Scorpius at first because he's afraid Jack may react badly.

You Can Be More: Aeryn is willing to shoot Crichton rather than let Harvey take over completely.

Buckwheat the Sixteenth: 'Taste this, bloodsucker!' Rygel tries to fly off in the Transport Pod and leave Crichton, Crais and Aeryn to die in combat with the Charrids; it's only Stark threatening him with a gun that forces him to remain. The sick little slug tortures the captured Charrid to death and enjoys it enormously. He's effective, too, managing to get the defiant critter to spill his guts about the Scarran Dreadnought. When he's posted by Aeryn to man the gun turret he's extremely reluctant, but once he's had a while to get used to it he has a great time.

Rygel IX led the charge at the battle of Katreen; Rygel considers him a fool because Dominars are too important to risk in combat.

The Man in the Iron Mask: Once again he's getting freaky, thanking Aeryn way too much for the goggles she gives him, and taunting Rygel that she likes him more than the Dominar. Perhaps he's developing a little crush. After Crais threatened him with a knife in **310**, 'Relativity' it's nice to see the tables turned, as blind Crais has to put himself in Stark's hands. Of course, since Talyn and Crais are sightless and Stark is monocular, it's demonstrably true that 'in the kingdom of the blind the one-eyed man is king'.

The Insane Military Commander: Why does Crais come down to Dam-Ba-Da with Crichton and Aeryn? It's not his fight after all. Could he genuinely consider himself part of the crew and one of the team? He doesn't exactly have the highest opinion of Stark.

Hi, Harvey: Harvey is becoming more confident: he plucks Crichton from Jack's mental interrogation, talks to him, suggests Furlow's involvement and then pops him back to Jack, all without Jack noticing. When he realises Crichton and Jack are about to try and expel him he tries to strike a deal, swearing he's only interested in survival and not in taking over or getting all the wormhole knowledge from Crichton. Crichton rejects his pleas for co-existence and so Harvey has no choice but to fight for control. When the 'to be continued . . .' caption flashes up it looks like he's won.

Big Baby: Talyn comes flying to the rescue of Crais, Crichton and Aeryn when they're pinned down by Charrids, even though he knows the solar flares will fry him in the process. He then retreats into the planet's shadow to recuperate.

The Ballad of Aeryn and John: Crichton doesn't want to return to Earth without Aeryn and she doesn't want him to either – maybe she is considering going with him? He is teaching her to read English.

Worlds Apart: Dam-Ba-Da has been levelled by the solar flares and is now a barren, uninhabited world. Furlow lied to Crichton about the frequency of the solar flares (**111**, 'Till the Blood Runs Clear') in order to keep him away so she could pursue wormhole research on her own.

Alien Encounters: A thousand cycles ago the Charrids invaded Hyneria. They killed billions and ate a million

Hynerian young. They were eventually repelled by millions upon millions of suicide bombers. It's unclear whether the suicide soldiers were volunteers or were forced.

The Charrids are allies of the Scarrans. Scarran Dreadnoughts are twice the size of PK Command Carriers. The Ancients are now settled on a new world but they are a 'dying race' and probably could not repel an alien attack.

Jack cannot read Crichton's mind deeply enough to tell whether he is lying or not; he can sense approaching solar flares; he is not susceptible to radiation. The Ancients would destroy Crichton and Jack if they knew they were intending to build a wormhole weapon.

Stats: Furlow has piloted her module through an unstable proto-wormhole four times and survived because of the Phase Stabiliser. This is the device Scorpius is trying to build but he still hasn't managed it, even though he's got the advantage of the equations from the neuro chip and a team of scientists. Furlow must be a frelling genius to do it on her own with the little data Crichton collected in 111, 'Till the Blood Runs Clear'.

Logic Leaps: Why did Green T Crichton not answer Jack's summons as well? Surely both Talyn and Moya could have been expected to turn up.

Bloopers: Furlow's facial scar changes size and shape alarmingly at a couple of points. Crais may be blinded but why does he not don goggles when next exposed to a solar flare? Just because he can't see it doesn't mean it won't further damage his retinas.

Backstage: Ben Browder pulled a hamstring while shooting this two-parter and was sent to a local doctor. When asked how he'd got his injury, he explained that he'd been sprinting across the sand, with a gun in one hand and a grenade in the other. When the doctor enquired about the gun and the grenade and Browder explained that he was attacking an alien base, she started thumbing through her Rolodex. 'I realised that they didn't tell her what I do for a living! I'm . . . [saying] that I'm attacking an alien base, and she's like, getting ready to call the police or a shrink or something!' Ben Browder told *SFX*.

The Verdict: Carleton Eastlake's first script for the show is action packed, has lots of nice touches and ends on a superb multiple cliffhanger – Rygel wounded, Talyn and Crais blinded, Jack unconscious, Crichton taken over by Harvey, Aeryn about to shoot him and all the while an invincible Scarran Dreadnought is on the way. The assault on the Dam-Ba-Da depot is amazingly violent and builds up Crichton and Aeryn into a near invincible killing machine – they polish off at least twenty Charrids without breaking a sweat. Furlow's return is welcome and funny; the new CGI look for the Ancients is so much better than the lamentable puppet of **116**, 'A Human Reaction'; for an episode concerned with wormhole technology the technobabble meter stays low and it's easy to understand what's going on. The fantasy sequence with Crichton battling Harvey is great and the funfair setting works well; nice stunt work with them hanging off the roller coaster, too.

315
Infinite Possibilities II: Icarus Abides

1st US Transmission Date: 3 August 2001
1st UK Transmission Date: 3 December 2001

Writer: Carleton Eastlake
Director: Peter Andrikidis
Guest Cast: Kent McCord (Jack Crichton), Magda Szubanski (Furlow),
Thomas Holesgrove (Alcar), Noel Hodda (Charrid Leader 2)

'It's a lucky or an unambitious man who goes when he's ready . . . Scorpius is gone, I'm at peace . . . I'm proud of my life, and I'm with you . . . I've never felt better.'

Crichton recovers, Harvey dies; Rygel continues to fight despite his wound; a Scarran scout sent ahead of the Dreadnought boards Talyn. Stark and Crais join forces, fool the Scarran into taking a neural transponder and thus give Talyn time to recover enough to shoot the critter with his internal guns.

Jack and Crichton convert the Phase Stabiliser into a Displacement Engine; it has no off switch, can only be used once, and 1.4 arns after activation it will meltdown. Furlow, who has been working with the Charrids all along, kills Jack but when the two Charrids hiding in the depot double-cross her she kills them too and tells Crichton and Aeryn that they killed Jack. She then steals the Displacement Engine and drives off with it. Crichton and Aeryn give chase causing Furlow to crash, which in turn activates the Engine. Knowing it'll be useless before she can sell it to the Scarrans, Furlow does a runner. The Engine is leaking radiation so Crichton has to close the lid, but in doing so he receives a lethal dose. He uses the Engine to destroy the Dreadnought and returns to Talyn, where he dies in Aeryn's arms.

Black T: 'I wouldn't change it for the world. You made me a better person.' Free of Harvey, and with all the wormhole knowledge unlocked, Crichton tells Aeryn that he can finally go home, mere minutes before receiving the dose of radiation that he knows will kill him. He flies the module, deploys the Displacement Engine, and returns to Talyn to die. He tells Rygel he's going to miss him but he can't have his stuff. Stark helps him pass by sharing some of his energy, and Crichton dies.

And you sobbed. Go on admit it. No shame in it.

You Can Be More: 'I would have gone to Earth.' Aeryn takes out a Charrid vehicle by dropping a grenade and then shooting it when the car drives over it; she doesn't want to kill the driver but he decides to fight rather than run, so she has no choice. The Aeryn of Season One wouldn't even have hesitated to shoot the Charrid instantly.

Aeryn breaks down the last of her barriers when she decides that she will go with Crichton to Earth. All her resistance to emotion and love is gone, eroded by two and a half cycles of Crichton's patience, kindness and love. And just when she's finally committed, open and happy the clumsy yotz goes and dies on her. No wonder she's a total wreck at the end. The emotional fallout will be terrible and how will she react when the inevitable reunion with Green T Crichton takes place?

Buckwheat the Sixteenth: Rygel the war hero fights on despite his wounds, although the discovery that the Charrids were never attacking properly, because they were in league with Furlow all along, somewhat detracts from his achievement. He tells dying Crichton: 'It will be hard not to think of you.'

The Man in the Iron Mask: Stark earns some respect from Crais by playing a dangerous bluffing game with the Scarran. He plays the part of menial, disaffected slave all too well and manages to save all their lives in the process. He displays no hint of his tendency to wig out either, so perhaps real pressure is what's needed to keep him focused. Crichton holds Stark's hand against his head after he's received his energy, and they seem to have some sort of unspoken understanding . . .

The Insane Military Commander: With the Scarran on Talyn killed, Crais and Talyn could leave – in fact Crichton orders them to – but Crais insists on staying and risking his life, and Talyn's, to help destroy the Dreadnought. Crichton replies, grudgingly: 'Damn it Crais, knock it off. You're gonna make me start liking you.' Crichton tells Crais to 'find the better part of yourself; you have to take care of them,' and Crais promises that he will. Indeed, perhaps he's already some way there already – his actions in this two-parter have been loyal and honourable to a fault.

Hi, Harvey: Harvey is beaten by Crichton and Jack, but as he dies he manages to seize control of Crichton long enough to convince Aeryn that Crichton is dead. She is just about to shoot Crichton when Jack stops her. The neural clone's last gambit fails and he dies, leaving Crichton's mind free. As he dies he tells Aeryn that next time she should 'be more decisive, shoot quicker. A soldier must not be weak. Weakness means defeat.' Of course Green T still has a Harvey, so there may indeed be a next time.

Big Baby: Talyn can use his neural transponder delivery system to immobilise a person, perhaps by electrocuting them. His impulse to panic and fire when in danger also seems to be better under control – he allows Crais to use him as bait and doesn't fire on the Dreadnought, even when targeted. Perhaps the neural graft (**310**, 'Relativity') has given him a cooler head courtesy of Crais.

Talyn has two Docking Bays.

The Ballad of Aeryn and John: When Harvey is finally expelled, Aeryn just can't keep her hands off Crichton – she's groping, kissing, hanging on to him for dear life even while he's discussing technical matters with Jack. Good grief, get a room!

Get Frelled: Crichton asks Furlow if it's always about the money and she queries whether there *is* anything else. 'I mean, how much sex can you have?' Crichton replies, 'I don't know, I haven't maxed out yet.'

Alien Encounters: Scarrans always send a reconnaissance scout, or a scout party, ahead of their Dreadnoughts.

Stats: Crichton does not perform a slingshot to open the wormhole, so the Displacement Engine must create it, but it still seems to require the presence of solar flares. The module circles the wormhole with the Displacement Engine doing whatever it does until the wormhole touches the surface of the star and then ejects a huge ball of burning star material. The target is burned up and swallowed by the wormhole until both target and wormhole burn out. This weapon is so powerful that Crichton reckons it could destroy a planet. He also claims he can now build a device to get him home and that Aeryn can come with him, which confirms that the liquidation problems being experienced by Scorpius are solvable.

Logic Leaps: OK, you're probably going to hate me for this but it's got to be said . . . why didn't Crichton just walk behind the Engine and close the lid by throwing something at it? A well-thrown shoe or gun could have closed the cover at no risk at all to Crichton. I don't want to take away from his noble sacrifice and all that, but come on, what a *dumb* way to die!!

Bloopers: Furlow's re-creation of Crichton's module has IASA and United States logos painted on it.

Backstage: David Kemper talked to *DreamWatch* about killing off the lead character on the show: 'It wasn't a fake . . . it wasn't a dream; he doesn't come back, he wasn't a clone, he wasn't half our hero or unworthy of living – he was Crichton . . . And we killed him.'

The Verdict: Heartbreaking and unbelievably cruel to the characters, this is top-notch drama. To have all Crichton and Aeryn's dreams come true, only to have him condemned to death minutes later, is horrible beyond words and has repercussions for Aeryn's character throughout the rest of the show's run. Claudia Black and Ben Browder act their socks off, really convincing us of how in sync these two are and how dreadful it is to be separated after everything they've been through. Also, we now know that Green T can be freed of Harvey and can conceivably build a wormhole device to take him home. Plus Furlow is still out there – she's lost her lab and her data but she's got all the necessary knowledge in her head to start again.

316
Revenging Angel

1st US Transmission Date: 10 August 2001
1st UK Transmission Date: 17 December 2001

Writer: David Kemper
Director: Andrew Prowse
Guest Cast: Tammy MacIntosh (Jool)

Note: *This episode features the crew of Moya.*

D'Argo is practising in the D'Argomobile when the self-destruct engages. He believes it is Crichton's fault and loses his temper, pushing Crichton into a pile of crates. Crichton is knocked unconscious. While he lies in a coma, near death, Harvey tries to give him a reason to live – revenge. Crichton turns to imaginary versions of his friends to ask their advice: Pilot recommends flight, Jool advises talking, and Chi suggests outsmarting D'Argo. In an imaginary Looney Tunes world D'Argo chases Crichton but always comes off worst, playing Wile E Coyote to Crichton's Road Runner. Eventually Crichton takes fantasy revenge on D'Argo, but he dies anyway until the thought of his love for Aeryn gives him reason to live, and he revives.

The D'Argomobile sends out an energy pulse that cripples Moya and traps the crew aboard as it counts down to self-destruct. D'Argo furiously throws his Qualta Blade from Pilot's Den into the depths of the ship. He later discovers that the ship responds to ancient Luxan and the self-destruct can be cancelled if the ship is given, you guessed it, a Qualta Blade.

Jool admits to D'Argo that it was she who caused the problem with the ship, but she somewhat makes up for it by wading through a sea of bat crap and finding the sword just in time. The ship is unlocked and now responds to D'Argo's commands.

Green T: Crichton's list of reasons to live: 'Earth, dad, pizza, sex, cold beer, fast cars, sex, Aeryn, love.' Marty Goldstein stole Crichton's bike when he was seven so Crichton went round to his house and gave him a bloody nose. He forgives D'Argo, in part because he doesn't even know why they're fighting, but also because nothing would ever make him take revenge on him. After his near death experience he goes to get some space – literally – by sitting outside the ship in a pressure suit.

I was a Teenage Luxan: 'I have nothing. Nothing! I have no wife, no son, no home, nothing! I have been forced to manufacture distractions in order to live.' D'Argo has been spending more and more time alone in the D'Argomobile, working out its control by trial and error, and has managed to lift off the Maintenance Bay floor four times. But it's just a distraction to keep him from going nuts. When he believes Crichton, who's winding him up anyway, has triggered the self-destruct he draws his Qualta Blade on him and succumbs to hyper-rage. He throws the sword away in disgust at his own actions and later apologises to Crichton, though he feels his apology is inadequate. 'I've so much rage inside, so many things. Sometimes I just need to control it better. It's a curse, John, a warrior heritage, my instincts.' He finds Jool's hair in the controls of the ship so he realises it's her fault before she tells him, but he doesn't confront her till she admits her mistake – he is touched by her attempt to make friends with him.

He is the son of Laytun, grandson of Reksa, and the great-grandson of Ka D'Argo Traytal. Luxans have a code that 'aggression against an ally entitles retribution'.

Everyone's Favourite Little Tralk: Chiana has another premonition and warns Jool about a piece of falling metal before D'Argo dislodges it. She hates Jool with a passion and has started to think of her as a child, but she still warns Jool not to admit her mistake to D'Argo in case he kills her. She suggests shooting the D'Argomobile to try and stop the countdown and she kisses and hugs D'Argo when the ship eventually acquiesces. Crichton thinks she is the 'sultana of survival'.

Jool in the Crown: 'I know that I can be difficult, that no one wants to spend time with me.' Jool takes good care of Crichton and even kisses him on the forehead as he lies in a coma, betraying how much a part of the crew she's become. She and Chiana argue all the time. Her culture passes on its history and languages at school, and she's disgusted that Luxans don't: 'It's savage. I'll wager there are no artists or chefs there either.' Despite this it's D'Argo she wants to make friends with. She tells him she likes him and she tried to learn about his ship to give them both something to talk about. She and D'Argo actually make friends, and he promises to give her the first ride in his ship when he's worked out how to fly it. This is the first episode where she's really likeable and Crichton is obviously warming to her, because in his imagination she's the one who recommends talking to D'Argo and considers that 'conflict is for barbarians'.

In the Driving Seat: Pilot accepts that he and Moya will probably die when the D'Argomobile self-destructs but advises the rest of the crew on ways of surviving the explosion. Jool is upset at the prospect of leaving him, and he and Moya later thank her for saving the ship. So Jool has two friends on board, at least.

Hi, Harvey: 'We are gathered here today to pay our final respects . . . to our dear friend, Commander John Crichton, a schmuck. Mule-headed, reckless, and probably brain-dead before I met him.' Harvey tries to keep Crichton alive because his death means Harvey's death too. What a contrast to **301**, 'Season of Death', when Harvey wanted to kill Crichton to be free. Revenge is the one ruling emotion of Scorpius's life, and Harvey has inherited that monomania, believing that revenge is the only emotion strong enough to keep a person alive through sheer force of will. Although he eventually rejects Harvey's advice, Crichton thanks him for it in a friendly manner, seemingly accepting that they are now allies.

A Ship, a Living Ship!: All of Moya's systems are frelled by the energy pulse that signifies the start of the self-destruct countdown. Moya is host to 'a panoply of harmless parasites, many serving symbiotic functions'. Among these are swarms of Hodian Trill-Bats whose copious dren lies in a huge lake at the bottom of Moya and spreads along her inner hull, helping seal small cracks. The pressure hatchway on Tier 16's treblin side can be pressurised and detached, acting as a lifeboat if Moya is destroyed.

The Ballad of Aeryn and John: Crichton's love for Aeryn is the thing that keeps him alive. He imagines her in lingerie.

then as Jessica Rabbit, Marilyn Monroe, Cleopatra, Dorothy (from *The Wizard of Oz*), Madonna, Pamela Anderson and what could be either Nancy Reagan or Hilary Rodham-Clinton. He's trying not to think about what she and Black T are up to on Talyn.

The Ballad of Chiana and D'Argo: D'Argo tells Chi he does not like to lose and she retorts, 'Well, then why'd you let go of me,' conveniently forgetting that she wanted him to.

Disney on Acid: Where to begin . . . the animated sequences are a lengthy and brilliant homage to the animated work of Chuck Jones, who died in February 2002, especially his Road Runner cartoons. In the animated sequences you can see the Starship Enterprise, the space station from *2001*, the Mir space station, a flying toaster, McDonald's arches and, in a cunning tribute both to Looney Tunes and Australia, all of animated D'Argo's toys are made by the Ozme company. Captain Kirk is still his touchstone, but not, perhaps, William Shatner. He says he doesn't want to stoop as low as to be like Harvey, because Kirk wouldn't stoop that low. Harvey's reply is: 'That was a television show, John. And he made Priceline commercials. But if you insist, then look to Kirk the way he really was – savage when he had to be.'

Crichton gives Harvey the Letterman list of reasons to live, taken from the top ten list on *The David Letterman Show*. There are mentions for, among others, *Forrest Gump*, *Basic Instinct* and *Natural Born Killers*.

Stats: The D'Argomobile is ancient Luxan and can be operated only with the use of a Qualta Blade, a Freedom text or an Orican's prayer amulet. It is voice activated and has two panels at the front of the ship which can turn clear to allow forward vision. The ship's systems include: power systems, telemetry functions, deception shroud, sonic accelerator, particulisation field, weapons cascade, and communications array.

Seen it all Before: Every time a Road Runner cartoon comes on television.

Logic Leaps: What are the chances that D'Argo's ship turns out to be ancient Luxan? And what was it doing floating free near the space station in **302**, 'Suns and Lovers'?

WHAT did you just say?: Now we have an explanation of why sometimes D'Argo's curses are heard as Luxan rather than translated through the microbes: the microbes have to be programmed with a specific language and ancient Luxan, which is the language D'Argo swears in even though he cannot actually speak it, is not in the microbes' program. Supplemental programs can be created, and Pilot compiles one from scraps of Ancient Luxan in Moya's database.

Backstage: David Kemper, Executive Producer and Head Writer, speaking in *Starburst*, said that, when they were going to do a cartoon episode, no one else, except Andrew Prowse, wanted to do it. 'A lot of people stepped away from that one. Other people got on board, but none of the powers wanted it done because it was a huge risk, a huge financial risk.' In another interview, this time in *Dream-Watch*, he continued, saying that when the episode began to take shape, 'we had a lot of people who had been saying, "This is a stupid idea, let's not do it," saying "Isn't this great? It's wonderful!" I'm really, really proud of it ...' Ben Browder also talked to *Cult Times* about this episode – an important one for Crichton's character as the audience doesn't know where the character is at this point. 'Taken outside the context of the series, the episode is OK, but within the context of the series it's very powerful. The whole metaphorical treatment of him being under siege and assault is clever and bold and brave and even entertaining.'

The Verdict: Just when 'Scratch 'n' Sniff' had convinced you that *Farscape* couldn't get any more out there, they follow up Black T's heartbreaking death scene with an all-out animated comedy episode in which the *other* Crichton dies too, although happily not permanently. This episode and **313**, 'Scratch 'n' Sniff' are extremely funny and light to offset the deep, dark character grimness happening on board Talyn. The animation is superb and the music fits so perfectly that Guy Gross, the composer, won the Australian Guild of Screen Composers 'Best Music For An Animation' Screen Music Award. This is one of the riskiest, funniest, most out there pieces of TV ever seen and any show that can pull it off is truly special. That's all folks!

317
The Choice

1st US Transmission Date: 17 August 2001
1st UK Transmission Date: 7 January 2002

Writer: Justin Monjo
Director: Rowan Woods
Guest Cast: Linda Cropper (Xhalax Sun), John Gregg (Talyn Lyczac), Stephen Shanahan (Tenek), Raj Ryan (Hotel Owner)

Note: *This episode features the crew of Talyn.*

Aeryn, in mourning for Crichton, leaves Talyn and takes a hotel room on Valldon, a world Stark claims has mystical properties that allow the living to contact the dead. What she doesn't know is that Xhalax is also on the planet, having been spared by Crais (**310**, 'Relativity'), and is plotting to mess with Aeryn's head. She hires someone to pretend to be Talyn, Aeryn's father, and to use a fake seer to convince Aeryn that Crichton's spirit is in pain. She then kills the Talyn impostor, forcing Aeryn to watch her father's death. Aeryn reveals that she never believed he was Talyn at all, which deflates Xhalax, who tells her that when the Peacekeepers caught her visiting young Aeryn they forced her to choose who she should kill to redeem herself – Aeryn or Talyn. She killed Talyn out of love for Aeryn and wants Aeryn to suffer because it will ease Xhalax's pain. Aeryn just manages to make a connection with her when Crais, thinking to rescue Aeryn, bursts in and shoots Xhalax.

Black T: Aeryn has visions of Crichton, which appear to be genuine. His spirit remembers the life they lived in **216**, 'The Locket'. It claims he never really believed he was going to die.

You Can Be More: 'I returned from the dead, why can't he?' Aeryn is broken and desperate, takes refuge on a planet of ghosts, rents a grotty hotel room and drinks herself silly. She never believed 'Talyn' was really her father, but she hoped he was. She condemns the PK life because, although the Peacekeepers think they are remarkable, 'We're not remarkable, we do nothing for love. Not one thing.' She psychoanalyses her mother pretty well, manages to get her to lower her weapon and for a moment it looks as though she might be her mother's salvation. After her grieving process is complete she retreats back inside herself, tries to reverse the evolution she's undergone throughout the series, and tells Crichton's spirit: 'Maybe I could have become something different if you'd lived ... But you are gone, and I am what I was bred to be.' Xhalax's last words to Aeryn are, 'Live, for me.'

Buckwheat the Sixteenth: Rygel was in love with a female called Kelor, back on Hyneria, but the relationship ended because his parents forbade it (this is the story told in the novel *Dark Side of the Sun*, except in that version the female was called Nyaella). His Thronesled can go very high indeed, but it becomes vulnerable to high winds at high altitude. Rygel goes to talk to Aeryn and for once he has no hidden agenda, he doesn't want anything from her, he's showing genuine concern and understanding: 'Self-sacrifice is not the answer ... I'm not trying to save you, or recreate with you ... Crichton loved you, Aeryn. He wouldn't want his death to lead you here.' He's looking forward to getting back to Moya.

The Man in the Iron Mask: 'If you've got a deity, you better make your peace with it now, because I'm going to lead you to the other side, real quick!' Stark's enraged that Crais spared Xhalax and if not for Rygel reasoning with him he would probably have shot him outright. He never believes Crais's explanation (see **The Insane Military Commander**) and instead thinks that he was planning to betray them all. He wants to take care of Aeryn because of the crush he has on her ('she's very beautiful; hair as dark as a Fellip berry'). She doesn't take kindly to it at all, threatens to knife his one good eye, and tells him that what makes it worse is that Stark thinks he's better than Crais, when he's not. He hears Zhaan's voice on Velldon and decides to leave Talyn and go in search of her. He leaves his mask for Green T Crichton, saying that only he will know what to do with it.

The Insane Military Commander: Crais claims he realised more Retrieval Squads would be sent after them if he killed Xhalax, so he cut a deal – her life in return for a message to High Command telling them that Talyn and his crew were dead. His desire for Aeryn is as transparent as Stark's, and she calls him on it, telling him that he now has his chance to take her from Crichton. 'And you know what, Bialar? If I squeeze my eyes closed tightly enough you could be someone else.' He claims because Talyn now has a large part of his psyche, only he can fly Talyn, but he later says that once he has offloaded Rygel and Aeryn on Moya he will find a new Captain for Talyn and leave.

Big Baby: Talyn has detected Moya in the Mannon Nebula.

The Ballad of Aeryn and John: Aeryn now remembers her life on the Favoured Planet (**216**, 'The Locket'). She recalls the times she and Crichton were together, in **112**, 'The Flax' and **116**, 'A Human Reaction', as well as more recently. She tells the seer, Cresus, that 'he loved me . . . he made me better'.

Worlds Apart: Valldon is a planet with 'dark powers' and is peopled with 'mystics and criminals', spirits and seers who can contact and sometimes even raise the dead.

Alien Encounters: There is a Diagnosian (**222**, 'Die Me, Dichotomy') on Valldon who pays good money for fresh corpses. Cresus is the most repulsive creature *Farscape* has ever given us, but the animatronic mouth is a real work of art. He says he normally fakes contact with the dead but his vision of Crichton may actually have been real. 'Talyn' claims that there are people called Sintars who can sometime make a spirit corporeal. Xhalax's leg became infected after Crais left her and she had to amputate it herself.

Get Frelled: Aeryn humiliates Crais by jumping on him and telling him to do her right there and then.

Stats: A PK device called a Blood Spectrometer allows you to check whether you are related to someone else or not with near 100 per cent accuracy.

Logic Leaps: How did Xhalax know Aeryn would go to Valldon? Where did she get all the money to pay her cohorts? Why did Aeryn choose to raise her father? What was Xhalax really playing at, anyway? Why did Stark recommend Aeryn go to Valldon and then warn that she shouldn't be left there because it's too dangerous?

Guest Stars: John Gregg has been a regular on *Medivac* and *Heartbreak High* but underneath that make-up he was also Lycett from the *Doctor Who* serial 'The Ark In Space'. Raj Ryan plays a recurring character in the *Dogwoman* TV movies.

Backstage: Claudia Black wanted to take centre stage for an episode and have something to really sink her teeth into, as well as to have something to put on her showreel. As she told *SFX*, during the 'Ophelia scene' (in the corridor with Stark and Crais), 'with director Rowan Woods. I said, "Well, I'm absolutely shitting myself because if I get this scene wrong, it's all gonna die; I've lost the whole episode." '

The Verdict: This episode looks a million dollars; the sets, make-up, costumes and puppets are all superlative, as is Claudia Black's performance. However the script is a bit muddled and seems like a first draft, needing one more pass to iron out the rough spots and internal inconsistencies. Part of the price you pay for having a show as risky as *Farscape* is that occasionally an experimental episode will not quite work as well as you'd have hoped; this is one such.

318
Fractures

1st US Transmission Date: 24 August 2001
1st UK Transmission Date: 14 January 2002

Writer: Rockne S O'Bannon
Director: Tony Tilse
Guest Cast: Tammy MacIntosh (Jool), Kate Beahan (Hubero),
Matt Doran (Markir Tal), Thomas Holesgrove (Naj Gil),
Alexandra Fowler (Voice of Orrhn)

Moya picks up a Transport Pod, believing it is from Talyn, but it contains a captured PK Tech and three escaped prisoners: a Scarran (Naj Gil), an androgynous Nebari (Hubero), a female Hynerian (Orrhn) and the disassembled remains of a Boolite. After half a cycle Moya and Talyn are reunited and Crais, Aeryn and Rygel come aboard Moya. The tech is locked up; Naj Gil stays with D'Argo, Orrhn with Rygel, and Hubero with Chiana. Crais and Jool attempt to put the Boolite back together again.

When a PK distress signal is sent from Moya the hunt for a traitor begins, but each escapee has stayed with his or her escort at all times. Naj Gil is found shot, another signal is sent and the PK Tech is mysteriously released. It transpires that Orrhn has made a deal with the Tech to betray Moya's crew – she has been having sex with Rygel and when he falls asleep afterwards she's been roaming the ship sending signals. There is a shoot-out in which Hubero and the Boolite are killed, and the Tech and Orrhn escape in a Transport Pod with Rygel as hostage. Using the D'Argomobile, Aeryn and Crichton board the Pod and kill the Tech. Rygel casts Orrhn adrift in space, and the Pod self-destructs.

Green T Crichton receives a posthumous message from Black T Crichton and decides that he is going to the Command Carrier to stop Scorpius developing wormhole technology. He doesn't ask for support, but just tells his shipmates what he plans to do and lets them decide for themselves whether to help or not. Aeryn and Crais stand by his side, Jool opts out, Moya, Pilot and Talyn register their disapproval, and Chiana just tells them they're all going to die.

Green T: 'We choose our own path, this one is mine. I'm going to the Command Carrier.' When planning for his reunion with Aeryn, the remaining Crichton changes out of his green T-shirt and into a black one, which is guaranteed to make it that much harder for Aeryn when she sees him. He's pleased to see Rygel, even seems OK with Crais being around, and is a bouncy happy puppy at the prospect of seeing Aeryn again. When she greets him with an emotionless 'Hello John' and walks off, and Crais tells him his double is dead, he works it all out in an instant and you can see on his face the realisation of the gulf that now lies between him and Aeryn. He tries to talk to her about it but she blanks him. He knows his plan to stop Scorpius offers only certain death, but it looks like he intends to go out in a blaze of glory. He gets a bag of Black T's stuff and carefully balances his new pistol against Winona, and finds that Winona's still his favourite.

Black T: 'OK, I'm gonna piss you off now, man. Be smart, don't push her, she takes time ... good luck, John.' Talyn's Crichton recorded a message for Green T and stored it in Stark's mask. It tells Green T about the events on Dam-Ba-Da, Furlow, the Scarrans, and tells him that he can unlock the wormhole knowledge in his mind. He also insists that Scorpius must be stopped at any cost. He tells Crichton not to push Aeryn, that she needs time. He plays one last game of Rock/Scissors/Paper, and both Crichtons choose scissors.

You Can Be More: Aeryn won't talk to Crichton about it, she won't talk to D'Argo about it. She's emotionless, functional and remote. The only time she's caught off guard is when she and Crichton come up with the same plan at the same time and she tells him the harpoon will hold in the Transport Pod 'just like the Budong'. But Green T wasn't there for **308**, 'Green-eyed Monster', and just for a moment she's completely thrown. She (rather conveniently) overhears the message from Black T and sees the two Crichtons choose scissors, reinforcing that they are still the same person. She is the first to stand by Crichton when he reveals his plan to stop Scorpius.

I was a Teenage Luxan: D'Argo the fashion guru: 'Far be it for me to say, but I've always thought the colour of that green shirt doesn't suit the shape of your body.' He reaches out to Crichton and it seems that their friendship is back on track at last. He tries to talk to Aeryn but gets nowhere. Surprisingly, he stands up for Naj Gil which rather gives the impression that he and the Scarran have been doing a bit of big, scary warrior-type male bonding. He can now fly his ship with precision and skill.

Buckwheat the Sixteenth: Rygel tells Crichton that he's in love with Orrhn even though he's only just met her and they've done little else but have sex. He plays the gracious Dominar and tells her it's all right for her to be focus of attention if he says it is. When he realises she's betrayed him he calls her a bitch and ruthlessly cuts her loose to die in space.

Everyone's Favourite Little Tralk: Chi has two more precognitive flashes, of the shootings of Naj Gil and Hubero; unfortunately she doesn't see who shot them. She has heard of Nebari androgynes but has never met one before. She tries to hide Hubero to prevent him/her being thrown off the ship along with the other escapees.

Jool in the Crown: Jool knows almost nothing about Scarran biology, is useless in a gunfight, and has taste in clothes that horrifies Chiana. She does know something about Boolite physiology though and can correctly distinguish between their mouths and their bumholes, even when they are in lots of tiny bits. She gets some Boolite in her eye during the gunfight and is now wearing an eye patch.

The Insane Military Commander: Crais is sympathetic to the remaining Crichton and helps Jool try and reassemble the Boolite. He's not exactly a sharpshooter, but he holds his own in the gunfight, even if he does resort to throwing bits of Boolite at the Tech. He yells when the Boolite's brain, eye and mouth land on his lap and start screaming.

Alien Encounters: Hynerians obviously can survive in space (**202**, 'Vitas Mortis'), as Rygel is fine for quite some time without his mask. Hynerians *are* 'body breeders' after all (**109**, 'DNA Mad Scientist'). Hynerian soldiers are considered lowly and unfit to fraternise with Royalty. Hyneria is broken up into provinces.

Some Nebari are born androgynous – neither fully male nor female. Most are taken away at birth but some survive in non-conformist colonies. When the Peacekeepers tried to return Hubero the Nebari authorities didn't want him/her back.

Boolites have high metal content and their body parts can survive as long as half a cycle independent of their bodies. The Boolite on the Transport Pod is in lots of tiny pieces but can be reassembled, and as soon as most of his brain is hooked up to what's left of his mouth he can speak, too.

When a Scarran is captured the Peacekeepers immediately remove the gland that allows them to project heat; it is located beneath their left breast.

Disney on Acid: Crichton calls Orrhn Barbarella even though she looks nothing like Jane Fonda. The Boolite is 'a little too *Naked Lunch*', which was a book by William S Burroughs that was filmed by David Cronenberg.

Get Frelled: All Hynerians fall asleep after 'pleasure' but Orrhn was faking, so while Rygel slept she got up to mischief. Poor old Rygel isn't quite the dynamite lover he thinks he is. Hynerian pillow talk: 'Growl like a Luxan.'

Stats: The Peacekeepers are testing a weapon that dissolves the bonds of metallic molecules and they put their prisoners in a Transport Pod to assess the effect of the weapon upon them. Black T claims the wormhole weapons could 'fry a whole solar system'.

Logic Leaps: The prisoners overpowered the Tech who was making pre-flight checks and escaped in a Transport Pod, presumably from a PK Leviathan. How did it not manage to catch up with them once it knew they were on the run, and they had been hit by the weapon?

Guest Stars: Alexandra Fowler was Zoe on *Neighbours* and Angela Hamilton on *Sons and Daughters*. Matt Doran was Damian in *Home and Away*, Mouse in *The Matrix* and will appear in *Star Wars Episode II: Attack of the Clones*. Kate Beahan is a regular on *Love is a Four-letter Word*.

Backstage: Crais's scream was improvised by Tammy and Lani, and they assumed it would be cut. Tammy got some paint in her eye and couldn't wear her contact lens at the end, hence the eye patch. Ben Browder commented to *Cult Times* on the reunion between Green T and Aeryn: 'It's a heartbreaking scene . . . when the one thing that he hopes for and loves most just . . . walks past him it's crushing to watch, but he has to pick up the pieces and move on . . .'

The Verdict: The whodunnit is pretty standard stuff, the real interest here comes from the reunion between the two crews and the way the escapees mirror Moya's crew so closely. Lots of nice scenes but nothing spectacularly special. Then again, after the lunacy of **316**, 'Revenging Angel' and the grimness of **317**, 'The Choice', a straightforward ship-bound runaround was probably a necessary breather before the inevitable high tension of the concluding four episodes.

319
I-Yensch, You-Yensch

1st US Transmission Date: 5 April 2002
1st UK Transmission Date: 21 January 2002

Writer: Matt Ford
Director: Peter Andrikidis

Guest Cast: Tammy MacIntosh (Jool), Thomas Holesgrove (Naj Gil), David Franklin (Lt Braca), Ben Mendelsohn (Sko), Anthony Hayes (Wa), Inge Hornstra (Essk), Salvatore Coco (Voodi)

Rygel and D'Argo arrange to meet Scorpius at a diner on a desolate planet. They tell him about Black T's encounter with the Scarrans and Charrids and claim that Crichton has decided to help Scorpius crack the wormhole problem. In return Crichton's shipmates are to be pardoned and returned to their homeworlds as full citizens. Scorpius agrees. Rygel insists there should be acceptable security measures and so Scorpius demonstrates I-Yensch bracelets: two people wear them and share each other's pain; if one dies the other dies. He demonstrates this by having D'Argo and Braca wear the bracelets. Scorpius suggests that Crichton and Braca should be thus linked, but Rygel insists that Scorpius wears the bracelet. Scorpius refuses and is about to leave when two gun-toting aliens, Sko and Wa, hold up the diner and shoot Braca in the leg, which in turn cripples D'Argo. They have been hired by the chef to burn down the diner for insurance, but they change their plan and decide to hold their hostages for ransom. Rygel and Scorpius join forces to outwit and defeat their captors, and in doing so build up a mutual trust. Scorpius agrees to wear the bracelet.

A medical transport ship encounters Moya and takes Naj Gil aboard. Jool wants to go with him but Chiana prevents her from doing so because she has a vision of herself in mourning. Moya and Talyn are approached by a PK Prowler and Marauder. Talyn shoots them, then panics and destroys the medical ship, killing six hundred innocents. The crew reluctantly decide that Talyn will have to be lobotomised and completely refitted, being reborn as a new, sane ship. Talyn responds to this decision by firing on Moya. However, he eventually relents and allows Crichton, Aeryn and Crais aboard. They shut him down, effectively killing his personality for ever.

Buck Rogers Redux: 'Some things you die for.' Crichton is tiptoeing around Aeryn, not offering advice unless asked for it, not making conversation at all. He even tells her she doesn't need to come with him to the Command Carrier, he's so anxious not to pressurise her.

You Can Be More: Aeryn slowly learns to work together with Green T Crichton, telling him that they have always worked well together in the past and there's no reason they can't do so again. She calls Green T 'Crichton', whereas she called Black T 'John'. She has a bad feeling about the Command Carrier but is determined to go anyway: 'We started this together, that's how we'll end it.' She is talking to him at least, and is able to thank him for offering to let her leave Talyn before he's shut down. She is the one who persuades both Moya and Talyn of the necessity of shutting the warship down; they both trust her because they know she loves Talyn.

I was a Teenage Luxan: The arrangement is for the meeting to take place without weapons; am I the only one surprised that D'Argo agreed to that? When he realises the Peace-keepers are under orders not to hurt him, he takes great pleasure in knocking three of them out. He has a thick skull.

Buckwheat the Sixteenth: This is undoubtedly Rygel's finest hour. It was he who assured his friends that Scorpius would negotiate, and volunteered to undertake the negoti-ations himself. He's not fooled by Scorpius's bluffs for one second and coolly appraises the robbers, divining their true motives and playing brilliantly on their stupidity and lack of planning. When instructed to kill a fellow hostage he shoots Scorpius full in the chest without knowing whether he is wearing armour or not because, as he gleefully tells Scorpius, he's a winner either way.

Everyone's Favourite Little Tralk: Chiana has a premon-ition of Peacekeepers, and tells Jool she saw herself in mourning for her so she mustn't go to the Medical Ship. It's unclear whether she was telling the truth or not, but either way she punches Jool to stop her leaving. She announces to Crichton that she's jumping ship at the next planet they encounter – she wants no part of their suicidal plan to attack Scorpius.

Jool in the Crown: Jool has no quarrels with Peacekeepers and they don't even know she exists, so she decides to leave the ship before they encounter the Command Carrier. However, she misses the shuttle to the Medical Ship and is then prevented from catching up with Naj Gil by Chiana.

The Insane Military Commander: Crais tries to stop Talyn firing on the Medical Ship but fails. It is he who suggests they shut Talyn down, and when he has pulled the final lever and killed his ship he is obviously deeply upset.

Nosferatu in Rubber: Scorpius refuses to wear an I-Yensch bracelet and is willing to walk away from negotiations rather than give in. He carries a single-shot pulse gun in his cooling system. He wears body armour at all times. Rygel believes that Scorpius is even more important than a Captain because he has no insignia on his uniform. The hostage situation sees him at his most cunning, scheming and manipulative but he's still a beginner compared to Rygel, who earns his respect.

A Ship, a Living Ship!: Moya is horrified at the decision to shut down Talyn and at one point even refuses to talk to Pilot. Aeryn is able to persuade her that it is for the best, but the ship remains deeply shocked and upset by the 'death' of her child.

Big Baby: Crais: 'You have not disappointed me, I don't hold you responsible, neither does Moya . . . you are very brave.' Talyn panics and succumbs to total paranoia. He realises his mistake in firing on the Medical Facility and instantly shuts down in shock, expressing complete remorse. When he understands the others are planning to shut him down he fires on Moya and severely damages her; he could have destroyed her, so the crew know he's still got some restraint, but he's a danger to himself and all those around him. He allows Crichton, Aeryn and Crais to board him and although he aims his guns at them on the bridge, Aeryn is able to persuade him to submit to their surgery. His biological parts are kept alive but all his mechanical elements have been shut down. He needs a total refit and when he is reactivated he will be a different creature. Aeryn: 'Talyn, you know you're sick . . . I don't want you to be frightened, you're not going to die, you'll be reborn . . . Please Talyn, let us take away your pain.'

The Ballad of Aeryn and John: Aeryn finally tells Green T how she feels: 'It was perfect, we were so perfect and you're just like him. You *are* him.' But Crichton reminds her that he wasn't there. 'I missed that dance.'

Alien Encounters: The robbers are a blue/purple species with weird vocalisations, like chimps or hyenas.

Get Frelled: Jool is *holding hands* with Naj Gil at the start. You don't think they've been . . . it's too horrible to contemplate.

Stats: The controls of the D'Argomobile are isomorphic – they use DNA particles and voice recognition to establish D'Argo's identity and they respond only to him.

Seen it all Before: In *Dog Day Afternoon* and countless films about robberies gone bad.

Logic Leaps: Talyn has just shot at his own mother and then shut down communications. So what do Crichton, Aeryn and Crais do? Fly at Talyn in a Transport Pod! As insane gambles go that's one of the daftest. At one point Sko takes Scorpius out of the main diner room and leaves Wa alone with Rygel and the others. Where were they? Was Scorpius caught short and escorted to the Gents?

Guest Stars: Salvatore Coco has been a regular on *Police Rescue* and *Heartbreak High*. Inge Hornstra was also on *Heartbreak High* as well as *Sweat*. Anthony Hayes was Molnon in **203**, 'Taking the Stone'. Ben Mendelsohn has been a regular on *The Henderson Kids*, *Prime Time*, *Fame and Misfortune*, and *Close Ups* as well as appearing in the films *Quigley Down Under* and *Vertical Limit*.

Backstage: For some reason Tammy MacIntosh is not in the main titles at this stage, but neither is she credited as a guest star.

The Verdict: After the cliffhanger ending to **318**, 'Fractures', *Farscape* again teases the audience by making us wait for the big confrontation we now know is inevitable. The hostage situation at the diner is not terribly original but it's livened up by the marvellous interplay between Rygel and Scorpius, the bizarre aliens and the I-Yensch bracelets linking D'Argo with poor old Braca.

The storyline with Talyn, on the other hand, is emotional and shocking, and leaves the audience feeling sorry for Crais and mourning the loss of a character who never even had any dialogue.

320
Into the Lion's Den I: Lambs to the Slaughter

1st US Transmission Date: 12 April 2002
1st UK Transmission Date: 24 January 2002

Writer: Richard Manning
Director: Ian Watson
Guest Cast: Tammy MacIntosh (Jool), David Franklin (Lt Braca),
Sean Taylor (Lt Reljik), Marta Dusseldorp (Henta),
Lenore Smith (Lt Lorel), Rebecca Riggs (Commandant Milon Graza),
Danny Adcock (Co-Kura Strappa)

Crichton, Aeryn, Jool, Crais and Chiana join D'Argo and Rygel aboard Scorpius's Command Carrier where they are given 'full diplomatic rights, immunities and courtesies'. Crichton and Scorpius are wearing the I-Yensch bracelets linking their nervous systems and ensuring that if one suffers or dies the other does too. The presence of Moya's crew is deeply resented by the crew of the Command Carrier, especially Lt Reljik, who persuades a friend to try and kill D'Argo. D'Argo survives, the attacker dies.

Scorpius threatens Reljik that he will be executed if any more attacks are made.

Jool, Chi, D'Argo and Rygel return to Moya but the ship is seized by a Retrieval Squad and brought to the Command Carrier on the orders of Commandant Graza, who challenges Scorpius's authority. He has her thrown off the ship and she promises to return with full sanction and shut down his project. She instructs Reljik to kill Crichton, and thus Scorpius; he fails. Scorpius shows Crichton his life story and manages to convince him that the Scarrans are a huge threat – Crichton is now unsure whether he should go through with his plan and stop Scorpius developing wormhole technology.

Scorpius agrees to bring Talyn aboard to be refitted and assigns Lt Lorel to assist Crais. Lorel was Crais's lover; she says she still loves him but has been told to spy on him – in fact this is a double bluff, and she really *is* spying on him.

Aeryn is reunited with an old friend and tries to convince her that she is not a traitor; she has little success.

Buck Rogers Redux: 'When my friends are threatened I am infamous for making really stupid moves!' Crichton is beginning to unlock the wormhole equations in his head – he can tell enough to know which research directions will pay off and which are dead ends. His plan A is to erase all of Scorpius's data, plan B is to steer him in the wrong direction, plan C is to give it up and run like hell. Crichton asks Harvey if the Scarrans are the threat that Scorpius claims and Harvey says they are. He also views Scorpius's personal history. These things combine to make him doubt his planned course of action: he is actually considering helping Scorpius stop the Scarran threat. When Aeryn points out that Black T Crichton sacrificed himself to stop wormhole technology getting into the wrong hands he replies, 'It's my shift now, he didn't know what we know.'

You Can Be More: Aeryn somewhat misses the easy camaraderie of being on a PK ship with friends and equals. Her best friend in those days was Henta, who remains a loyal PK and instinctively despises Aeryn now. She throws a drink in Aeryn's face in the officer's lounge but later on she is willing to sit and talk with her, at least giving her a chance to present her case. She claims that Aeryn could have come back after Crais went rogue, but Aeryn admits she didn't want to come back. Aeryn has not abandoned all elements of the PK code: 'I kept loyalty, sacrifice, honour.' She tells Crichton she will back him whatever course of action he decides on.

I was a Teenage Luxan: D'Argo has had the rings in his collarbones removed and is given full details of Macton's whereabouts and current assignment (Macton is the brother, and the killer, of D'Argo's wife Lo'Laan – **110**, 'They've Got a Secret'). He tries not to kill the PK who attacks him, but it is unavoidable.

Buckwheat the Sixteenth: Rygel has been given a full breakdown of the political situation on Hyneria. He discovers that the usurper, Bishan, is in disfavour and there is much dissent against his rule. Rygel is planning to return, raise an army, and retake the throne.

Everyone's Favourite Little Tralk: Chi did not jump ship after all, although mainly because they were too far from a suitable planet. Once on the Command Carrier she tries her old tricks, turning on the sex appeal, flirting with Reljik, stirring up trouble. Luckily D'Argo steps in before she can start a fight.

She has another precognitive flash, of Pilot screaming, just before the Retrieval Squad turns up.

Jool in the Crown: Why does Jool come to the Command Carrier? The Peacekeepers don't even know she exists, but by accompanying Crichton and the others she declares her presence, openly allies herself with wanted criminals and places herself needlessly in the firing line. Either she's very stupid or she's very brave. When D'Argo is attacked she dives right in and lands a few good punches herself – a far cry from the wimpy scream queen who came aboard the ship at the start of the season. Her hair is shocking red, a reflection of her deep anxiety at being on a PK ship.

The Insane Military Commander: Crais was not a good PK even when he was still Captain – he had formed an emotional attachment to Lt Lorel and regrets not taking her with him when he defected to Moya. His ex-crew despise him for abusing his power and running out on them, leaving them to be commanded by Scorpius, who they hate even more.

Nosferatu in Rubber: 'At last the rift between us is finally bridged.' Scorpius is in a difficult position. His crew resent him, High Command is about to withdraw support for his project, and he suspects Crichton is stalling for time. He has a trick up his sleeve though – he has located Earth. It is just over sixty cycles' travel away at top speed. If Crichton betrays him Scorpius swears he will keep him alive just long enough to see Earth completely destroyed.

Hi, Harvey: Harvey is now a staunch ally of Crichton's because he has decided he wants to survive, and to do that he needs to keep Crichton alive. He modifies Crichton's energy signature so that Scorpius cannot tell when he is being lied to. He says he does not share Scorpius's passions or fears, only his intellect. His belief in revenge (**316**, 'Revenging Angel') hints otherwise.

A Ship, a Living Ship!: Moya would rather die than accept another Control Collar. An immobiliser pulse hits her just as she is entering StarBurst and she is badly damaged. She is now among the Command Carrier's fleet.

Big Baby: Crais wants Talyn to have a complete cognitive systems replacement and for all Talyn's weapons to be removed before he is revived. Talyn is in a hangar on the Command Carrier and Crais and Lorel are working to have him repaired and restored.

Alien Encounters: The Peacekeepers have decided upon a policy of appeasement towards the Scarrans and are trying to put on a show of strength at the same time as opening negotiations. The Luxans have signed a treaty with the Peacekeepers under which they retain autonomy but pledge to help fight any Scarran invasion. Every time the Peacekeepers approach a world in the Uncharted Territories and propose they join the alliance, they meet one of two responses – fear of Peacekeepers or laughter at the fact that they haven't been able to capture the legendary Moya and Crichton. They consider that Scorpius's project may be seen as provocative and intend to have it shut down so as not to give the Scarrans an excuse to invade. Scorpius claims that appeasement equals suicide and the new policy will only ensure a swifter invasion and a total defeat.

Seen it all Before: The rocket pack scene was straight out of the old Republic serial, *King of the Rocketmen*. The introduction of Commandant Graza is an interesting move, and she promises to be a recurring figure in the future, but she's so very reminiscent of Servalan from *Blake's 7* – she adds one more parallel between two shows that already have a great deal in common.

Disney on Acid: Crichton called the I-Yensch bracelet 'Dick Tracey's neural bracelet', after the old comic strip. He also refers to Scorpius as 'Grasshopper' – a reference to the TV show *Kung-Fu*, and 'Bram Stoker's nightmare'. Stoker wrote *Dracula*.

Stats: Co-Kura Strappa is working on generating an external field to stabilise the wormhole before entry. To this end they have transformed the Command Carrier's hull into a huge wave repeater but they cannot find the correct resonant frequency to stabilise the wormhole. The anaesthetic mist in the Restorative Chamber interferes with surveillance devices. If a pulse pistol is fired in the generator room the blast bounces back as if on a piece of elastic, and kills the shooter. Rocket packs are used to enable maintenance of the generator stacks. Command Carriers contain about forty huge hangars which house planetary terrain reconstructions for use in combat training.

Guest Stars: Lenore Smith was a regular on *The Restless Years* and *The Flying Doctors*. Marta Dusseldorp has appeared in *Innocence* and *Paradise Road*.

The Verdict: This episode muddies the waters greatly, making Crichton realise his vendetta against Scorpius has far wider implications, and showing us how desperate Scorpius is to retain his command and stop the Scarrans, even if it means defying his superiors for their own good. The effects are great, the sense of scale conjured in the Command Carrier is awesome, and there's a real feeling of danger for our heroes. There's so much happening, so many plot strands and set-ups, that it promises to be that rarest of things – a two-parter in which the second episode outstrips the first.

321
Into the Lion's Den II: Wolf in Sheep's Clothing

1st US Transmission Date: 19 April 2002
1st UK Transmission Date: 28 January 2002

Writer: Rockne S O'Bannon
Director: Rowan Woods
Guest Cast: Tammy MacIntosh (Jool), David Franklin (Lt Braca),
Marta Dusseldorp (Henta), Lenore Smith (Lt Lorel),
Danny Adcock (Co-Kura Strappa)

'I understand the power ... Scorpius is attempting to harness, ... the horror ... if anyone wields this weapon ... I now know that I am the only individual capable of stopping it.'

Crichton decides that the only course of action left open to them is to destroy the Command Carrier. Crais betrays this plan to Scorpius, who locks up Jool, Chi, Rygel and D'Argo as a guarantee of Crichton's continued assistance. However, Crais is playing a double bluff – he realises that the best way to destroy the ship and still allow all the people on board to escape, is to board Talyn and initiate StarBurst while still in the hangar. This will cause the Carrier to implode slowly but irrevocably, giving the crew time to make their escapes. It will also result in the certain deaths of Talyn and Crais. Crichton agrees to provide a diversion. He fetches his WDP from Moya and takes Scorpius with him on a ride through the wormhole. While the crew of the Carrier listen to the broadcast of the journey, Crais and Aeryn overpower the men guarding Talyn and Crais boards. When Crichton and Scorpius return to the Carrier, Crais broadcasts his farewell to the ship and triggers StarBurst. Aeryn helps rescue her shipmates, who escape to Moya on D'Argo's ship. Henta tries to kill Aeryn for helping destroy the Carrier, but is burned to death before she can pull the trigger. Aeryn steals a new Prowler and escapes to Moya. Crichton uses the Aurora Chair to erase all the wormhole knowledge from Co-Kura Strappa's mind. He meets Scorpius on the disintegrating hangar floor and they tell each other the combinations to remove the I-Yensch bracelets. Scorpius walks away into the crumbling ship and Crichton flies back to Moya in the WDP. Back on the ship he transcribes the wormhole equations into a book, as his shipmates make plans to return to their homes.

Buck Rogers Redux: 'One evil at a time, that's the best I can do.' Crichton could gamble that Commandant Graza would shut down Scorpius's research and end the entire wormhole project. He could just leave. But he's not willing to bet on Graza beating Scorpius in a fair fight so he decides they have to be entirely certain and thus must destroy the Carrier. He takes a lot of convincing that Crais is on his side, he really believes Crais has betrayed them and even Aeryn vouching for Crais does little to convince him; it's only when he realises the scale and the cost of what Crais is proposing that he finally accepts it, and later Crichton seems to regret that he didn't express his appreciation.

He dares Scorpius to drive through a wormhole with him even though he knows it's an absurd risk. He even seems willing to let Scorpius escape the Carrier with him in his WDP. He discovers that the way to gain access to the wormhole equations in his head is to zone out and let his subconscious take over his writing, then the equations pour out of him.

You Can Be More: It is Aeryn that Crais goes to when he's taken action, knowing that she trusts him and will help him convince Crichton of his sincerity. She does just that, and the depth of her regard for Crais is clear when she says goodbye to him just before he blows up Talyn. Even as the Carrier falls apart, before she rescues her friends, she pauses to help some children and Peacekeepers evacuate. She faces down Henta and tells her that she's satisfied she's done the right thing – destroying Scorpius's work will save millions of lives.

She now has a new Prowler.

I was a Teenage Luxan: 'We all knew the time would come when we'd split up. At the beginning I would never have believed it could take so long.' D'Argo agrees that he, Rygel, Jool and Chi should all leave the Carrier, but that's before they learn of Crichton's new plan to blow it up. He manages to get hold of schematics of the Carrier detailing the changes made since Crais was in charge. How on Earth does he manage to do that?

Buckwheat the Sixteenth: 'Don't think I'm going to miss you, any of you. I'm not! Well . . . maybe a little.' Surprisingly it is Rygel who first backs Crichton's plan, detailing his fear of wormhole weapons and claiming that it's in his own interest to help because if he did reclaim his throne he could never hold it against a PK force that had such weapons.

Everyone's Favourite Little Tralk: Chiana plans to find the Nebari resistance and join up with her brother, Nerri.

Jool in the Crown: Jool is upset at the prospect of leaving Moya and the disintegration of the crew.

In the Driving Seat: Pilot seems upset that Jool is leaving, showing the regard he's come to have for her.

The Insane Military Commander: So farewell then, Captain Bialar Crais. He plays a very dangerous game and it's only by making outrageous demands of Scorpius that he convinces the leather-clad loon that he's genuine in his betrayal of Crichton. It is his decision to sacrifice himself, and he does it with nobility, courage and not a little fatalistic humour. It's a superb send-off for a great character. He hits Lorel and gets rid of her before he acts, and it's unclear whether he does this because he no longer trusts her or because he wants to save her. He accuses Scorpius of stealing his entire life when he stole his command, calls him an abomination and takes great pleasure in knowing that he is destroying him.

Nosferatu in Rubber: 'I may not be getting off this ship, John. Goodbye, Crichton.' Scorpius is so convinced that Crichton has doomed them all to Scarran defeat that he accuses him of committing a great evil, and who's to say he's wrong: 'Commander John Crichton, generations will know that name. Because of you the Scarrans will soon destroy us.' He lets Crichton think he's decided to go down with the ship, but he took Braca somewhere beforehand, so it's safe to assume he made his escape and is plotting other ways to take the revenge that sustains him. He gives Crichton the bracelet release code first, perhaps so that Crichton might continue to believe he died on the ship. Had Crichton kept the bracelet on he would have been fully aware of Scorpius's survival. When travelling through the wormhole, Scorpius is totally fazed, calls the experience 'indescribable', says he's 'never felt so connected' and staggers a bit when he gets out of the WDP.

Hi, Harvey: Harvey beats Crichton at chess, draughts and Go Fish. He's noticeably more friendly, quirky and daft in this two-parter, perhaps reflecting Crichton's increased control now that he has a real purpose.

A Ship, a Living Ship!: Moya is obviously upset at Talyn's demise but accepts it; she always knew her child was destined for a violent end and appreciates that it will be a heroic one.

Big Baby: So farewell, Talyn. Blown to smithereens, but at least going out in a blaze of noble glory and self-sacrifice, dying to save the galaxy and Moya.

Disney on Acid: Scorpius goes into 'Captain Queeg mode'; this refers to the book and film *The Caine Mutiny* in which a naval vessel is terrorised by an insane captain. Crichton quotes *Star Wars* when he tells Scorpius, 'Flying through wormholes ain't like dusting crops, farm boy.'

Stats: 'It's not just science, it's *never* just science, it's a weapon!' The Command Carrier is over a metra long and contains fifty thousand men, women and children. Crichton tells Scorpius that he thinks there is a reason why his unshielded module lets him survive wormholes when Prowler pilots don't. He then flies through a demonstrably unstable wormhole full of Rantath Flux, and emerges unscathed. Since he had no Phase Stabiliser on board then the module *must* have particular properties. Linfer implied that Crichton only survived his initial journey because he was lucky enough to create a stable wormhole. That now seems questionable.

Logic Leaps: Crais convinces Scorpius that Aeryn was the only one of Moya's crew not conspiring with Crichton to destroy the Command Carrier. Scorpius then lets her roam the ship freely. Is he daft, or what?

The Verdict: On the down side, the subplot with Henta seems to fizzle out and doesn't really provide the exploration of an alternative Aeryn it promised, and the rest of the crew are sidelined as the focus shifts entirely to Crichton, Aeryn, Scorpius and Crais. On the other hand, Ben Browder again puts in his bid to be considered best actor on TV, and Lani Tupu gets to go out in a blaze of glory, and gives Crais real nobility as he finally reaches the end of his quest for redemption.

Spectacular effects, big explosions, a majestic score, and a decisive victory for the good guys won at great cost – this is epic stuff, and pushes the limits of what we normally see on TV, achieving cinematic scope.

322
Dog with Two Bones

1st US Transmission Date: 26 April 2002
1st UK Transmission Date: 31 January 2002

Writer: David Kemper
Director: Andrew Prowse
Guest Cast: Tammy MacIntosh (Jool), Kent McCord (Jack Crichton),
Melissa Jaffer (Old Woman)

Rygel: 'Talyn rests where he belongs, Scorpius has no ship,
we're all unhurt, healthy, and no one's trying to kill us! It
means finally we can go . . . home!'

Moya has collected Talyn's remains and wishes to dump
them in the Leviathans' sacred resting place. A female
Leviathan whose three children have all been captured by
PK hunters has been driven mad by her loss, has killed her
pilot, and determines to prevent Moya laying Talyn, a half
PK ship, to rest there. She has killed three Leviathans
already and rams Moya, severely damaging her. Eventually
Moya asks her crew to kill the insane Leviathan and they
use the D'Argomobile to do so. Talyn is laid to rest.

As Moya's crew prepare to go their separate ways,
Crichton daydreams about returning to Earth and marrying Aeryn. A mysterious old woman whom they rescued
from the Command Carrier uses herbs to show Crichton
the truth of his fantasies, and he confronts the reality:
Aeryn would be unhappy; the Peacekeepers would follow
and destroy everyone. He realises he must abandon his
dream of returning home. As Aeryn prepares to leave
Moya he declares his love for her and asks her either to
stay with him or to let him come with her. She resists but
eventually agrees to trust to fate, and they toss a coin. He
calls it wrong, she leaves. As he floats in his WDP outside
Moya, gathering his thoughts, Harvey manifests and
unlocks a memory in Crichton's subconscious: while he
was seeing visions of Peacekeepers killing all his friends on
Earth the old woman told him that Aeryn is pregnant.
However, before he can return to Moya and chase after

Aeryn, a wormhole appears and Moya, along with Jool and the old woman, is sucked through it. The wormhole vanishes and Crichton is left alone, floating in his WDP, out of fuel and miles from help . . .

Buck Rogers Redux: 'When I was a kid I dreamed of outer space and then I got here and I dream of Earth. Lately none of my dreams work.' He dreams of taking Aeryn and his friends home with him and fantasises about marrying Aeryn and settling down. Only when he's really truthful with himself does he acknowledge that his friends wouldn't fit in, Aeryn would be miserable, and the Peacekeepers would follow. He no longer considers returning to Earth an option. 'I am *so* tired of running . . .'

Crichton has a cousin, Susan.

You Can Be More: While on the Command Carrier Aeryn heard about an ex-PK unit that specialises in protecting people and preventing terrorism by assassinating people. She resolves to leave Moya and join this unit. Jool points out to her that this would be a step backwards in her personal evolution but Aeryn doesn't want to hear it.

I was a Teenage Luxan: 'Revenge is a feast best served immediately.' D'Argo loads up his ship with supplies and heads off to take revenge on Macton, who is posted a long way away. He has mastered his ship's weapon systems. Before he leaves he tells Crichton, 'Anything positive I do with the rest of my life will be because of you.'

Buckwheat the Sixteenth: Rygel also heads home, presumably in a Transport Pod.

Everyone's Favourite Little Tralk: Chi is overcome with grief at Talyn's burial. She would love Crichton to come with her as she hunts for Nerri and the Nebari resistance, but the fact that he looks like a PK would probably hinder her search. She tells him she loves him and leaves, also presumably in a Transport Pod.

Jool in the Crown: Jool is still on Moya when she is sucked down the wormhole, but Moya was intending to help her find her home world. She hugs Chiana as Talyn is laid to rest, and gives sage advice to Aeryn too – never has she been so personable and nice.

In the Driving Seat: Pilot is unable to persuade Moya to back down in the face of the rogue Leviathan's attacks, and at one point Moya takes control herself.

Hi, Harvey: 'Having chosen our partnership above all else, your well-being is now irrevocably mine.' Harvey pops up to unlock Crichton's subconscious memory of the old woman's revelation and then vanishes again, having given Crichton his gift.

A Ship, a Living Ship!: Moya explicitly asks her crew to kill another Leviathan so that Talyn can be laid to rest. This ruthlessness is surprising, but is much admired, at least by Rygel. Chiana once asked Zhaan how she managed to get on with Moya so well, and Zhaan replied that the secret was just to be completely honest at all times. Moya is by no means the largest Leviathan out there – the rogue is much bigger.

Big Baby: Rygel: 'Talyn was special, a joy to his mother and a credit to his species, both of them ... We lay Talyn, offspring of Moya, to rest in his sacred ground.' There's very little of Talyn left when he's dumped in the sacred space, but we can be pretty sure that he didn't survive the StarBurst on the Command Carrier: no surprise returns from the dead for he and Crais, they're definitely toast. (Then again, who knows what will be pulled out of the hat in Season Four?).

The Ballad of Aeryn and John: As Aeryn is packing her Prowler, Crichton tells her he's coming with her and provokes a fierce confrontation. Aeryn's finding it difficult: 'You see you died, I watched that happen, and yet you're still alive. I have to go ... guarantee you won't die in my arms again.' By leaving, she's also granting Crichton's wish that she won't die in his arms either.

His anger at being called Crichton by Aeryn ever since she got back to Moya (see **319**, 'I-Yensch, You-Yensch') spills out and he tells her to call him John. He also tells her that this time she has to say goodbye because if she goes it's the last time they'll ever see each other. There's shouting, shoving, tears ... When asked whether she loves 'John Crichton? Not him, not me, John Crichton,' Aeryn admits that she does.

He kisses her and she says it tastes of yesterday and he all but gives up because he can't compete with a perfect dead version of himself.

Aeryn says that, if the fates meant for them to be together, they will be, but Crichton responds 'Running away is not fate, Aeryn. Running away is running away.' He says that if fate is so important they should toss a coin. Aeryn protests that it is too late for her to go back to who she was, and, if Crichton loves her, he won't make her say goodbye and he won't make her stay. But then she thinks again, and so they toss a coin ... Aeryn: 'We're in the hands of fate now, we have to trust in that. Fly safe. Goodbye John Crichton.'

Alien Encounters: The old woman is some kind of shaman, and has a third eye in the middle of her forehead – a standard symbol of second sight. She's still on Moya when the ship is wormholed, so we can expect her to crop up again in Season Four.

Get Frelled: Crichton's dreams of Chiana on Earth involve her sleeping her way through all his friends and, yeuch, his dad! Dream D'Argo also gets lucky, with two babes, at Crichton's imaginary wedding.

Stats: A Leviathan can kill its pilot by starving it of nutrients. Although D'Argo's ship only responds to his DNA, other people can pilot it wearing gloves if D'Argo has previously smeared all the controls with some sort of bodily secretion. The ship has devastatingly powerful weaponry which takes everyone by surprise – it entirely disintegrates the rogue Leviathan without breaking a sweat.

Seen it all Before: The massacre at Crichton and Aeryn's imaginary wedding, with all the crew being shot down in slo-mo by faceless helmeted Peacekeepers, strongly recalls the final episode of *Blake's 7*.

WHAT did you just say?: Rygel refers to his 'tiny, shiny, heiny'. He's definitely been around Crichton too long!

Guest Stars: Melissa Jaffer appeared in *Farscape* as old Nilaam in **202**, 'Vitas Mortis'.

Backstage: A scene set on Earth in which Pilot makes a living in a carnival as 'Lobster Boy From Space' – don't let your children get too close!!! He's Weeeeird!! Count his arms! – was cut from the finished episode.

The Verdict: Following the example set by *Buffy* Season Four, and capping the intense final battle with a more contemplative, surreal season closer, this is the episode the whole season has built to. It addresses all the issues raised in the opening voiceover and resolves some of them – most importantly Crichton gives up all hope of ever returning home. The fantasy scenes of the crew on Earth, Aeryn and Crichton's wedding and all that ensues are superbly evocative, believable and, when they all die, heartbreaking. It's beautifully directed and the sequences where Crichton's imagined earthbound conversations interweave with his real-world conversations with his shipmates are superbly handled. The old woman is unsettling and her motives are unclear – why not just tell Crichton outright that Aeryn was with child? The cliffhanger is astonishing mainly because it comes *entirely* out of the blue: there was no build-up to the appearance of the wormhole at all, and no explanation given whatsoever. It's a totally random event that happens in a split second and then is gone, leaving Crichton and no doubt the audience to exclaim, incredulously, 'You have *got* to be kidding!' The combination of the situational cliffhanger with the emotional revelation of Aeryn's pregnancy, makes this a doubly potent season finale.

Finally, just consider the title of **301** – 'Season of Death'. This year we have seen Aeryn dead (**301**, 'Season of

Death'), Zhaan die, (**304**, 'Self Inflicted Wounds II: Want for the Wheel'), Chiana (**306**, 'Eat Me'), D'Argo (**306**, 'Eat Me'), Rygel (**310**, 'Relativity'), Crichton dies twice (**315**, 'Infinite Possibilities II: Icarus Abides' and **316**, 'Revenging Angel'), Crais and Talyn (**321**, 'Into the Lion's Den II: Wolf in Sheep's Clothing'). The only regular characters who have not died in some way this year are Moya, Pilot, Scorpius, Stark and Jool. Truly this was the Season of Death. But, as Ben Browder said to *TV Zone*, 'on *Farscape* we usually have to kill people two or three times to keep them in the ground.'

Appendix One: Back and Back and Back to the Future, Again

Before the final four episodes of Season Three were broadcast it had already been announced that Seasons Four and Five had been commissioned, guaranteeing at least 44 new episodes of *Farscape*. But David Kemper may not be satisfied even with that boon: 'Personally, I think it's a six-year show . . . it could end at the end of year four or year five. But I think it needs to go six years to fully explore the themes we're exploring and getting to.' (*DreamWatch*)

More immediately he's got firm plans for Season Four: 'I know the last four episodes of next year already . . . I'm really excited because I normally don't know them in such detail this early and I've cracked them – I feel pretty good about that.' (*Starburst*) And to *DreamWatch*, he said that Season Four will make people 'go "Holy crap! How did they do that? Why did they do that? It's unbelievable!" We're gonna do some things that really throw people for a loop next year.' Andrew Prowse adds: 'Season Four will be lighter in tone. We couldn't actually get much darker . . . so what we've figured on is, well Crichton's liberated from a lot of stuff and he's going to be much more of an adventurer in Season Four.' (*SFX*).

Rockne S O'Bannon shares Kemper's enthusiasm: 'I'm totally stoked. Season Four is shaping up as an especially wild chapter in the *Farscape* saga . . . I guess if I were to crystallise the upcoming season, I'd refer to it as '*Farscape Extreme*'.' (*DreamWatch*)

There are significant behind-the-scenes changes for the coming year, as well. Andrew Prowse, whose association with the show goes right back to **101** 'Premiere', which he directed, is becoming a full producer. The writing staff are undergoing a major overhaul, with four new staff writers being brought on board to inject new ideas and talent: American-based Emily Skopov (who's written for *Andromeda* and *Xena: Warrior Princess*) and Mark Saracini (who's written for *The Sopranos*, *The X-Files*, *E-Z Streets* and *JAG*); and Aussies Michael Miller (who's written for *Wildside*, *GP* and *Water Rats*) and Chris Wheeler (head writer on *Going Home*).

Also adding to the new feel is a new ratio, as the show begins shooting in a widescreen format to even further increase its cinematic scope.

Which leads on to the movie . . . will *Farscape* go to the big screen? Negotiations have begun, and discussions are being held about how best to approach it – should it fit into regular continuity like the first *X-Files* movie or should it be a stand-alone 'missing adventure'? Time will tell, but it's already clear that cast and crew are very keen on taking the show to a multiplex sooner or later.

Appendix Two: Publications

There are three official guides to Farscape, one covering each season. They are heavy on interesting backstage info. They are published by Tor books in the US, and Titan Books in the UK.

There is also a bi-monthly official *Farscape* Magazine published by Titan Publishing. It contains original fiction, news, interviews and in-depth analyses of particular episodes.

There have been three original novels published to date by Boxtree in the UK and Tor in the US. They are:

Book One – *Dark Side of the Sun* by Andrew Dymond

This book is set during the few stand-alone episodes at the start of Season Two. The basic premise is elegant – Crichton has been recycling the Dentics that absorb his tooth decay. Moya cannot process the human bacteria and has developed a necrotising infection as a result. There are some nice sci-fi trappings to this tale of a trade collective bartering with Moya's crew for the medicine needed to cure Moya, but it gets bogged down in an unengaging Rygel love story before going totally off the deep end with some bizarre occurrences.

Trivia: Rygel uses his sweat to make holes in the wall of his room, creating the secret exit he uses to escape when locked in. Dymond seems to get Moya confused with the Lexx (from the show *Lexx*) and states that she secretes foodstuffs for the crew and sometimes lands on planets to eat.

Book Two – *House of Cards* by Keith RA DeCandido

This book is set during Season Two, after **214** 'Beware of Dog'. In terms of characterisation and dialogue this book rings true to the series and is the best of the three. On a gambling planet the individual crew members have to get out of a nasty situation Rygel dumps them in – by losing Moya in a card game.

Trivia: Crichton has a sister. His full name is John Robert Crichton Jr.

Book Three – *Ship of Ghosts* by David Bischoff

I would review this book but I had to give up after fifteen pages because it's dreadful and I just didn't have the stamina to wade through another 242 pages. Sorry. I tried.

The March 17–24 2001 edition of *The Ultimate TV Cable Guide* featured a one-off five-page *Farscape* comic strip produced by Wildstorm, written by Marv Wolfman and drawn by Robert Teranishi, Sandra Hope, Richard Friend, Scott Williams and Mark Propst. This was a preview of Wildstorm's full comic book launch and can be read at: www.tvguide.com/magazine/issues/010319/farscape.asp. The full book finally launched a year later with the two-parter 'War Torn', also by Marv Wolfman with art by Robert Teranishi, Heath Aiken and Al Gordon. This tells the tale of two warring planets. Crichton, Zhaan and Chi go to one, D'Argo, Rygel and Aeryn to the other. As war approaches they realise that all is not as it first appeared . . .

The art is great, the characters well realised and the story is a good introduction to the strip.

Appendix Three: Web

There are three official *Farscape* websites. The first is at www.farscape.com but it is low on content. It contains a synopsis and cast lists for all episodes, a couple of screensavers, links to merchandise producers and brief character profiles. The Sci-Fi Channel's *Farscape* site (www.scifi.com/farscape) is far more comprehensive and contains reams of interesting material. There are logs for each episode, journal entries from Crichton, back stories for various races and individuals, as well as a message board, movie clips and wallpapers. The BBC also maintains a *Farscape* site at www.bbc.co.uk/cult/farscape, which has episode reviews, a message board, interviews, games, and character profiles.

For fan-maintained sites none come close to The Snurcher's Guide (www.snurcher.com), which contains a comprehensive analysis of every episode, annotations, interview snippets, complete ratings for both UK and US transmissions and a wealth of information. Farscape World (www.farscapeworld.com) has comprehensive synopses and reviews, news, forums, fan fiction, articles and screen grabs. The Tourist's Guide to the Uncharted Territories (www.perriverse.dreamhost.com/farscape) is good as well, as are Farscape Weekly (www.farscapeweekly.com), Kieriahn's Farscape Starcharts (www.kieriahns.com), Karlsweb (www.karlsweb.com), and finally The Society Against Cruelty to Crichton (www.scaper.com).

On Usenet, UK fans congregate at uk.media.tv.sf.farscape, while US fans hang out at alt.tv.farscape.

Finally, I can be reached at www.sixesandsevens.net/unchartedterritory, where I will post any addenda, changes, corrections or fun feedback I receive.